Windows™ 3.1

SELF-TEACHING GUIDE

Keith Weiskamp
Saul Aguiar

John Wiley & Sons, Inc.
New York ▲ Chichester ▲ Brisbane ▲ Toronto ▲ Singapore

Ami Professional is a trademark of Lotus Corporation.
Corel Draw is a registered trademark of Corel Systems Corporation.
Crosstalk for Windows is a trademark of Digital Communication Associates, Inc.
Excel is a trademark of Microsoft Corporation.
Helvetica is a trademark of Adobe Corporation.
Microsoft is a trademark of Microsoft Corporation.
Microsoft Word is a trademark of Microsoft Corporation.
Novell Network is a registered trademark of Novell Corporation.
PageMaker is a registered trademark of Aldus Corporation.
PC Paintbrush is a trademark of ZSoft Corporation.
PostScript is a trademark of Adobe Corporation.
Times is a trademark of Adobe Corporation.
Windows Notepad is a trademark of Microsoft Corporation.
Windows Write is a trademark of Microsoft Corporation.
WordPerfect for Windows is a trademark of WordPerfect Corporation.

Library of Congress Cataloging-in-Publication Data

Weiskamp, Keith.
     Windows 3.1 self teaching guide / Keith Weiskamp, Saul Aguiar.
        p. cm. -- (Wiley self-teaching guides)
     Includes index.
     ISBN 0-471-55870-2 (paper)
       1. Microsoft Windows (Computer program)   I. Aguiar, Saul.
  II. Title. III. Title: Windows three-point-one self-teaching guide.
  IV. Series.
  QA76.76.W56W452 1992
  005.4'3--dc20   91-33055
                                                        CIP

Printed in the United States of America

10 9 8 7 6 5 4 3 2 1

Contents Overview

Contents

3   The Program Manager at Work, 67

4   Putting Windows to Work, 109

5   Using the Control Panel, 133

6   Managing Your Files and Disks, 181

7   Printing with Windows, 235

10 Working with Write, 325

11   Working with Paintbrush, 351

Preface

Welcome to Microsoft Windows 3.1—the graphics user interface (GUI) that turns your PC into a powerful, easy-to-use tool. In the past, using the PC involved memorizing cryptic DOS commands. Windows 3.1, on the other hand, adds a rich interface to your computer so that you can get your work done easier, faster, and better. In addition, Windows allows you to take advantage of the more advanced memory management capabilities of 386 and 486 PCs. With Windows, you can run multiple applications at the same time and easily switch between them.

To help you learn Windows and be more productive with this GUI, *Windows 3.1 Self-Teaching Guide* takes you inside Windows using a practical "hands-on" approach. Here are some of the major highlights:

▲ Covers the major applications of Windows, including the Program Manager, File Manager, Print Manager, and the Control Panel

▲ Shows you how to use the powerful new features of Windows 3.1, such as TrueType fonts, the Screen Saver, object linking and embedding, and the Object Packager

▲ A special appendix is provided to help you install and set up Windows 3.1

▲ Provides coverage of the useful desktop accessories

▲ Explains how operations can be performed with the keyboard and the mouse

Who Should Use This Book

If you have never used Windows, or if you have been running a previous version, such as Windows 3.0, you'll be amazed at the powerful features available in Windows 3.1. We've taken great care to show how to use the most important features of Windows 3.1 so that you can be more productive and have more fun using your PC.

This book is much more than a rewrite of the users manual. In fact, it is especially designed for people who like to learn at their own pace. You'll find numerous visual cues, hands-on reference sections—such as the **Quick Task Summaries** at the end of each chapter—and question and answer sections. All of the examples provided are designed to help you perform useful operations from managing files to running applications.

Why This Book Is Unique

This book is organized to help you learn Windows 3.1 step-by-step. Each chapter provides a number of hands-on features:

▲ Throughout the book, you'll find numerous **Tips** that show you how to get the most out of Windows and take advantage of undocumented features.

▲ Interactive **Check Yourself** sections are including in each chapter as a learning aid. These sections provide questions, instructions, and answers to help you test your knowledge as you work through the chapters.

▲ A **Practice What You've Learned** section is included at the end of each chapter to help you review the procedures and techniques presented in the chapter.

▲ Each chapter also provides a **Quick Task Summary** that you can use to review the commands and techniques presented in the chapter. You'll find that each summary serves as an excellent reference guide.

What's Inside

What's Inside

This book progresses from the basics to more advanced topics. The step-by-step approach will help you put previously learned skills to use quickly.

Chapter 1: *Getting Started* introduces the basic features of Windows, including Windows operating modes, equipment requirements, the Program Manager, and the main Windows applications and accessories. The second half of the chapter presents a quick tour to help you get started using such interface components as the mouse, windows, icons, menus, and dialog boxes.

Chapter 2: *Building Your Windows Skills* presents the basic techniques for working with Windows. You'll learn all about the Windows desktop, document and application windows, icons, control menus, dialog boxes, and more. This chapter serves as a useful reference guide that you'll want to use whenever you need to brush up on a basic technique.

Chapter 3: *The Program Manager at Work* shows you how to use the heart of the Windows environment. The Program Manager is the main application window that allows you to run and organize your applications.

Chapter 4: *Putting Windows to Work* presents a hands-on introduction of techniques for working with documents. Here, the Write application is used to show you how to create, open, and save documents, locate documents, perform basic editing operations, and use the Clipboard to transfer data between documents.

Chapter 5: *Using the Control Panel* covers basic techniques for using the Control Panel to set up and customize your Windows environment. Some of the topics covered include selecting colors, setting the system date and time, setting up a screen saver, installing fonts and printers, and setting up the mouse and the keyboard.

Chapter 6: *Managing Your Files and Disks* shows you how to use the File Manager to manage your DOS files. Here, you'll learn a variety of techniques for performing file- and directory-related operations such as viewing directories, renaming files and directories, searching for files, and moving, copying, and deleting files.

Chapter 7: *Printing with Windows* shows you how to get the most out of Windows' printing features. You'll learn how to install, set up, and remove printers, and how to change the default printer. The second part of the chapter covers the Print Manager application, which allows you to control how your documents are printed.

Chapter 8: *Working with Non-Windows Applications* shows you how to set up non-Windows applications so that they can be run in the Windows environment. You'll learn how to use the PIF Editor to customize the operating environment for your non-Windows applications.

Chapter 9: *Using Desktop Accessories* presents the major built-in accessories, including Clock, Notepad, Calendar, Calculator, Cardfile, Macro Recorder, and the useful Object Packager.

Chapter 10: *Working with Write* explores the useful word-processing application called Write. You'll learn a number of useful tips and techniques for working with Write documents, including how to use Windows' object linking and embedding features to add pictures to a Write document.

Chapter 11: *Working with Paintbrush* shows you how to use the interactive drawing and painting program called Paintbrush.

Chapter 12: *Using Terminal* introduces the Terminal application to help you communicate with other computers.

Contacting the Authors

As you are using this book, you might have questions or comments that you would like to pass along to us. We'd like to encourage you to do so (although we can't always answer every letter). The quickest way to reach us is through CompuServe. (The ID is 72561,1536 for Keith Weiskamp.) You can also reach us by mail at 7721 E. Gray Rd., Suite 204, Scottsdale, AZ 85260.

Getting Started

Welcome to the Microsoft Windows (version 3.1) environment. In this book we'll show you what Windows can do and how to use it most effectively. A good way to learn about the basic advantages of using Windows is to examine some of the problems it's designed to solve.

We'll start by discussing the basic reason Windows was created—to simplify the way users interact between programs and DOS. Next, we'll discuss the basic components of Windows, including the following:

▲ **Graphical User Interface (GUI)**

▲ **The basic features of Windows**

▲ **Windows operating modes**

▲ **The hardware and software needed to run Windows**

▲ **The applications and accessories provided with Windows**

▲ **The powerful new features provided with Windows 3.1**

Why Windows?

For years, users have criticized the PC because it lacked an easy-to-use interface (in other words, a way for users to communicate easily with the computer). DOS was one of the first PC operating systems and quickly became the most widely used operating system for IBM and compatible PCs. Although DOS provided features that most users needed, it had two major drawbacks: It was difficult to use, and it could run only one program at a time.

When PCs became more available and affordable, more nontechnical people began to use them and began to demand a simpler, more intuitive way to control the way the computer worked, other than the capabilities available with DOS.

As PCs continued to evolve, manufacturers began to focus on the ease-of-use concept by introducing computers that sported a *Graphical User Interface (GUI)*. A GUI helps to simplify the use of a computer by presenting users with graphic symbols, called *icons*, that can be used to make selections. A GUI also relies on a system of *menus* that make it easy for users to identify and choose available programs, commands, and options.

The Apple Macintosh was one of the first computers to support a GUI. The GUI quickly caught on with users of all levels because it made use of the easy-to-understand electronic desk metaphor (Figure 1.1). Under this approach, multiple files and programs could be opened at the same time. Here, the computer screen simulates an actual desk, where everything is at your fingertips.

As IBM PCs and compatible systems increased in processing power and memory capacity, it became increasingly possible to provide a GUI that could run efficiently on top of DOS. Eventually, the demand for a standard, Mac-like PC GUI led to the development of Windows. With this environment, you don't need to memorize cryptic commands, such as XCOPY A:\BACKUP*.* C: /S.

Instead, commands are performed by choosing them from menus or by clicking icons. Also, Windows can manage more than one program at a time. This feature prevents you from wasting time by continuously loading and quitting programs as you switch from one task to another.

▼ *Figure 1.1. The Electronic Desk*

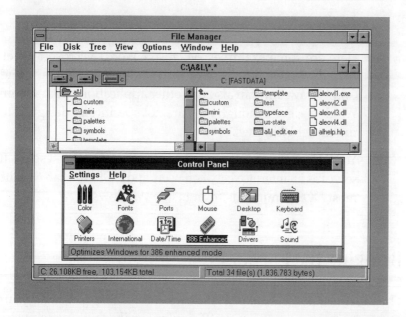

Because most Windows applications follow a standard design philosophy, they operate consistently. Whether you're running a word processor, a spreadsheet, or a database, the basic techniques for performing tasks (such as opening, closing, and printing files) are the same. Once you learn the basics, you won't have to search through manuals to learn commands for different programs.

Windows also allows you to easily move data between applications. Finally, Windows provides special applications that let you write documents, create pictures, and even maintain an electronic equivalent of a 3 by 5 cardfile of names, addresses, or other organized information.

CHECK YOURSELF

This book provides a number of hands-on exercises (like the one shown here) to help you test your skills as you progress. We call this the "learn-by-doing approach."

1. For your first task, take a moment to discover some of the Windows applications that are available to you.

2. Do you need DOS to run Windows?

ANSWERS

1. Here are some examples: Microsoft Word, Microsoft Excel, Ami Professional, Crosstalk for Windows, PageMaker, and Corel Draw. You can also run other applications from within Windows, even though they are not specifically designed to run under Windows.

2. Yes. Windows is not an independent operating system. It serves as an interface between users and DOS. You can execute most DOS commands from inside Windows.

Breaking the Barriers

The most unique feature of Windows is its ability to put all your computer's memory to work. (If you're familiar with versions of Windows before version 3.0, you're probably aware that they could not break the DOS 640K barrier.) The new memory access capabilities of Windows means that you work more efficiently. In fact, if you use a computer with 1Mb of memory or more, you can load multiple applications simultaneously and switch between them. If you use a 386- or 486-based computer, you can even run multiple applications at the same time. This feature is called *multitasking*.

Windows 3.1 also sports a whole new look over the 3.0 version. When you first see the new Windows environment, you'll discover visually appealing icons, 3-D buttons, new colors and fonts, and easy-to-use dialog boxes, menus, and windows—all provided to create an attractive and easy-to-use system.

What's Available

When you first use Windows, you'll quickly understand how this software package got its name. Areas of the screen are divided into separate *windows*, with each window representing a different application or category of use.

The heart of Windows is a control window called the *Program Manager*. This component is so important that we've devoted an entire chapter to it (see Chapter 3). From this window, you can run other Windows applications to perform a wide range of operations from managing your files to setting up your working environment. As Figure 1.2 shows, the Program Manager provides a window at startup, called Main, and a set of icons that represent different categories of applications. The Main window contains the following components:

▲ File Manager

▲ Control Panel

▲ Print Manager

▲ Clipboard Viewer

▲ MS-DOS Prompt

▲ Windows Setup

▲ PIF Editor

▼ *Figure 1.2. The Program Manager*

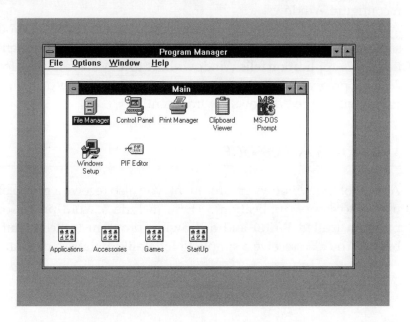

The powerful *File Manager* application lets you perform file and disk-maintenance operations (moving or deleting files, searching for files or directories, renaming files, and so on). The *Control Panel* lets you easily customize how Windows is set up. For example, you can set up a screen saver, customize colors, and even select date and time formats.

The *Print Manager* schedules and controls how files are printed. It lets you "send" a file to the printer and then return to your work in an application program. The Print Manager provides data to the selected printer at a rate the printer can handle.

The *Clipboard Viewer* is a temporary storage area that you use to transfer information between Windows applications. The Clipboard is always available. So, you can cut or copy information from an application, store the information in the Clipboard, and later transfer the information to another application.

The *MS-DOS Prompt* accesses the DOS command interpreter so you can easily execute DOS commands. When this feature is used, you can type in the name of an MS-DOS command or a non-Windows application.

The *Windows Setup* application can be used at any time to change the hardware under which Windows runs. If you change one or more hardware devices for your computer system, such as installing a new VGA display, you should run Windows Setup to reconfigure Windows.

The last component in the Main group, the *PIF Editor,* lets you set up non-Windows applications to run under Windows. Essentially, this application tells Windows how to allocate resources for running programs (applications) that are not specifically designed to run within the Windows environment.

Windows Accessories

As part of the Windows environment, you also receive a group of useful accessory applications. These include a word-processor program (called Write) and a drawing program (called Paintbrush). You also receive a simple Rolodex-like database program (called Cardfile), an electronic Calendar that can sound an alarm, and a Calculator that allows you to transfer results of calculations to other programs.

What's Available

You also get a Notepad program that you can use to save information temporarily and a Terminal program that automatically dials telephone numbers and transfers files to or from another modem-equipped computer. You can also use the Terminal program to transfer files between two computers using a simple RS-232 connection. Many of these accessory applications are shown in Figures 1.3 and 1.4.

Windows also provides a Clock program that displays the system time. In addition, a specialized program called Recorder lets you record your commands for reuse. You'll also find two applications, Media Player and Sound Recorder, for controlling multimedia devices. In case you need a break from the daily grind, Windows even provides two games: Solitaire, the card game; and Reversi, which resembles a simplified version of Go.

▼ *Figure 1.3. Calculator, Calendar, Cardfile, and Clock*

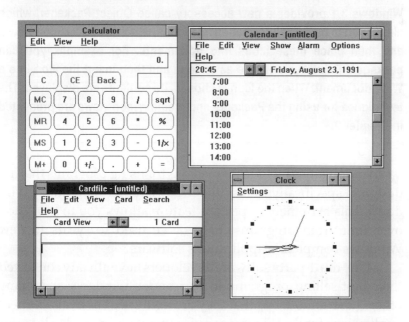

▼ *Figure 1.4. Paintbrush, Notepad, and Terminal*

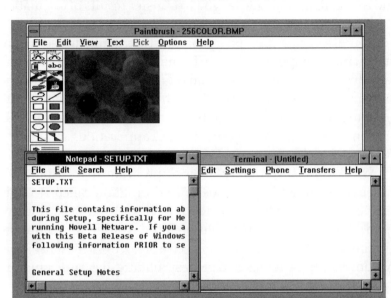

TIP

Windows 3.1 provides a new accessory called Object Packager, which allows you to package information into icons, which are called icon views, and then place these icons into documents. For example, you can package a Paintbrush picture as an icon and then insert the icon into a Write document. When the icon is chosen, its contents are displayed. The techniques for using the Packager and creating icon views are presented in Chapter 9.

Windows also includes provisions for using programs that are designed specifically to run under DOS, rather than under Windows. This extremely important feature allows you to transition over time from programs that you've used for years to new Windows-compatible applications software.

Many third-party software developers have already converted their best-selling programs to run under Windows and many others have announced that they are doing so. The availability of applications for the Windows environment is expected to increase rapidly in the next few years. The point to keep in mind is that

Windows includes provisions for running these DOS-based applications from within Windows.

What's New in Windows 3.1?

If you are familiar with the previous version of Windows (version 3.0), you might be wondering what's different about Windows 3.1. Because many of the changes are internal, you won't see them, although you'll probably notice that Windows 3.1 runs faster on your system than its predecessor. There are, however, some new features that you'll want to explore right away.

New File Manager

The File Manager has been greatly improved to make it easier for you to manage your disks and files. The key component of the File Manager, the directory window, has been redesigned to help you view multiple directories and perform operations such as copying, moving, and deleting files. You'll learn all about the new File Manager in Chapter 6.

StartUp Group

In addition to the standard Main, Accessories, Games, and Applications group windows, Windows 3.1 provides a StartUp group that you can use to automatically run applications when Windows starts up. With this feature, you simply place a program item icon in the StartUp group; Windows will then load and/or run the program for you each time it starts.

TrueType Fonts

Older versions of Windows' screen fonts were bit-mapped and scaled pixel by pixel. The net result was that fonts looked jagged on the screen and were inefficient to update on the screen. A new font scaling technology, called *TrueType Fonts*, has been incorporated into Windows 3.1 to help improve the display quality and performance of fonts.

Screen Saver

Windows 3.1 also provides a useful screen saver. This feature, which is selected from within the Control Panel, allows you to display a picture or a moving pattern on the screen after your computer has been sitting idle for a while. The screen saver is discussed in Chapter 5.

New Properties

Three new properties have been added for program items. One of the properties, called *Working Directory*, allows you to specify the name of the directory where you want an application to store and read its files. The second property, *Shortcut key*, allows you to define a shortcut key for launching an application. The third property allows you to set up an application so that it will run as a minimized application when it is chosen.

Object Linking and Embedding

When Windows 3.0 was released, a new feature was incorporated called *dynamic data exchange* (DDE). The goal for DDE was to provide a system whereby Windows users could easily share data between applications. Unfortunately, Microsoft left the details about implementing DDE up to the people who designed Windows applications.

Windows 3.1 takes this technology one step further and provides a way that you can actually link Windows document files without relying on features that are specific to a particular application. For example, you can insert a drawing from Paintbrush into a Write document so that the files become linked.

Why is this linking capability so important? It allows you to make changes to a source document, with the changes then reflected in other documents that the source document is linked to. The data in documents, such as a picture created by Paintbrush or a chart created by Excel, are treated as objects that can be embedded or linked in other files. As you begin to work with Windows 3.1, you'll find that this linking feature opens up many possibilities.

To support this *OLE (Object linking and embedding)* technology, a new accessory application has been added, called Object Packager. We'll explore this application in Chapter 9.

What's New in Windows 3.1?

TIP

After installing Windows 3.1, you should contact vendors of your Windows 3.0 applications to see if new versions are available. By obtaining software updates, you'll be able to take advantage of new Windows 3.1 features.

New Dialog Boxes

As you begin to work with Windows 3.1, you might notice that a number of dialog boxes have been changed (from the 3.0 version) to make them more consistent and efficient. For example, the standard Browse dialog box has been improved so that you can easily select drives and filter the files that are listed in a directory search. A Help button has also been added to many dialogs so that you can quickly get help on the operation you are performing.

Understanding Operating Modes

To install and make full use of Windows, you need to know about the operating modes that it supports. With early releases of Windows (before version 3.0), special versions of the program were introduced to support different hardware platforms. For example, if you used a PC with an 80386 processor, you needed Windows

386. Fortunately, Windows 3.1 has integrated the different operating modes into one product.

The operating modes that Windows support come in two flavors: standard mode and 386 enhanced mode. The first operating mode is the *standard mode*, which is the normal operating mode. When you run this mode, you can access extended memory (up to 16Mb), load multiple applications, and switch between them. Keep in mind that you need a PC with an 80286, 80386, or 80486 processor to operate in standard mode.

The most powerful operating mode is the *386 enhanced mode*. You'll need an 80386 or 80486 processor to run this mode, which is designed to take advantage of the power and flexibility of the 80386. One of the more important features of this mode is that it provides support for *virtual memory*. With a virtual memory system, a computer can access more memory than it actually has, which lets you run very large programs and run multiple programs simultaneously.

TIP

When Windows starts, it automatically selects what it determines to be the most efficient operating mode for your hardware configuration. However, you can also specify a different operating mode when Windows starts. You can determine which mode is in use by choosing the About command from the Help menu in any application.

What You Will Need

Windows 3.1 is designed to run on XT and AT-class machines that use the Intel 80286, 80386 or 80486 family of microprocessors (or their equivalent). Windows prefers 386/486 processors because these have advanced memory-management hardware features that are not available on the 80286. Windows also expects a hard disk and runs best with at least 2Mb of main memory. Windows also works best with a mouse (either serial or bus type). (Windows

3.1 can operate without a mouse and be controlled through key-board commands, but the use of a mouse adds significantly to the friendliness of the Windows environment.)

CHECK YOURSELF

1. Take a few minutes to review the requirements for running Windows. If you use a PC with an 80286 processor, how much memory can you access? How much memory can you access with an 80386 PC?

2. How much hard disk space does Windows require?

3. Do you need to install a mouse in order to run Windows?

4. What are the differences among the standard and 386 enhanced modes?

ANSWERS

1. Up to 16Mb can be accessed directly by both processors. With an 80386 you can actual access up to 64Mb; however, any memory above 16Mb is accessed as virtual memory.

2. 6Mb to 10Mb of free disk space is needed.

3. No. However, you'll find that a mouse greatly enhances Windows' ease of use.

4. Standard mode is designed for the 80286 processor, and the 386 enhanced mode is designed to take advantage of the memory-management features of the 80386.

The Windows Quick Tour

Before you get to work in Windows, you should familiarize your-self with several of its basic components, such as the mouse, the menus, the icons, and the windows themselves. Use the quick tour of these components in this last section to prepare yourself to start using Windows. (Chapter 2 provides more detailed information about working with these components.) Let's start with the Program Manager.

Introducing the Program Manager

When Windows starts, it automatically loads and runs the Program Manager shell unless you have customized Windows to run a different shell, such as the File Manager. As Figure 1.5 shows, the Program Manager contains a number of components.

Desktop. The *desktop* is the screen area where the Program Manager runs. When you are running multiple programs that have been minimized, you'll see the icons for these programs on the desktop.

Work area. The *work area* is defined by the border of an active application window, such as the Program Manager.

▼ *Figure 1.5. The Program Manager and Its Components*

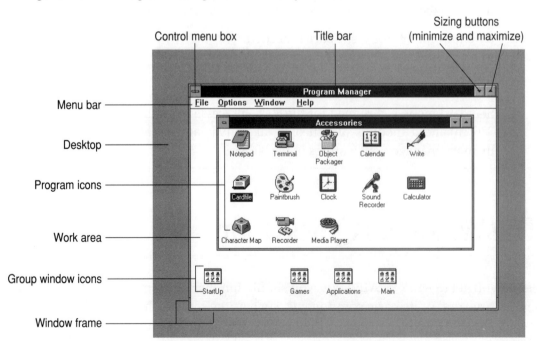

Window frame. The *frame* is the border (all four edges) of a window. A window can be moved and resized by selecting different edges.

Title bar. The *title bar* displays the window's name. This bar also indicates whether a window is active.

Menu bar. The *menu bar* is displayed directly below the title bar and contains the set of menu commands for an application window.

Control menu box. The *control menu box* is always displayed in the upper-left corner of a window or dialog box. When activated, it lists a set of commands for controlling the window or dialog box.

Sizing buttons. These two arrows appear in the upper-right corner of a window. When chosen, the down arrow button *minimizes* a window (reduces it to an icon), and the up arrow button *maximizes* a window (enlarges the window to fill the full screen).

Group window icons. Inside the Program Manager's window is a set of icons that represent groups of applications. When one of these groups is opened, a window is displayed to show the contents of the group. Each group contains a set of Windows applications and sometimes non-Windows applications.

Program icons. These icons represent the items (programs or applications) that are stored in a group window. If you double-click on a program icon, Windows will launch the application for you.

A Look at the Mouse

To make the best use of Windows, you should understand the function and the operation of the mouse. As you slide your mouse around your desk, notice that the standard *pointer*, a single arrow, moves in the same direction on the screen. To select an object or a menu, simply move the pointer (also called the *mouse cursor*) on top of the object. Next, press the left mouse button while the mouse cursor is over the object. The process of moving the mouse cursor to a position and pressing the left mouse button is called *clicking an object.* We will use this term throughout the book.

On certain occasions you may wish to move an object. To do so, position the mouse cursor on the object, press the left mouse button, and hold the button down while you move the mouse cursor to the new location. This action is called *dragging an object*, because you seem to drag it across the screen.

You can also choose commands by placing the mouse pointer over an icon, a button, or a menu item and then pressing the mouse button twice in quick succession. This technique is called *double-clicking the mouse.* In many situations, a double-click corresponds to the process of using the keyboard to highlight an item and pressing the Enter key.

The standard mouse cursor (arrow) isn't the only pointer you'll encounter while using Windows. In fact, eight types of pointers are provided, as shown in Figure 1.6. The pointer that displays on your screen will correspond to the task that you are currently performing. For example, if you are waiting for a task to finish, the hourglass pointer displays. In this respect, the pointer serves as a useful visual cue.

TIP

Windows is designed to work with both the mouse and the keyboard. If you don't have a mouse installed, you can still operate Windows (although the mouse is the preferred input device for selecting, choosing, and sizing operations). As we present different mouse techniques, we'll also show you how to use the keyboard alternatives.

▼ *Figure 1.6. Mouse Pointers*

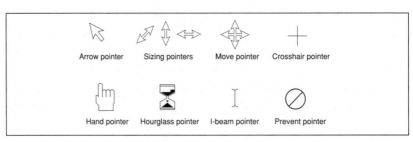

Windows

In general, a *window* is a rectangular section of the screen that represents a means of communication between you and a task. Every application that you run has its own corresponding window. As Figure 1.7 shows, an application window contains four main control components: a frame, a title bar, a Control menu, and a menu bar. The *frame* defines a window's edge, and the *title bar* displays the window's title. The *Control menu* provides a set of commands for manipulating a window. This menu is typically used to perform such tasks as changing the size of a window, moving the window, and closing the window. The *menu bar* provides the menus for controlling the application.

The window displayed in front or on top of other windows is called the *active window*. The active window represents the task currently responding to commands from the user. If you are using the default colors, the active window can also be recognized because its title bar is highlighted, while the title bars for other open windows are the same color as other parts of the window. To select a different window, simply move the pointer to a location anywhere in the window to be selected (excluding the size buttons

▼ *Figure 1.7. An Application Window*

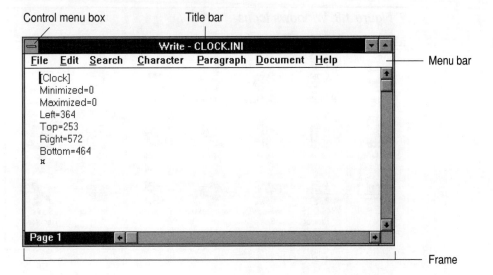

in the window's top-right corner), and press the left mouse button. When a new window is selected, the previously active window moves into the background and its title bar changes color.

In Chapter 2, we'll present a number of different techniques for processing windows using the keyboard and the mouse.

TIP

By default, an active window is displayed with a blue title bar. An inactive window is displayed with a white title bar.

Icons

An icon is a small picture that represents some task or operation. Figure 1.8 illustrates the icons associated with the standard Windows tools. All of these tasks or programs can be started by using the mouse to double-click on them. If you click the mouse button once, a pop-up menu appears that lets you alter the appearance and the location of the icon.

You can arrange your desktop by moving icons around so that they display in a different order. To move an icon, click on the icon and drag it to a new location.

▼ *Figure 1.8. Windows Icons*

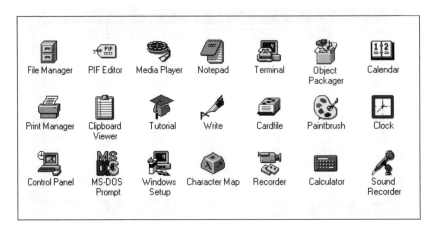

CHECK YOURSELF

1. What pointer indicates that a window can be moved?

2. Practice using the mouse to move an object, such as a window.

3. How can you tell which task is assigned to a window?

4. What is the difference between clicking the mouse and double-clicking the mouse?

ANSWERS

1. Windows displays the pointer that contains four arrows (up, down, left, and right).

2. To move an object, first select it by positioning the pointer on it and clicking and holding the left mouse button. Drag the mouse while the left button remains pressed.

3. The window's title indicates which task is assigned to the window. For example, when you run the File Manager application, the window that appears has the title shown in Figure 1.9.

▼ *Figure 1.9. The File Manager Window*

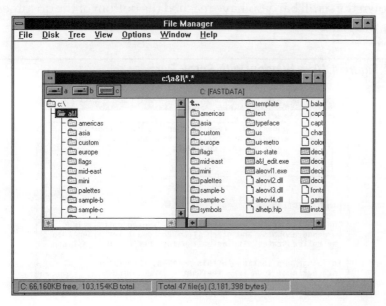

4. A single click selects (highlights) an item. A double-click chooses a command (performs an action).

Scroll Bars

Most Windows applications provide *scroll bars* that appear along the bottom and the right side of a window. If you position the pointer over one of the small *scroll arrows* that indicate either up and down or left and right, and then hold down the left mouse button, you can scroll around what appears to be a larger area behind the window. These scroll arrows act like buttons that can be pressed to move the information in the window. Scrolling allows you to view a document or a picture that is much larger than the screen or the window (Figure 1.10).

Scroll through a window and notice that a small box appears to slide along the scroll bar. This *scroll box* indicates the approximate location of the current window in the full document. For example, if the scroll box for the up/down scroll bar is positioned at the very top of the slot, you are viewing the top of the document or the picture. As you press the down arrow, the scroll box will slowly move down the scroll bar. When the box will not move any farther down the scroll bar, you have reached the bottom of the document or the picture.

▼ *Figure 1.10. A Window with Scroll Bars*

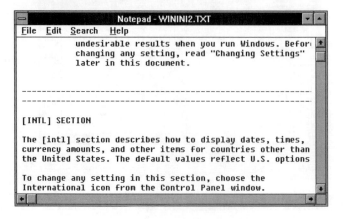

TIP

Chapter 2 presents a number of shortcut keys to help you scroll through windows by using the keyboard.

After you've used Windows a while, you will develop an intuitive feel for the size of a document by noting the speed at which the scroll box moves when you press the scroll arrows. The scroll box will move quickly through a short document (it may even appear to jump), and may barely move while you click on the scroll arrows for a very large document.

All of the information just presented about up/down scrolling also applies to a left/right scroll box and scroll arrows. (If a document or a picture is no wider than the width of the window, the left/right scroll bar will not appear.)

Title Bars

Figure 1.11 illustrates a typical screen with several windows. You can quickly tell the function or application of each window by reading the contents of the title bar. This aspect of Windows shows how the program provides a consistent and friendly interface to the user. If the title bars were not present, you would have to identify the application in each window by looking at the contents of the window. As we mentioned earlier, the title bar of the active window is highlighted.

The Menu Bar and Drop-Down Menus

The last major component of a typical window is the menu bar. As you can see in Figure 1.12, the *menu bar* provides several categories of actions that can be taken within that window. Move the pointer to one of the items on the menu bar, press the left mouse button, and watch the item expand into a *drop-down menu*. Choose one of the commands on this menu by moving the pointer to the item and clicking on it.

▼ *Figure 1.11. Desktop with Multiple Windows*

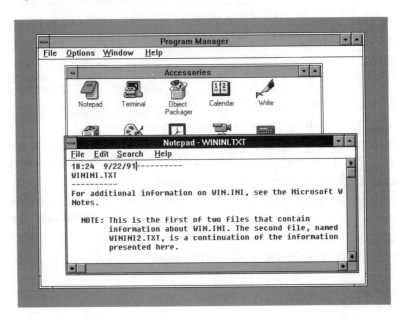

▼ *Figure 1.12. Menu Bar for a Typical Window*

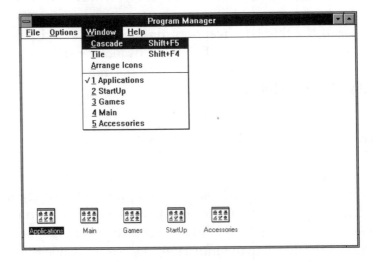

Drop-down menus can contain other information, in addition to commands. For example, you may see keystroke information along the right-hand side of the command, such as Alt+F4, which in this case means that the particular option can be chosen when you are in that window by pressing the Alt key and the F4 function key at the same time. This is called a *keyboard shortcut sequence*. Keyboard shortcuts can be invoked at any time when you're in the window, even if the drop-down menu isn't visible.

Sometimes you'll see commands displayed at half-intensity in a drop-down menu (Figure 1.13). These commands appear dimmed because they aren't currently available. (If you choose any of these disabled options, Windows ignores your request.) Notice that some commands in the drop-down menu have three dots (...), called an ellipsis. When you choose a command that contains an ellipsis, Windows displays a *dialog box*, which contains suboptions or asks for additional information required to complete the command. Dialog boxes are discussed next.

Dialog Boxes

Dialog boxes appear whenever you need to make multiple selections associated with an action. One frequently used dialog box is the one that appears each time you choose the Open command in the File menu for an application such as Notepad (See Figure 1.14). The dialog box requests information, in this case the name of a file, so that Windows can perform an operation.

▼ *Figure 1.13. A Menu with Disabled Items*

▼ *Figure 1.14. The Open Dialog Box*

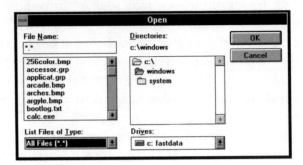

Dialog boxes are very useful because they provide many types of controls, such as buttons, text boxes, scroll menus, and check boxes that you can use to select options and enter information. You'll learn an assortment of techniques for working with dialog boxes in Chapter 2.

PRACTICE WHAT YOU'VE LEARNED

In this chapter you've learned why Windows was developed and how it provides a useful interface to DOS, the PC's operating system. You've also learned about the basic components that Windows provides, including icons, windows, menus, and dialog boxes.

1. Take a few minutes to review the hardware installed in your computer. If you don't know the type of PC you have (80286, 80386, 80486), consult your owner's manual. Make a list of your computer's components, such as a mouse, printer, video board, monitor, printer, and so on.

2. If you have a mouse installed but you don't know how to use it, practice by running one of the programs, such as a game, that comes with Windows. This will help you develop basic skills, such as moving the pointer, and selecting and dragging objects.

2

Building Your Windows Skills

The greatest advantage in using Windows rather than working directly with DOS is the ability for you to communicate easily with your computer. In fact, you'll find that you only need to learn a few basic techniques in order to perform a variety of operations, from opening windows to selecting dialog boxes. Before you start using the basic Windows features, such as the Program Manager and the File Manager, you should develop some basic skills for working with windows, menus, dialog boxes, and control menus.

This chapter will explain how to:

▲ **Use the Windows desktop**
▲ **Work with windows and menus**
▲ **Use scroll bars to view data in windows**
▲ **Work with icons**
▲ **Use control menus to move, resize, and close windows**

▲ Work with dialog boxes

▲ Use interface features such as check boxes, option buttons, text boxes, and list boxes

Starting with the Desktop

The world of Windows begins with the *desktop*—the place where all of the application windows, menus, icons, and dialog boxes are displayed. When Windows starts up, it displays the Program Manager application on the desktop. The Program Manager is the main application, but you can open up other applications on the desktop at any point during your Windows session.

TIP

Windows can also be set up so that the File Manager serves as the main shell and appears at startup instead of the Program Manager. Chapter 6 shows you how to set up Windows in this manner.

CHECK YOURSELF

Start at the DOS prompt. Make sure you are in the directory where Windows is installed.

1. Start Windows.

2. What are some of the components on the desktop?

3. Close the Program Manager window by pressing Alt+F4. What happens to the desktop?

ANSWERS

1. Type WIN and press the Enter key.

2. The major component is the Program Manager, which is represented as a window. You should also see a set of icons at the bottom of the Program Manager's window. These icons represent the group windows selected during Windows Setup, and include Applications, Main, Accessories, StartUp, and Games.

3. By closing this window, you are effectively shutting down Windows (the desktop).

Starting with the Desktop

What's in a Window

Windows divides the desktop into rectangular screen regions, called *windows*. These windows are used to run applications, such as Microsoft Excel and Word, and to display the documents used with these applications. These windows give you much more flexibility and power than the standard DOS screen, and they're easy to use.

Two kinds of windows are provided: *application windows* and *document windows*. An application window is used to run applications, and a document window displays the documents associated with an application. As Figure 2.1 shows, an application window consists of a title bar, a menu bar, a frame, a Control menu box, sizing buttons, and optional scroll bars. The Program Manager window introduced earlier is an example of an application window.

A document window doesn't require a menu bar because it only displays the data associated with an application. For example, if you use a word processor application to create a document named BUDGET, the text that you compose displays in a document window named Budget.

Figure 2.2 shows a sample document window created by the File Manager application. Notice that the menu bar is missing; the commands to control the application are provided with the File Manager's application menu.

▼ Figure 2.1. An Application Window

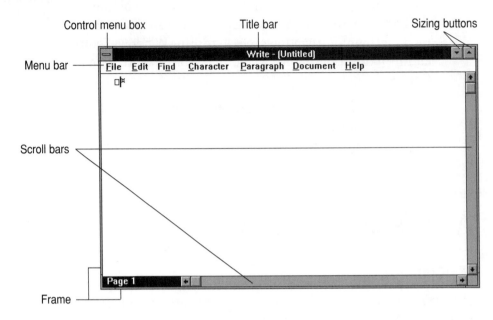

▼ Figure 2.2. A Sample Document Window

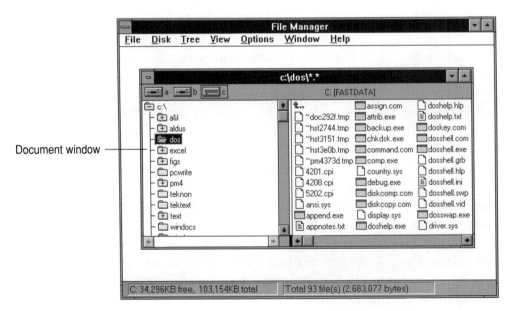

TIP

Many Windows applications allow you to have multiple document windows open for an application, although only one can be active at a time. In such a case, the commands provided by the application's menu bar only affect the active document window.

CHECK YOURSELF

1. Double-click on the Accessories icon from the Program Manager application window. What type of window is displayed?

2. Choose the Notepad icon displayed in the Accessories window. What menu items appear in the window's menu bar?

3. Click on the small rectangle in the upper-left corner of the Notepad window. What happens?

4. Click and hold the mouse button down at the lower-right corner of the Notepad window. What happens?

5. Click on any edge of the Notepad window frame and try to drag it off the screen. What happens?

6. When multiple windows are displayed, how can you tell which window is the active window?

ANSWERS

1. A document window; the window doesn't have a menu bar.

2. File, Edit, Search, and Help.

3. The Control menu for the window (application) appears. This menu provides the basic commands for processing the window.

4. The cursor changes to a diagonal double-headed arrow, indicating that you can size the window.

5. The window cannot be dragged off the edge of the screen.

6. The active window is displayed on top of all the other open windows and its title bar is highlighted.

Scrolling through Windows

If you're an experienced DOS user, you're probably well aware of the frustration of performing a command, such as DIR, and seeing your data pass by on the screen before you have a chance to read it. With Windows, you don't have to worry about this problem because many of the windows provide special scroll bars to help you view your data.

Figure 2.3 shows a window with labeled scroll bars. Notice that the window contains a horizontal and a vertical scroll bar. The scroll bar track contains a small box, called a *slider* or *scroll box*, which is used to quickly scroll through a window. To move the slider, position the pointer on it, hold the mouse button down, and drag the slider.

To scroll through the window vertically one line at a time or horizontally one character at a time, use the up, down, right, or left scroll arrows. Windows also supports other keyboard shortcuts for quick scrolling and cursor navigation. These key sequences are listed in Table 2.1.

TIP

Here's a quick method for scrolling through a window, one screen at a time: click the pointer directly above or below the slider. You can also use this technique to scroll the window horizontally.

▼ *Figure 2.3. A Window with Scroll Bars*

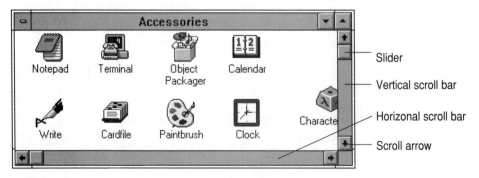

▼ *Table 2.1. Keys for Scrolling through Windows*

Key Combinations	Operation
PgUp	Scrolls up one window at a time
PgDn	Scrolls down one window at a time
Ctrl+PgUp	Moves text cursor to first line in window
Ctrl+PgDn	Moves text cursor to last line in window
Ctrl+Home	Scrolls to beginning of window
Ctrl+End	Scrolls to end of window

What's in a Window

CHECK YOURSELF

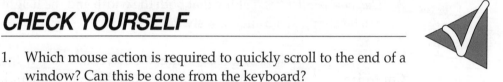

1. Which mouse action is required to quickly scroll to the end of a window? Can this be done from the keyboard?

2. Point to one of the scroll arrows and hold the mouse button down. What happens?

3. How can you tell when you have scrolled to the middle of a window? How can you tell when you have scrolled to the end of a window?

ANSWERS

1. Drag the vertical slider to the bottom of the window. Press Ctrl+End on the keyboard.

2. The window continues to scroll until you release the mouse button.

3. When you've scrolled to the midpoint of a window, the vertical slider is positioned in the middle of the window. The vertical slider moves to the bottom of the window when you have scrolled to the end.

Changing a Window's Size

What can you do if you need more space on your desktop to view multiple windows? This problem is easy to solve because you can change the size of a window by using the mouse or the keyboard.

Move the pointer to any edge of the window frame: top, bottom, left, or right. Depending on where you move the pointer, it will change to show how the window can be resized. In each case, the pointer will display with two heads. The following three pointer types appear in Figure 2.4:

▲ *Vertical pointer heads* show that the window's height can be changed.

▲ *Horizontal pointer heads* show that the window's width can be changed.

▲ *Diagonal pointer heads* show that both the width and the height can be changed simultaneously.

To change a window's size using the keyboard, open the Control menu (press Alt+Spacebar) and choose the Size command. Next press the arrow keys to change the size of the window. When you press an arrow key, a dashed outline shows you the actual size and location of the window while it is being resized. When you're done, press the Enter key to save the window's new size. You can cancel the sizing operation and return the window to its previous size by pressing the Esc key.

TIP

To change both the horizontal and the vertical dimensions of a window from the keyboard, choose the Size command and press two arrow keys simultaneously to select a corner. For example, press the up arrow and the right arrow to select the top-right corner of the window. Next, press the right arrow to stretch the window to the right, or the up arrow to stretch the window upward. Remember to press the Enter key when you finish resizing the window.

Maximizing and Restoring a Window

You can also quickly expand a window so that it takes up the full desktop. This technique, called *maximizing a window,* can be performed in one of two ways:

▼ *Figure 2.4. Pointer Types for Window Sizing*

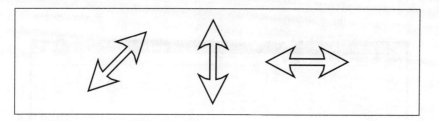

1. Click on the up arrow button (maximize button), as shown in Figure 2.5.

2. Choose the Maximize command from the window's Control menu.

In either case, first make sure the window you want to maximize is currently selected. (We'll explain how to select windows shortly.)

After a window has been enlarged, a new button appears in the upper-right portion of the window. As Figure 2.6 shows, this button is called the *restore* button. You can click on it to restore an enlarged window to its previous size. (You can also restore the window's previous size by choosing the Restore command from the Control menu.)

▼ *Figure 2.5. Using the Maximize Button*

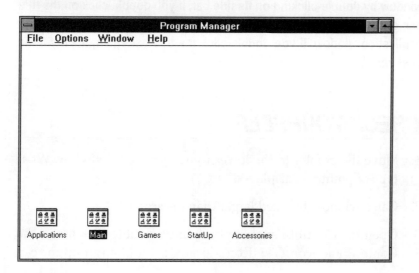

▼ *Figure 2.6. The Restore Button*

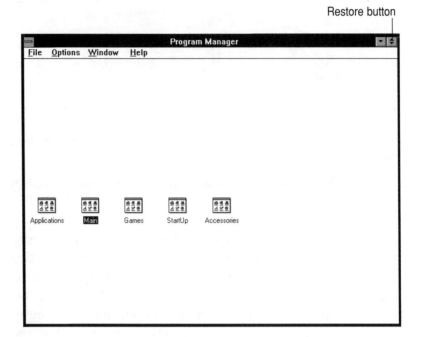

TIP

You can also maximize a window or restore a maximized application window by double-clicking on its title bar. If you double-click on the title bar of a document window, it will fill to the size of the controlling application window. If you double-click the title bar again, it will fill the desktop.

CHECK YOURSELF

1. Move the pointer to the lower-right corner of a window. What type of pointer is displayed?

2. Can a window be sized larger than the screen?

3. Open the Control Panel application by double-clicking on the Control Panel icon. (This icon is located in the Main group and can

be located by first double-clicking on the Main group icon.) What happens if you try to maximize the Control Panel window?

4. Press the Esc key while resizing a window. What happens?

ANSWERS

1. A diagonal pointer.

2. No.

3. The window cannot be maximized.

4. The resizing operation is canceled, and the window returns to its previous size.

What's in a Window

Moving a Window

No matter what application you run in Windows, you'll occasionally want to move application and document windows around on the desktop to easily view more than one window. Fortunately, moving a window is even easier than changing a window's size. To quickly move a window, drag the title bar at the top of the window until the window reaches the position you want, and release the mouse button.

From the keyboard, open the Control menu (press Alt+Spacebar) and choose the Move command. Move the window with the arrow keys in the same way you use these keys to change a window's size. When you finish moving the window, press the Enter key to anchor it.

CHECK YOURSELF

1. Open the Notepad application, choose the Move command from its Control menu, and move the window with one of the arrow keys. What happens if you try to use the window before pressing the Enter key?

2. Try to move a window off the screen. What happens?

ANSWERS

1. You cannot use the window until you press the Enter key or click the mouse button to anchor it. You can also cancel the operation by pressing the Esc key.

2. The window moves off the desktop.

Reducing a Window to an Icon

When windows are opened, they are always displayed with a title, a frame, optional scroll bars, and so on. Although you can open multiple windows and move them around to better arrange your desktop, you may find that the desktop becomes cluttered with windows. Of course, you can always close the windows not currently in use; however, if you plan to use them later, you'll have to open them again.

To help you manage the desktop, Windows lets you reduce a window to an icon. You can choose the icon later to open the window. The best part about this feature is that when an application window is converted to an icon, the application is still running in memory.

Follow these steps to reduce a window to an icon:

1. Select the window using the mouse or the keyboard.

2 Click on the down arrow button (minimize button) in the upper-right corner. (The minimize button is directly to the left of the maximize button. See Figure 2.7.) If you're using the keyboard, choose the Minimize command from the Control menu.

After a window is reduced to an icon, or minimized, the icon appears at the bottom of the screen. Use the mouse or the keyboard to select the icon and move it around. To restore the icon to a window, double-click the icon, or highlight it, press Alt+Spacebar to bring up the Control menu, and choose the Restore command.

▼ *Figure 2.7. The Minimize Button*

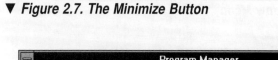

Minimize button

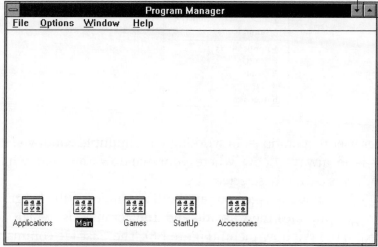

CHECK YOURSELF

Open the Notepad application, and enlarge the window to its full size by clicking the maximize button. Convert the window to an icon by clicking the minimize button.

ANSWER

You can minimize a window that has been enlarged in this way. Before minimizing a window, you don't need to restore the window to its previous size by clicking the Restore button or by choosing the Restore command from the window's Control menu.

Tips for Working with Multiple Windows

Occasionally, you'll want to display multiple windows on your desktop at the same time. After all, you can use multiple windows to transfer data between applications (such as Microsoft Word and Excel), edit multiple documents at the same time, and perform

▼ *Figure 2.8. The Window Menu*

other useful operations. In working with multiple windows, the key is to always know where your windows are and which window is currently selected.

To help you manage your application windows, the Program Manager provides the Cascade and Tile commands, which are listed in the Window menu (Figure 2.8). The Cascade command staggers open windows so that each window's title bar is visible (Figure 2.9). The Tile command displays the windows in a smaller size, arranged as if they were tiles (Figure 2.10). This format lets you view the contents of all open windows simultaneously.

▼ *Figure 2.9. Windows Displayed in the Cascade Format*

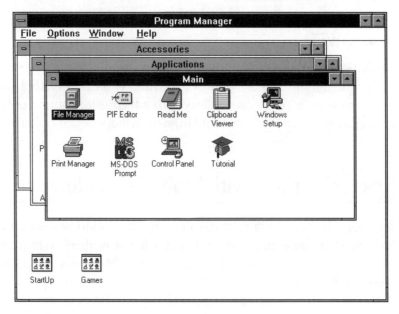

▼ *Figure 2.10. Windows Displayed in the Tile Format*

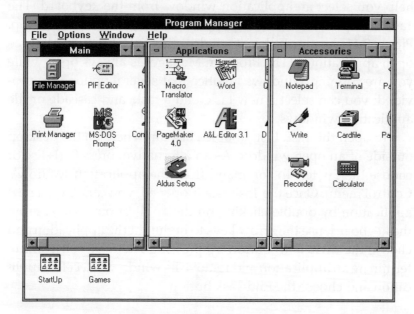

TIP

Windows applications that support multiple document windows typically provide a menu bar entry called Window so that you can select one of the open windows. If you choose this menu entry, you'll find a list of the currently opened windows, and the active window will have a check mark next to its name.

Selecting an Application Window

To use an application window that is open but is not the active window, you must first select its window by clicking on it with the mouse. However, this can be difficult if one or more windows are hidden behind the currently active window.

Windows provides a useful controller, called the *Task List*, to help you select an application window from the keyboard. The Task List presents all of the applications open on the desktop. Figure 2.11 shows a Task List window that lists the names of three open applications. (The Program Manager is always open while you are running Windows.) Notice that several options are provided: you can select a new task, end a task, and cascade or tile application windows.

To open the Task List, double-click anywhere on the desktop outside of an open window. As an alternative, press Ctrl+Esc or choose the Switch To command from the application window's Control menu. Once the Task List is opened, you can select a new application by double-clicking on the application's name. From the keyboard, use the arrow keys to highlight the application and choose the Switch To button by pressing Alt+S. If you want to terminate an application and remove its window, select the application and choose the End Task button.

Selecting Windows with the Keyboard

Using the mouse to select a window is relatively easy, as long as you know where the window is. Selecting a window from the keyboard is a little trickier: If the window you want is covered by another window, you need to use the Task List or cycle through the windows displayed on the desktop. You can cycle through open windows in two ways: to cycle through your application windows, press Alt+Esc. To cycle through document windows, press Ctrl+Tab.

▼ *Figure 2.11. The Task List*

TIP

To select applications that have been minimized to icons press Ctrl+Esc.

Closing a Window

When you're finished using an application window, you can close it by choosing the Exit command from the window's File menu. This action terminates the application and closes the opened files associated with that application. You can also close a window by choosing the Close command from the Control menu. In either case, a warning dialog box will appear (Figure 2.12) if you try to close a document window that you've changed but not yet saved.

TIP

As a shortcut, double-click on the window's Control menu box to close the window. You can also use the shortcut keys Ctrl+F4 to close a document window, and the keys Alt+F4 to close an application window.

CHECK YOURSELF

1. Move the mouse to the right edge of a window. Which cursor is displayed?

2. What is the difference between the Size and Move options provided in the Control menu for each application window?

▼ *Figure 2.12. A Warning Dialog Box*

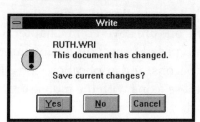

3. Open a few document windows. What happens when you press Ctrl+F6?

4. What happens when you double-click on the desktop outside of a window?

5. Which key do you press to cancel moving or resizing a window?

6. True or false? Document windows usually contain menus.

ANSWERS

1. The right and left double-headed arrow.

2. The Size option is used to resize a window, and the Move option is used to move a window.

3. The Windows program will cycle through the document windows.

4. The Task List is displayed.

5. The Esc key.

6. False.

Icons

If you've ever used a Macintosh computer, you already know how useful icons can be. Windows uses icons to represent many types of objects, such as programs, directories, document windows, disk drives, and so on. In this chapter, our discussion of icons corresponds to the icons found in the Program Manager. Other Windows applications, such as the File Manager, use other types of icons for other objects, including files, directories, and disk drives. The File Manager icons are covered in Chapter 6.

The two main types of icons you'll encounter in the Program Manager are group icons, and application icons (Figure 2.13). You can select any of these icons with the mouse or the keyboard and move them around.

▼ *Figure 2.13. Two Types of Icons*

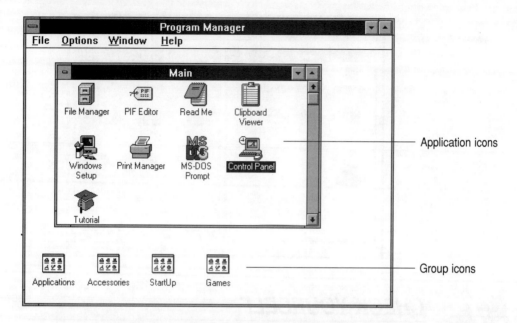

Application icons

Group icons

Application icons are used by the Program Manager to represent Windows applications, such as Paintbrush, PIF Editor, and Clock. They are stored in group windows. They can be moved between group windows, but they can't be moved out of the Program Manager window. Figure 2.14 shows some of the application icons provided with Windows.

After an application has been started, it can be reduced to a minimized application icon. This type of icon is displayed on the desktop outside of Program Manager's window borders. Windows doesn't allow you to put this type of icon into another window. As you've seen, minimized application icons are created by minimizing a window.

Group icons represent the documents or groups associated with an application. They always appear at the bottom of the application window that they're assigned to. For example, when using the Program Manager, you'll find a set of group icons at the bottom of the window with names such as Main, Applications, StartUp, and so on. When you choose a group icon, a group (document) window displays.

▼ *Figure 2.14. Windows Application Icons*

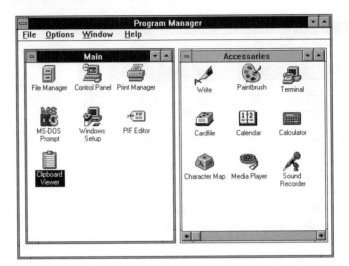

CHECK YOURSELF

1. Try to drag a running application icon that has been minimized, such as the Calendar, inside a window. What happens? What happens if you move the window?

2. What type of icon is the Terminal?

ANSWERS

1. The application icon moves into the window, but it still resides on the desktop. If you move the window, the icon will not move with it.

2. An application icon.

Selecting and Moving Icons

There's a subtle but important difference between selecting an icon and choosing it. When you select a group icon or a minimized application icon, it becomes highlighted and you can move it, activate it, or access its Control menu. (An application icon does not have a Control menu unless it has been minimized.) When you choose an icon, on the other hand, you open the application, and the application window appears.

Icons

To select an icon using the mouse, click on the icon. To use the keyboard, press Alt+Esc to select a minimized application icon, or press Ctrl+Tab to select a group icon. (Each time you press Alt+Esc or Ctrl+Tab, a different minimized application icon or group icon is selected.)

Once you select an icon, you can move it by dragging it with the mouse. If you don't have a mouse, access the icon's Control menu by highlighting the icon and pressing Alt+Spacebar for a minimized application icon or Alt+Hyphen (-) for a document icon. After the Control menu appears, choose the Move command and position the icon using the arrow keys. (This technique is the same one you used to move a window.)

TIP

To neatly arrange the icons on the desktop, open the Task List by double-clicking anywhere on the desktop or pressing Ctrl+Esc. Choose the Arrange Icons button, as shown in Figure 2.15.

▼ *Figure 2.15. Using the Task List Dialog Box*

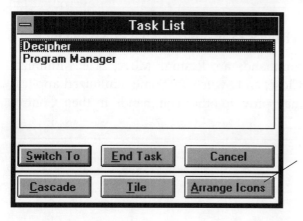

Use this button to neatly organize your icons.

Activating an Icon

The easiest way to choose an icon is to double-click it. The pointer changes to an hourglass while the application is loading. If you're using the keyboard, select the icon and press the Enter key.

TIP

With Windows 3.1, you can now assign a shortcut key to a program icon so that the application represented by the icon can be launched when the shortcut key is pressed. Follow these steps to assign a shortcut key:

1. Select the Program Manager as the active application.
2. Select (highlight) the icon you want to assign a shortcut key.
3. Choose the Properties command from the File menu.
4. Enter the shortcut key in the Shortcut Key text field.
5. Click the OK button or press Enter

CHECK YOURSELF

1. Drag an icon with the mouse. How does the pointer change?

2. Select an application icon that has been minimized, such as Write, and press Alt+Spacebar to display the icon's Control menu. Which commands are provided with the menu?

ANSWERS

1. The pointer changes to an outline of the icon being moved.

2. The basic commands are Restore, Move, Size, Minimize, Maximize, Close, and Switch To. Some minimized application icons may provide other commands in their Control menus.

Accessing Menus

Each application window has its own set of menus, which are grouped in a *menu bar system*. Figure 2.16 shows the two key components of a menu bar system: a menu bar and a drop-down menu associated with each menu bar entry.

The menu bar is used to open a specific menu, and the drop-down menu lists the commands associated with a menu bar entry. Using a mouse, you open a drop-down menu by clicking on a menu bar entry. For example, to open the File menu in the Program Manager you click on the File item. You don't have to hold the mouse button down to keep the menu open. When the menu is open, choose a command by clicking the pointer on the command's name.

To open a menu from the keyboard, press Alt or F10 to select the menu bar. Next, use the arrow keys to highlight the menu entry, and press the Enter key or the Down arrow to display the menu.

Here are some tips for using menus and choosing commands:

▲ To close a menu and return to the current application, press Alt or F10.

▲ To close a menu but remain on the menu bar, press the Esc key.

▲ Menu commands with underlined letters can be chosen by pressing the Alt key and the key for the underlined letter.

▲ Some menu commands provide keyboard shortcuts, which allow you to choose the commands without opening the menu.

▼ *Figure 2.16. A Menu System*

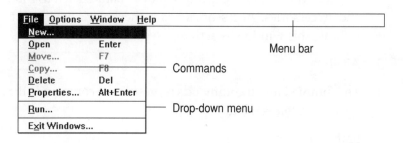

These shortcuts will be listed to the right of the command names in the menu.

▲ Sometimes a menu command name will change because of the context in which a menu is being used. The Undo command used in applications such as Word for Windows is one such example.

CHECK YOURSELF

1. Open the Options menu within the Program Manager window. Which commands does it provide?

2. Choose the Accessories icon to open the Accessories group window. Now open the Window menu to see the commands available. Which option has a checkmark?

3. Which two keys do you press to open the Program Manager's File menu?

4. Why are some menu commands dimmed?

5. Which shortcut key do you press to choose the Cascade command in the Program Manager's Window menu?

ANSWERS

1. To open the Options menu, click on the Options item, or press Alt+O. The commands listed are Auto Arrange, Minimize on Use, and Save Settings on Exit.

2. To choose the Accessories icon, double-click on it. The commands are Cascade, Tile, and Arrange Icons. Below the dividing line, you'll find the group window names such as Main and Accessories. Accessories has a checkmark next to it to indicate this window is active.

3. Alt+F.

4. The dimmed menu commands represent the commands that are currently disabled.

5. Shift+F5.

▼ *Figure 2.17. The Move Program Item Dialog Box*

```
┌─────────────────────────────────────────────┐
│ ▬        Move Program Item                   │
├─────────────────────────────────────────────┤
│ Move Program Item:    DOS Prompt   ┌───────┐ │
│ From Program Group:   Main         │   OK  │ │
│                                    └───────┘ │
│ To Group:                          ┌───────┐ │
│ ┌─────────────────────────────┬──┐ │ Cancel│ │
│ │Accessories                  │ ±│ └───────┘ │
│ └─────────────────────────────┴──┘ ┌───────┐ │
│                                    │  Help │ │
│                                    └───────┘ │
└─────────────────────────────────────────────┘
```

Working with Special Menu Commands

Usually, when you choose a menu item, Windows performs a command. Some menu items are displayed differently because they perform functions other than simply activating a command. For example, you've already seen that a dimmed item represents a command that is currently unavailable. The other three types of menu items include a menu item with an ellipsis (…), a menu item with a checkmark, and a menu item with a right-pointing triangle.

A menu item with an ellipsis indicates that a dialog box appears when the command is chosen. Figure 2.17 shows the dialog box that appears when the Move command is chosen from the Program Manager's File menu. The dialog box appears because Windows needs more information from the user in order to carry out the command.

When a checkmark appears next to a menu item, as shown in Figure 2.18, the command is active. You'll see this feature whenever you work with menus containing commands with on and off settings, such as the Paragraph menu provided with the Write application. For example, when the Left command in the Paragraph menu has a checkmark, the left alignment style is currently selected.

▼ *Figure 2.18. A Menu Showing a Selected Command*

When a triangle appears next to a command, the command represents a *cascading* menu. When you choose that command, a second level of menus is displayed.

CHECK YOURSELF

1. Open the Program Manager's File menu. Which menu items have an ellipsis?

2. If a menu command is dimmed, how can you choose it?

3. Which Program Manager menus provides checkmark options?

ANSWERS

1. To open the Program Manager's File menu, click on the File item in the menu bar, or press Alt+F. These menu items have an ellipsis:

   New, Move, Copy, Properties, Run, Exit Windows

2. You need to perform another command (such as open a file) or select something (such as mark a paragraph) to the use command. For example, if you are using an application such as Write, and you want to choose the Save As command from the File menu, you must first open a file using the Open command before you can choose the Save As command.

3. The Window and Options menus.

Using the Control Menu

The Control menu is represented by the small rectangle in each application and document window. This menu is common to all applications, and it always contains the first six commands listed in Table 2.2.

▼ *Table 2.2. The Control Menu Commands*

Using the Control Menu

Command	Description
Restore	Restores the current window to its previous size after it has been enlarged or reduced.
Move	Allows you to move a window by using the arrow keys.
Size	Allows you to change the size of a window by using the arrow keys.
Minimize	Allows you to convert a window to an icon.
Maximize	Allows you to enlarge a window to its maximum size.
Close	Closes a window.
Switch To	Allows you to select a different application from the Task List (application window only).
Next	Allows you to switch among document windows and icons (document window only).

As you've seen, the easiest way to access the Control menu for a window is to click on the Control menu box icon. Remember to click only once—if you double-click, you'll close the window.

If you're using the keyboard, select the application window and press Alt+Spacebar. After the menu opens, choose commands by highlighting them with the Up and Down arrow keys and then pressing the Enter key. To close the menu, press the Alt key.

CHECK YOURSELF

Run Notepad and then minimize it to an icon.

1. Select the Notepad application icon.

2. Open Notepad's Control menu. What commands are available?

3. Which command in the Control menu displays a dialog box when selected?

4. Which keyboard shortcut chooses the Close command in the Control menu?

ANSWERS

1. Click once on the Notepad icon. (Don't double-click, or you'll start the application.)

2. The commands listed in the Control menu are Restore, Move, Size, Minimize, Maximize, Close, and Switch To.

3. Switch To.

4. Alt+F4.

Accessing the Control Menu for Icons and Dialogs

Windows provides a Control menu for minimized application icons and dialog boxes, as well as for windows. As Figure 2.19 shows, the Control menu for dialog boxes is typically much shorter. You can easily open the Control menu for either type of object by using the procedure we just discussed for accessing a window's Control menu. In the case of an icon, simply click the mouse on the icon once, or highlight the icon with the keyboard and press Alt+Spacebar. For a dialog box, click the Control menu box displayed in the upper-left corner, or press Alt+Spacebar.

Mastering Dialog Boxes

In addition to windows and menus, the other key ingredients to the Windows environment are dialog boxes. Windows uses dialog boxes to request and provide important information.

Dialog boxes are typically displayed as warning messages or linked with menu commands. For example, if you try to quit a Windows application without saving the work you have been doing, a special dialog box asks if you want to save the changes you made to documents during your session. As an example of a menu option dialog, when you choose the Open command from the Notepad

▼ *Figure 2.19. The Control Menu for a Dialog Box*

application's File menu, a dialog box asks you to enter the directory and the filename for the file you wish to open (Figure 2.20).

The techniques for controlling dialog boxes are easy to learn because dialog boxes and windows share some common features. For example, all dialog boxes provide Control menus to help you close and move them.

CHECK YOURSELF

1. Choose the Move command from the Program Manager's File menu. What is the name of the dialog box that is displayed?

2. Click on the title bar of the dialog box and drag the mouse. What happens?

3. While the dialog box is open, press the Tab key. What happens?

4. Can you change the size of a dialog box?

5. Can you minimize a dialog box?

▼ *Figure 2.20. The Open Dialog Box*

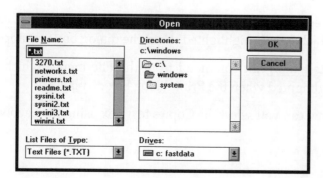

ANSWERS

1. Move Program Item.

2. The dialog box moves.

3. One of the items in the dialog box is selected.

4. No.

5. No.

Selecting Dialog Options

Before we explore the different types of dialog boxes and the dialog box options, let's look at how you select the items in a dialog box.

Only one item in a dialog box, whether it's a text box, a button, or a menu list, can be active at a time. This item will either be highlighted, outlined with a dashed line, or will contain a blinking cursor. Before you can work with an item, you must select it. If you're using a mouse, simply click on the item. With the keyboard, either press the Tab key to move the selection in a forward direction, or press Shift+Tab to move the selection backwards. You can also select an item that has an underline by pressing the Alt key and the key for the letter. For example, in the Open dialog box shown in Figure 2.20, press Alt+D to select the Directories list menu.

CHECK YOURSELF

1. Open the Write application.

2. Select the Open command from the Write application's File menu. Which item is highlighted when the dialog box first appears?

3. Select the Print command from the File menu. Which item is highlighted when the Print dialog box displays?

4. How can you select the Copies text box using the keyboard?

ANSWERS

1. Double-click on the Write icon. (This icon is stored in the Accessories group.)

2. The File Name text box.

3. The All button in the Print Range group.

4. Press Alt+C.

Using Warning Dialog Boxes

The warning dialog boxes are the easiest to use because they provide only a few options. This dialog box contains two types of selection items: command buttons and a check box.

CHECK YOURSELF

In addition to the Exit Windows dialog box, name three other warning dialog boxes that Windows uses?

ANSWER

The Notepad warning dialog box, the Format Complete dialog box, and the Error Deleting File dialog box are a few examples. (The last two are associated with the File Manager application.)

Command Buttons

Command buttons carry out an operation. As you work more with dialog boxes, you'll discover three types of command buttons. The first type, such as the OK button, simply performs an action without requiring any additional information. The second type of command button, which is marked with an ellipsis (...), opens another dialog box. Finally, command buttons marked with the symbols >> expand the current dialog box by presenting more information that doesn't fit in the dialog box.

TIP

When a command button is dimmed, you can't choose it.

Check Boxes

Check boxes are different from command buttons because they don't actually initiate an operation. The check box options in a dialog box are grouped by category. Figure 2.21 shows the Terminal Preferences dialog box displayed by the Terminal application. Notice the two groups of check boxes: Terminal Modes and CR -> CR/LF. In each group, you can select as many of the check boxes as you want. When an item is selected, an X appears in the box. If an item is dimmed, you can't select it.

To select a check box with the mouse, click on the check box. To use the keyboard, highlight the item by pressing the Tab key. The highlighted item is enclosed by a dashed box. To place or remove a check mark, press the Spacebar.

▼ *Figure 2.21. The Terminal Preferences Dialog Box*

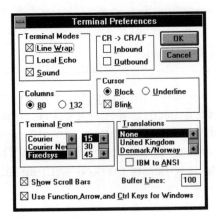

TIP

You can select check box items that contain an underlined letter by pressing the Alt key and the key for the underlined letter. For example, you can choose the Left Margin option in Figure 2.22 by pressing Alt+L.

CHECK YOURSELF

1. Start the File Manager application by double-clicking on the File Manager icon in the Main group window. Next, choose the Properties command in the File menu. What check boxes are provided?

2. Which keyboard shortcut selects the Hidden check box?

3. True or false? Check boxes can be represented by either a square or a circle.

ANSWERS

1. Read Only, Archive, Hidden, and System.

2. Alt+I.

3. False. Check boxes are represented with a square, and option buttons are represented by a circle.

▼ *Figure 2.22. The Page Layout Dialog Box*

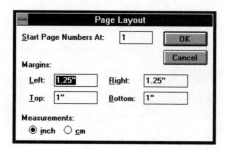

Using Menu Option Dialog Boxes

Figure 2.23 shows a typical menu option dialog box with its components labeled. Notice that these dialogs are much more complex than warning dialog boxes. In addition to selection buttons and check boxes, they contain other selectable objects, such as option buttons, list boxes, text boxes, and menu boxes.

An *option button* is similar to a check box but only one option button in a group can be selected. A *list box* provides you with a list of choices that you select, using the mouse or the keyboard. A *text box* is a single-line rectangular box where you enter information, such as a filename. A *menu box* is a single-line rectangular box that displays a menu. It's also called a *drop-down list box*.

 ## *CHECK YOURSELF*

1. Which menu commands in the Program Manager's File menu produce menu option dialog boxes?

2. Open the Properties dialog box. (Select the Properties command.) Which text boxes do you see?

3. Which dialog box accessible from the Program Manager provides a list box?

4. True or false? The Run Minimized option in the Properties dialog box is an option button.

ANSWERS

1. New, Move, Copy, Properties, and Run.

2. Description, Command Line, Working Directory, and Short-cut Key.

3. The Task List.

4. False; it's a check box.

▼ *Figure 2.23. A Menu Option Dialog Box*

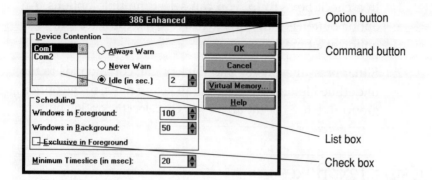

Option Buttons

Option buttons differ from check boxes because you can select only one of the options in the set. Figure 2.24 shows a dialog box with option buttons. Notice that only one option in the group can be selected, and the selected option contains a black dot.

CHECK YOURSELF

1. What's the difference between a check box and an option button?

2. How can you select an option button from the keyboard?

▼ *Figure 2.24. A Dialog Box with Option Buttons*

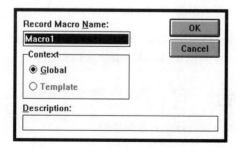

ANSWERS

1. In a check box group, you can select multiple options. An option button is mutually exclusive—you can select only one option at a time.

2. Either press the Alt key and the key that corresponds to the underlined letter, or press the Tab key to move to the option group and then use the arrow keys to select the option button.

Using Text Boxes

Text boxes provide an interactive prompt so that you can enter text, such as a filename or a date (see Figure 2.25). The text that you type is used by the dialog box to perform its operation.

You enter text into a text box in the same way you enter text into a window. You can use any of the arrow keys as well as the Delete and Insert keys. You can also use the mouse to select text. To select the entire text block, click and drag the mouse inside it. To select text from the keyboard, hold down the Shift key and press the right or left arrow keys to select the region of text.

When text is highlighted in a text box, you can delete the text by pressing the Delete key or the Backspace key.

CHECK YOURSELF

1. Choose the Run command from the Program Manager's File menu. Enter the text *Write* in the Command Line text box, and double-click the mouse inside the box. What happens?

2. Open a dialog box that has a text box containing text. How is the text formatted when the dialog box opens?

ANSWERS

1. The entire text box is selected.

2. The text is highlighted.

▼ *Figure 2.25. A Dialog Box with a Text Box*

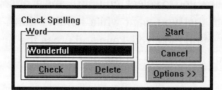

Using List Boxes

A list box functions like a menu because it provides the names of options that can be scrolled and selected using the mouse. Figure 2.26 shows the Open dialog box associated with the Write application's File menu. Although this dialog box provides only scrollable list boxes, some dialog boxes provide both scrollable and non-scrollable list boxes. The scrollable list boxes can be operated using the same techniques that you use to scroll through windows.

To choose an item in a list, either double-click on the item or highlight it by clicking once and then choose the appropriate command button. For example, to open a file with the Open dialog box, click on the desired filename in the Files list, and then click the OK button. Remember that if the item you want is not listed, click the scroll arrows or move the arrow keys to locate the item.

To select an item from the keyboard, move the arrow keys or press the key for the first letter of the item. Select the highlighted item by pressing the Enter key.

▼ *Figure 2.26. The Open Dialog Box*

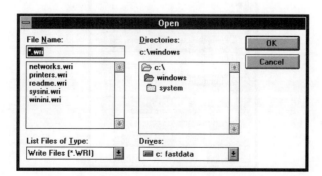

TIP

Some list boxes allow you to select multiple items at once. To do so, either click on each item that you want while holding down the Ctrl key, or highlight the item using the arrow keys and press the Spacebar. You can also deselect items by clicking on them or pressing the Spacebar.

Drop-Down List Boxes

In addition to the standard list boxes, some dialog boxes provide a variation called a drop-down list box. (Figure 2.27 shows an example.) To choose the drop-down list box, click the arrow at the right of the box. You can then drag the scroll box to select an item.

To open a drop-down list box from the keyboard, press Alt+Down arrow. Use the up and down arrow keys to highlight the item and press the Enter key.

Closing Dialogs

There are two basic methods for closing a dialog box. If you don't want to carry out the options you've selected, select the Cancel button. To accept the options and carry out the command, select the OK button.

▼ *Figure 2.27. A Dialog Box with a Drop-Down List Box*

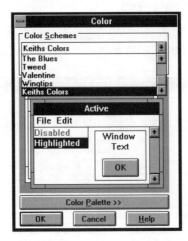

QUICK TASK SUMMARY

Task	Procedure
Start Windows	Use the command WIN at the DOS prompt
Scroll through a window	Use the scroll sliders; or Press PageUp, PageDn, etc.
Resize a window	Click on a window border and drag mouse; or Use Size command in Control menu
Move a window	Click and drag window's title bar; or Use Move command in Control menu
Maximize a window	Click window's maximize button; or Use Maximize command in Control menu
Minimize a window	Click window's minimize button; or Use Minimize command in Control menu
Select application windows	Press Alt+Esc
Select document windows	Press Ctrl+Tab
Display the Task List	Double-click on desktop; or Press Ctrl+Esc
Close a window	Press Ctrl+F4—document; or Press Alt+F4—application
Select an icon	Click once on the icon; or Press Ctrl+Tab—document; or Press Alt+Esc—application
Select the menu bar	Press Alt or F10
Open a menu	Click on menu item; or Press Alt and underlined letter for menu
Open a Control menu	Click on Control menu box; or Press Alt+Spacebar
Open icon's Control menu	Click once on icon; or Select and press Alt+Spacebar
Cancel dialog box	Click Cancel button; or Press Esc
Arrange icons	Use Arrange Icons (Window menu)
Exit Windows	Choose Exit Windows (File menu); or Double-click on Program Manager's Control menu box

PRACTICE WHAT YOU'VE LEARNED

In this chapter you've learned about all of the major interface components of Windows, including windows, icons, menus, and dialog boxes. You'll find yourself returning to this chapter whenever you need to brush up on the basic techniques for using Windows.

1. Start Windows by executing the following command at the DOS prompt:

    WIN

2. Double-click on the Accessories icon.

3. Click on the window's title bar, hold the mouse button down, and drag the window to the right.

4. Release the mouse button and double-click on the icon.

5. Click on the Card item in the menu bar.

6. Choose the Autodial command in the Card menu.

7. Click on the Control menu box in the upper-left corner of the dialog box.

8. Press the Alt key.

9. Click on the Use Prefix check box.

10. Choose the Setup button and then click on the Pulse option button in the Dial Type group.

11. Click the Cancel button.

12. Minimize the application by selecting the down arrow icon in the upper-right corner.

13. Double-click on the icon.

14. Exit by selecting the Exit command from the File menu.

15. Point at the left border of the Accessories window.

16. Drag the border to the right.

17. While holding down the mouse button, press the Esc key.

18.   Press Ctrl+F4.

19.   Select the Exit Windows command in the Program Manager's
File menu.

20.   Select Cancel.

ANSWERS

1.   Windows loads and you see the Program Manager and Main
windows.

2.   The Accessories window opens and a set of application icons
appears.

3.   The window moves to the right.

4.   The application loads and displays a window with the title
bar - (Untitled).

5.   The Card menu displays.

6.   The Autodial dialog box displays.

7.   The Control menu for the dialog box displays.

8.   The Control menu disappears.

9.   An *X* appears in the check box.

10.   The Tone option button is deselected, and a black dot appears in the Pulse option button. Recall that only one option
button at a time can be selected in a group.

11.   The dialog box disappears, and the options you selected
aren't saved.

12.   The application turns into an icon, and control returns to the
Program Manager.

13.   The application restarts.

14.   Cardfile terminates; control returns to the Program Manager.

15.   The mouse cursor changes to a two-headed arrow.

16.   The size of the window changes.

17. The window returns to its previous size.

18. The Accessories window closes.

19. The Exit Windows dialog box is displayed.

20. Control returns to the Program Manager.

3

The Program Manager at Work

Now that you've successfully installed Windows and learned the basic skills for controlling the program, you're ready to put it to work. When Windows starts, the first application that opens is the Program Manager. You can think of the Program Manager as your portal into and out of the Windows environment.

This chapter explores what the Program Manager can do for you and covers these major topics:

▲ **The main components of the Program Manager**

▲ **How to use the basic commands provided with the Program Manager**

▲ **Techniques for using the keyboard**

▲ **How to use the Program Manager's Control menu**

▲ **How to launch applications**

▲ **How to create and manage group windows**

▲ How to create and manage program icons
▲ How to move and copy program icons from one group window to another

The Program Manager—
A Close Look

The Program Manager is the heart of the Windows environment. It always appears after you start Windows unless you set up Windows differently, and remains in control until you exit the program. The Program Manager allows you to run your applications and to arrange them into units called *groups*.

Figure 3.1 illustrates how a typical Program Manager window looks. Notice that the window contains the title bar with the text *Program Manager*, and a menu bar. In addition, several icons appear in the window, and each of them corresponds to a group of programs.

▼ *Figure 3.1. The Program Manager Window*

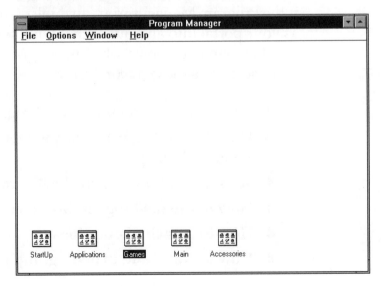

To open a group and view the applications that are stored in the group, double-click on the icon for that group or select the group to highlight it and choose the Open command from the File menu. When you start Windows, you'll see icons for Main, Accessories, StartUp, and Games. You may also see icons for Applications if programs were present on your disk when Windows was installed.

The Program Manager— A Close Look

TIP

To open a program group from the keyboard, press Ctrl+F6 repeatedly until the desired program group is highlighted. Then press Enter.

When you open a group icon, a new window appears. This window, called a *group window,* contains the program item icons for that group. For example, if you open the Accessories group, a new group window titled Accessories appears. In this window, you'll see program icons for the applications Write, Paintbrush, Terminal, Notepad, Recorder, Cardfile, Calendar, Calculator, Clock, Object Packager, Media Player, Sound Recorder, and Character Map. (Figure 3.2). Later in this chapter, we'll discuss a number of techniques for selecting program icons and launching applications.

In the top-left corner of the Accessories window (and all other windows), notice a small square with a dash inside it; recall that this is the Control menu box for the window. Click on it once to see the Control menu (Figure 3.3). Move the mouse cursor to the line that contains Close, and click the left mouse button once. The

▼ *Figure 3.2. The Accessories Group Window*

▼ *Figure 3.3. Opening the Control Menu*

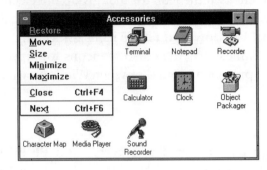

Accessories window disappears and you return to the Program Manager window.

TIP

For a faster way to close a window, move the pointer to the Control menu box and double-click on it. You can also close the window by pressing Ctrl+F4.

CHECK YOURSELF

1. Open the Main group window (if it's not currently opened). What do you see?

2. Open the Control Panel application. What happens?

3. Minimize the Control Panel application.

4. Restore the Control Panel application. What happens?

5. Close the Control Panel. What happens?

6. How can you tell the difference between a program item icon and a group window icon?

ANSWERS

1. Double-click on the Main group window icon and a window appears with the title bar Main. This group window contains the main applications that Windows 3.1 provides.

2. Double-click on the Control Panel icon. The application appears in its own window.

3. Click on the down arrow in the upper-right corner. An icon labeled Control Panel displays in the bottom-left corner of the desktop.

4. Double-click on the icon. The Control Panel starts again.

5. Double-click on the Control Panel's Control menu box. Control returns to the Program Manager.

6. Group icons are located at the lower edge of the Program Manager. They always look like a window with items inside. A program item icon resides inside a group window, and typically depicts the type of function that the application performs.

Working with the Menu System

The three main menus provided with the Program Manager—File, Options, and Window—are always available to help you control your group windows and the program items stored in the group windows. With a few commands, you can perform a variety of operations.

File menu. This menu provides access to the commands New, Open, Move, Copy, Delete, Properties, Run, and Exit Windows. All of these options (except the last one) are provided to help you manage group windows and program items. You can perform several major operations from this menu, including:

New...	
Open	Enter
Move...	F7
Copy...	F8
Delete	Del
Properties...	Alt+Enter
Run...	
Exit Windows...	

▲ Create and delete groups (New and Delete)

▲ Change the contents of a group (Copy and Move)

▲ Run an application (Run)

▲ Add a new program item to a group window (New)

▲ Delete a program item from a group (Delete)

▲ Select an icon for a program item (Properties)

▲ Assign a shortcut key to an application (Properties)

▲ Set the working directory for an application (Properties)

▲ Exit Windows (Exit)

Options menu. This menu provides three options—Auto Arrange, Minimize on Use, and Save Settings on Exit—to help you control how the Program Manager operates. You can toggle any of these options between their active and inactive states by clicking on them with the mouse, or by highlighting the option and pressing Enter. A checkmark is displayed next to an option that is active.

TIP

By default, Save Settings on Exit is active so that Windows will save its settings when you end your Windows session. You should keep this option active unless you want to exit Windows without saving your current settings.

Window menu. This window provides access to the Program Manager's group windows. The Window menu also provides these three commands:

▲ Cascade

▲ Tile

▲ Arrange Icons

to help you manage your work area.

CHECK YOURSELF

1. True or false? The Program Manager window is an application window.

2. Which window appears in the Program Manager when Windows first starts?

3. Choose the Minimize command in the Program Manager's Control menu. What happens?

4. Is a group window considered to be an application window or a document window?

5. How are group windows different from other windows?

ANSWERS

1. True; however, keep in mind that the Program Manager serves as a shell to manage group windows, such as Main, Accessories, and Applications.

2. Main.

3. Windows converts the application to an icon, and places it at the bottom of the desktop.

4. Document window.

5. Group windows organize application icons, instead of simply displaying data. The applications stored in group windows can be launched from the Program Manager.

Working with the Keyboard

Windows allows you to perform all Program Manager-related commands, such as creating and deleting group windows, moving and copying program items between groups, and starting applications, from the keyboard.

You can open menus in several ways. Press the Alt key to highlight the File keyword on the menu bar. Now press the right arrow key to highlight the Options keyword. Press the left arrow key to move the highlight in the opposite direction. When a keyword is highlighted, press the Enter key to display its menu.

A second way to open a menu is to press Alt+Spacebar. The Control menu opens, and you can use the left and right arrow keys to select other menus. (These menus automatically open when their keyword is highlighted.)

A third method for opening a menu is to press the Alt key and the key for the underlined letter in the keyword. For example, press the Alt key and the W key at the same time to open the Window menu.

After a menu appears, you can select a command by scrolling the highlighted bar up and down, using the up and down arrow keys. When the desired option or command is highlighted, press Enter to choose it. A second way to choose an option is to use the underlined shortcut letter or number. For example, the Window menu in Figure 3.4 shows numbers in front of each group name. In this case, press the number 1 to open the Accessories group.

TIP

To close a menu, press the Alt key. (This is equivalent to moving the pointer away from the menu keywords and pressing the left mouse button.)

CHECK YOURSELF

1. Which keys select the Games group from the Program Manager's Window menu?

2. What happens if you press Shift+F4?

3. Press the Enter key inside the Program Manager Window. What happens?

4. True or false? Pressing Alt+A brings up information about the Program Manager.

▼ *Figure 3.4. Using the Window Menu*

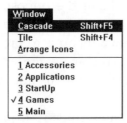

ANSWERS

1. Alt+W and then the number 4. (The number may vary depending on how many groups you have.)

2. Your windows display in a tile format.

3. The group that is highlighted opens.

4. False. The correct sequence is Alt+H followed by the A key.

Using the Control Menu

Earlier in this chapter, we mentioned the function of the Program Manager's Control menu. Now we'll look at the commands in this menu in more detail.

The Restore command is used to resize a window to its normal size. If the window is an icon, the Restore command expands it into a full window. If the window had been expanded to take up the full screen, it's reduced to its previous size, so that other objects can be viewed.

The Move and Size commands are provided for keyboard users. If you choose Move, a four-headed arrow appears on the screen. You can then move the window to another part of the screen by using the arrow keys. When you've repositioned the window at the new location, press Enter to anchor the window.

The Size command allows you to use the arrow keys to expand or reduce the entire window either vertically or horizontally. Choose Size, and use the arrow keys to move the four-headed arrow to one of the borders of the window that you want to move. Next use the same arrow keys to move the border in the new direction. (A low-intensity outline indicates the new location for the border.) When the outline reaches the desired size, press the Enter key.

The Minimize and Maximize commands are used to control window size. The Minimize command always reduces a window to an icon. Conversely, the Maximize command always expands a window to its maximum size.

The last two options in the Control menu are Close and Switch To. The Close command closes the window entirely and exits Windows. The Switch To command brings up the Task List dialog box so that you can choose other open applications.

CHECK YOURSELF

1. Open the Control menu for the Program Manager.

2. Choose the Move command.

3. Move the window to the right and down using the keyboard.

4. Anchor the window.

ANSWERS

1. Click on the Control menu icon, or press Alt+Spacebar.

2. Click on the Move option, or press the M key.

3. Press the right arrow key a few times, and then press the down arrow key.

4. Press the Enter key.

Running the Program Manager as an Icon

The Program Manager provides a feature called Minimize on Use in the Options menu so that you can easily access the Program Manager when running other applications. If you select this option, Windows automatically reduces the Program Manager to an icon and places it along the bottom of your desktop with any other minimized icons. To reopen the Program Manager window, double-click on the minimized icon.

If the Minimize on Use option is not active and you want to return to the Program Manager, you must either move your current application so that you can see enough of the Program Manager's window to select it, or use the Task List. The Task List

▼ *Figure 3.5. Using the Task List*

shown in Figure 3.5 is accessed by choosing the Switch To command from an application's Control menu.

Arranging Group Windows and Icons

As you start opening more group windows and rearranging your work area, you might have trouble locating groups and program icons. Fortunately, the Program manager provides a few commands and settings to help you better manage your work area.

Organizing Group Windows

Because group windows are document windows, you can move and resize them with the mouse or the keyboard. When a group window is resized so that all of its program icons aren't visible, the window will be displayed with one or two scroll bars. You can then scroll through the window to locate its program icons.

The Program Manager provides two commands—Cascade and Tile—to help you better arrange your group windows,. Whenever you choose Cascade from the Window menu or press Shift+F5, the currently open group windows are arranged so that the active window is in front and the title bars of the others are visible behind it (Figure 3.6). The Tile command (selected through the Window

▼ *Figure 3.6. Viewing Windows in the Cascade Format*

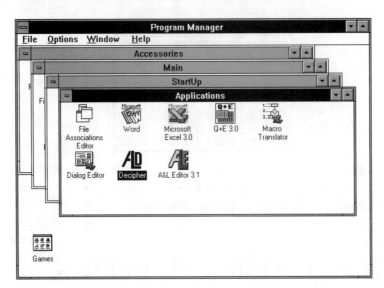

menu or by pressing Shift+F4) resizes the open windows so that they're positioned side by side (Figure 3.7).

These commands can't be automatically set; they operate only when you choose them. For example, if you open two groups and then press Shift+F4, the windows are tiled. If you then open a third group, it covers some area of one of the other windows. You'll need to press Shift+F4 again to retile the windows.

Arranging Icons

The Arrange Icons command in the Window menu arranges the group icons within Program Manager so that you can easily view as many as possible. This option comes in handy when you need to resize the Program Manager window so that it only occupies part of the screen. If the Program Manager window becomes tall and thin, the icons are rearranged one above the other; if the window is sized as wide but not tall, then the icons are rearranged in a horizontal orientation. If the window is too small to show all of the icons, it will show as many as possible.

▼ *Figure 3.7. Viewing Windows in the Tile Format*

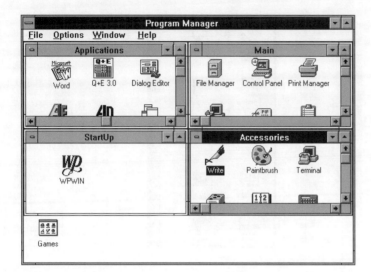

The Arrange Icons command can also be used to arrange the program icons in a group window. To perform this operation, open a group window and then choose the Arrange Icons command.

TIP

If you resize the Program Manager's window or a group window, and you can't easily locate the window's icons, choose the Arrange Icons command and the icons will come into view.

Arranging Icons Automatically

When the Auto Arrange option in the Options menu is active, Windows rearranges the icons within groups to fit in the window. For example, if you open the Accessories group and resize the window to be taller and narrower, Windows automatically rearranges the icons to fit (if possible), as shown in Figure 3.8.

▼ *Figure 3.8. Arranging Icons Automatically*

CHECK YOURSELF

How can you make Windows automatically rearrange icons each time the Cascade or Tile command is used to display windows?

ANSWER

Choose the Auto Arrange option in the Options menu.

Quick Group Selection

If you are having trouble locating a group icon in the program Manager's window or you don't want to move or close an opened window to access the group icons, you can use the Window menu to choose a group. The Window menu assigns numbers to each program group. To open a particular group, press Alt+W to open the Window menu, and then press the appropriate number to activate the group.

TIP

Each time you create a new group, the group is added to the Window menu and assigned a new number. When a group is deleted, it is removed from the menu.

Launching Applications

Now that you've seen how to open groups and arrange your work area, you're probably wondering how you can launch (start) an application from the Program Manager.

Here is the easiest way to start an application:

1. Open the group window where the program icon is located.
2. Double-click on the program icon.

When a program icon is activated, Windows loads and runs the DOS program file associated with the icon.

TIP

To see what program file is associated with a particular program icon, select the icon and choose the Properties command from the File menu. The program file for the icon is listed in the Command Line text box, along with the path to the file. A program file must have one of the following extensions: EXE, COM, BAT, or PIF.

Using the Run Command

The Run command provides an easy way to launch an application from the keyboard. Press Alt+F to open the File menu, and then use the arrow keys or press the *R* key to choose the Run command. A dialog box will appear (Figure 3.9), requesting the command line

▼ *Figure 3.9. The Run Dialog Box*

for starting the program. Enter the full path and the filename of the application, and choose the OK button (or press the Enter key). If the Program Manager can't find the file, it provides a warning message. To abort this command at any time, press the Esc key.

To use the Run command, you need to know where the application you want to run is stored on your hard disk. The full pathname for the program file should be entered in the Command Line text box. To help you locate a file, the Run dialog box provides a Browse button that brings up the Browse dialog shown in Figure 3.10. Notice that this dialog box provides two scrollable lists so that you can manually examine the current directory and other directories to locate your file.

You can also use the File Manager to locate a hard-to-find file by following these steps:

1. Run the File Manager application.

2. Choose the Search command from the File menu. This command displays the dialog box shown in Figure 3.11.

▼ *Figure 3.10. The Browse Dialog Box*

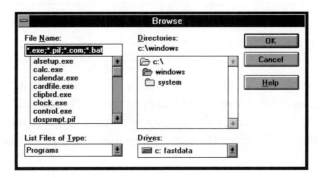

▼ *Figure 3.11. The Search Dialog Box*

```
┌─────────────────────────────────────────────┐
│ ─                   Search                   │
├─────────────────────────────────────────────┤
│  Search For:   │ Test.*              │  ┌────────┐ │
│                └─────────────────────┘  │   OK   │ │
│  Start From:   │ C:\A&L              │  └────────┘ │
│                └─────────────────────┘  ┌────────┐ │
│                ⊠ Search All Subdirectories│ Cancel │ │
│                                         └────────┘ │
│                                         ┌────────┐ │
│                                         │  Help  │ │
│                                         └────────┘ │
└─────────────────────────────────────────────┘
```

3. Enter the name of the file you want to locate. You can use the DOS wildcard symbols * and ? if you don't know the exact file-name.

4. Select a drive and path for starting the search.

5. Click OK.

The File Manager will then attempt to locate the file for you. If the file is found, a dialog box is displayed with the file's name and directory path.

CHECK YOURSELF

How can you find out which command is associated with the Cardfile application?

ANSWER

Open the Accessories group window, highlight the Cardfile icon, and choose the Properties command. The CARDFILE.EXE file name appears in the Command Line text box.

Running Minimized Applications

An application can be set up to run as a minimized icon. When you double-click on an icon that has been set up to run minimized, it will appear as a running icon on your desktop instead of as an application window.

When you use the Run command to launch an application, choose the Run Minimized check box to run the application as an icon. You can also set up a program item to run as a minimized icon by changing its property. Here are the steps to follow:

1. Select the program item by clicking on it once.
2. Choose the Properties command from the File menu.
3. Turn on the Run Minimized check box.
4. Click the OK button.

When you later double-click on the icon, it will run as a minimized icon.

Launching Applications with a Shortcut Key

You can also set up an application so that it launches when you press a shortcut key. To set up a shortcut key, follow these steps:

1. Select the desired program icon.
2. Choose the Properties command from the File menu.
3. Click on the Shortcut Key text box and press a key.
4. Click the OK button.

For shortcut keys, the Program Manager reserves the key sequences Ctrl+Alt+X, where X is any standard key. For example, if you press p as the shortcut key, you'll need to press Ctrl+Alt+p to launch the application.

Running Applications at Startup

The Program Manager can be set up to launch one or more applications for you when Windows starts up. This feature is especially useful if you have a certain application, such as Word for Windows or Excel, that you always run after you start windows.

To set up an application for auto-startup, use these steps:

1. Locate the program icon for the application you want to set up.
2. Click on the icon and drag it to the StartUp group icon.
3. The application will now be assigned to the StartUp group.

If multiple program items are placed in the StartUp group, the Program Manager will run them in the order they are arranged (from left to right) in the group window. The program item in the top-left corner is loaded first followed by the other programs listed in the first row.

Running an Application with a Document

Often you'll want to run an application and have it load a document file automatically, as soon as the program starts. If you are using the Run command, enter the name of your program followed by the name of the file you wish to load. For example, the command line PBRUSH.EXE RIBBONS.BMP would instruct Windows to run Paintbrush and load the file RIBBONS.BMP.

TIP

A program item (icon) can also be set up so that it loads a document file when you start the application with the mouse. This technique is explained later in this chapter.

Creating and Managing Group Windows

The more you work with the Program Manager, the more you'll appreciate the flexibility and usefulness of group windows. You can perform these and other operations with group windows:

▲ Reduce a group window to an icon

▲ Create and delete group windows

▲ Change the contents of group windows

▲ Change group window names

▲ Control how group windows are displayed

CHECK YOURSELF

1. What is the difference between group windows and group icons?

2. What are some of the program groups provided with Windows?

3. What are some of the program items that are installed automatically by Windows?

4. True or false? Each group window has its own Control menu.

5. Open the Main group window (if it's not currently open). Try to move the window outside the Program Manager window. What happens?

6. True or false? A group icon can be moved outside the Program Manager.

7. Close the Main group window by selecting the Close command from its Control menu. What happens to the window?

ANSWERS

1. A group window is a document window managed by the Program Manager, and contain icons that start applications. Group icons are minimized group windows, and usually display at the bottom of the Program Manager window.

2. Main, Games, Accessories, StartUp, and Applications.

3. File Manager, Control Panel, Clipboard, Notepad, and Write are a few examples.

4. True.

5. Windows won't let you move a group window outside the Program Manager.

6. False.

7. The window closes, but it doesn't completely disappear like other document windows because Windows converts the closed group window to an icon.

Creating a Group

Windows makes it easy for you to create either type of program object: a program group or a program item. Only one command is required for creating either type of object—the New command in the File menu. When this command is chosen, the dialog box shown in Figure 3.12 is displayed. For now, we'll be using the Program Group option.

Here are the steps required to create a new program group:

1. Choose the Program Group option in the New Program Object dialog box and click the OK button.

2. Using the dialog box shown in Figure 3.13, enter a description for the group in the Description text box.

3. Click the OK button to create the group.

Windows uses the text you enter in the Description text box to name the program group. This is the name you see when the group is displayed as an icon or a window. You should try to limit the

▼ *Figure 3.12. The New Program Object Dialog Box*

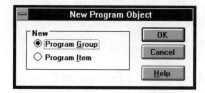

▼ *Figure 3.13. The Program Group Properties Dialog Box*

Program Group Properties		
Description:	Windows Applications	OK
Group File:		Cancel
		Help

length of your names so that your work area doesn't become too clutterd.

Notice that we've ignored the Group File text box up to now. You don't need to enter a group filename in the Program Group Properties dialog box; Windows creates one for you automatically. (The default file extension for a program group file is GRP.) You can enter your own filename if you want; however, you should use the extension GRP when naming the file.

TIP

The group (GRP) files are stored in the main Windows directory. Each group you create is stored as a file. If a group file is accidently deleted, Windows will no longer display the group.

After you've created a group, you can transfer program items to it by moving them from other groups or by using the New command from the File menu to create new program items.

CHECK YOURSELF

1. Create a program group named Database.

2. What happens after you create the program group?

3. What happens if you leave the Group File text box blank when you create a program group?

4. True or false? If you include your own group filename, it should have the extension GRP.

ANSWERS

1. Choose the New command from the File menu. Choose the Program Group option button in the New Program Object dialog box and click OK. Enter the name Database in the Description text box. Click the OK button in the Program Group Properties dialog box.

2. The new group window appears in the bottom of the Program Manager's window.

3. Windows automatically provides the necessary filename and assigns it the extension .GRP.

4. True.

Creating a Read Only Group

After a group has been created and set up in the Program Manager, you can change its attributes to make it a read-only group. This feature allows you to protect a group so that its program items cannot be changed. Although you'll need to use the File Manager to perform this operation, the procedure is quite simple:

1. Using the Program Manager, select the group you wish to change and choose the Properties command from the File menu.

2. Examine the Group File text box in the Program Group Properties and make a note of the filename used for the group.

3. Run the File Manager application.

4. Use the File Manager directory window to locate the group file. Click on the file to select it.

5. Choose the Properties command from the File menu to display the dialog box shown in Figure 3.14.

6. Click on the Read Only check box to turn this attribute on.

7. Click the OK button.

8. Return to the Program Manager.

▼ *Figure 3.14. Changing the Attributes of a File*

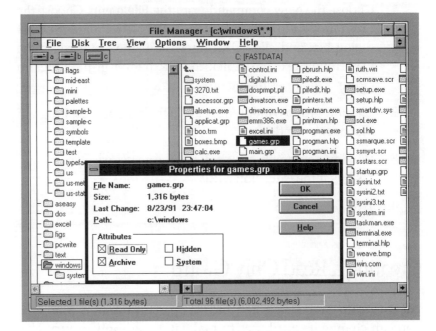

After setting the Read Only attribute, Windows will display a warning message if you try to change the contents of the group. For example, Figure 3.15 shows the message that is displayed if you try to move a program item from the Games group, which has been set up as a read-only group.

Deleting a Group

To delete a program group, first make sure that the group is displayed as an icon and not as a group window; otherwise you could delete a program item by mistake. Highlight the group icon and then choose the Delete command from the File menu or press the Del key. A dialog box appears (Figure 3.16) to confirm that you want to delete the group. To confirm the delete operation, click the Yes button. If you don't want to delete the selected group, click No or press the Esc key.

▼ *Figure 3.15. Warning for Copying an Item to a Read-Only Group*

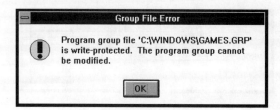

Creating and
Managing Group
Windows

TIP

When a group is deleted, Windows physically deletes the group (GRP) file for the group. However, the files for the program items stored in the group are not actually deleted. If you accidently delete a group you can rebuild it by creating a new group with the same name and then using the New command to add the program items that were in the group. The technique for adding program items to a group is presented later in this chapter.

Changing Group Properties

You've now learned how to open, create, and delete groups. The Program Manager also allows you to rename a group or define a different group file for the group. To change either of these properties, highlight the group and then choose the Properties command from the File menu. As Figure 3.17 shows, the Program Group Properties dialog box provides two text boxes for setting a group's properties.

To change a group's name, highlight the text in the Description text box and enter the new name. Keep in mind that the text you enter will be used to name the group icon.

▼ *Figure 3.16. Warning for Deleting a Group*

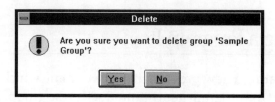

▼ *Figure 3.17. Program Group Properties Dialog Box*

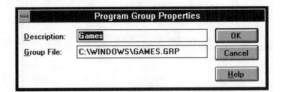

Creating and Managing Program Items

The Program Manager provides a number of options for creating and managing program items. Here are some of the operations you can perform using the commands in the File menu:

▲ Add a program item to a group

▲ Include parameters, such as the name of a document file, that you want to load when an application starts

▲ Change the icon assigned with a program item

▲ Delete a program item

▲ Move or copy program items from one group to another

▲ Specify a shortcut key and a working directory for a program item

▲ Change the DOS executable file associated with a program item

▲ Change the name of a program item

In this section, we'll explore these and other basic techniques for working with program items.

Creating a Program Item

Before creating a new program item, determine which group you want to put the program item into and select the group. If you want to put the program item into a new group, first use the New command to create the group. (The techniques for creating a new group were covered earlier in this chapter.)

Creating and Managing Program Items

To add a new program item to a group, follow these steps:

1. Choose the New command from the Program Manager's File menu.

2. Choose the Program Item option in the New Program Object dialog box and click the OK button.

3. Using the Program Item Properties dialog box shown in Figure 3.18, include a description for the program item in the Description text box. This text is used to name the program item.

4. Type the name of the DOS file to be associated with the program item in the Command Line text box. Remember that,when you later double-click on the program item icon, the file associated with the icon is executed by the Program Manager. The file must have one of the following extensions: EXE, COM, BAT, or PIF.

5. Type the name of a directory in the Working Directory text box. This directory will be used by the program to read and write its files. This feature is optional.

6. Select a shortcut key for the program item by using the Shortcut Key text box. This feature is also optional.

7. Click the OK button or press Enter to create the program item.

After you complete these steps, the Program Manager automatically selects an icon for your new program item and places the icon

▼ *Figure 3.18. Program Item Properties Dialog Box*

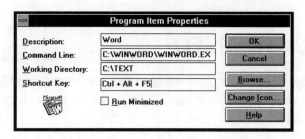

in the current group window. You can also choose an icon by clicking the Change Icon button in the Program Item Properties dialog box. (We'll show how this feature is used later in this chapter.)

TIP

Make sure you specify the proper directory path and filename for a DOS executable file in the Command Line text box. If the program isn't located in a directory that's automatically searched by DOS (via the DOS PATH command in the AUTOEXEC.BAT file), then you need to specify the full pathname. For example, if you were installing a program called BLINK.EXE, located in the directory C:\MYSTUFF, you would enter the following in the Command Line box:

```
C:\MYSTUFF\BLINK.EXE
```

This information tells Windows exactly where to search for the desired program.

Including a Document with a Program Item

When you enter a program filename in the Command Line text box, keep in mind that you can also include a document name. If you use this technique, Windows automatically loads a file when the application starts. If you are setting up an application that can open multiple documents when it starts up, you can specify more than one document in the Command Line text box. For example, if you are using EXCEL, you could load multiple documents by using a command line similar to this one:

```
EXCEL.EXE \WORK\BUDGET1 \WORK\BUDGET2
```

CHECK YOURSELF

What steps would you take to create a program item named *Text Editor* that activates the program WRITE.EXE and loads the document file NOTES.WRI?

ANSWER

First, access the Program Item Properties dialog box. Type Text Editor in the Description text box, and type WRITE.EXE in the Command Line text box. Type NOTES.WRI in the Command Line text box after the filename WRITE.EXE, leaving a space between the two files. Click the OK button.

Creating and Managing Program Items

Selecting an Icon for a Program Item

If you don't like the default icon that Windows selects for you when creating a program item, or if you wish to change the icon for an existing program item, you can easily select a different icon by using the Program Item Properties dialog box. Here are the required steps:

1. Select the program icon.
2. Choose the Properties command from the File menu.
3. Click the Change Icon button.

Windows then displays the Change Icon dialog box shown in Figure 3.19.

The dialog box highlights the icon currently associated with the program item. Keep clicking one of the scroll arrows to locate the icon you want to use. Then double-click on the icon of your choice or click once to highlight the icon and click the OK button.

TIP

If you have an application whose icon you like and you want to use it to set up another application, you can access the icon by typing the filename for the application in the Change Icon dialog box. To view the list of application icons that Windows 3.1 provides, type PROGMAN.EXE.

Using Browse to Locate a Program File

If you don't know the pathname for a program, click the Browse button in the Program Item Properties dialog box to look through

▼ *Figure 3.19. Selecting an Icon*

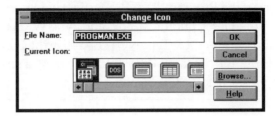

your list directory names. When the dialog box shown in Figure 3.20 displays, you can select a directory and a filename. By default, only files that have the extension EXE, COM, PIF, or BAT are listed. To select a different directory than the default one, use the list box on the right-hand side. Each time you double-click on a directory (folder icon), the contents of the selected directory is displayed in the left-hand list box.

TIP

The techniques for using the Browse dialog box are discussed in more detail in Chapter 4.

After you find the correct filename, double-click on the file to select it. The Command Line text box in the Program Item Properties dialog box will then be updated with this new filename.

▼ *Figure 3.20. Using Browse to Locate a File*

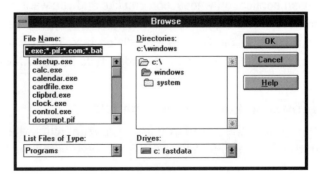

CHECK YOURSELF

1. Create a new program item called *Editor*.

2. Assign the program item to the file WORD.EXE.

3. View the icon that is associated with the program item.

4. Which icon displays?

5. Change the icon to the text icon (the one that portrays a screen of text).

6. Finish creating the program item.

7. What will happen if you now double-click on the new icon?

8. True or false? You can use the Browse button to locate a file and a directory to assign to a new program item.

ANSWERS

1. Type the name Editor in the Description text box in the Program Item Properties dialog box. (Follow the steps presented in this section to access this dialog box.)

2. Type WORD.EXE in the Command Line text box.

3. Choose the Change Icon button. Windows may give you a warning because it can't find a path for the application WORD.EXE.

4. The default icon.

5. To select the text icon, type the program filename PROGMAN.EXE in the Change Icon dialog box. You'll then see the set of Windows icons. Keep clicking the right scroll button until the text icon is displayed, as shown in Figure 3.21.

6. Click the OK button in the Change Icon dialog box, and click OK in the Program Item Properties dialog box.

7. Windows tries to load the program WORD.EXE. If this file isn't in the current directory, or its path hasn't been previously defined by the PATH command, Windows won't find the file.

8. True.

▼ *Figure 3.21. Selecting the Text Icon*

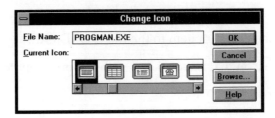

Deleting a Program Item

To remove a program item from a group, select the program item icon and then choose the Delete command from the File menu. Figure 3.22 shows the warning dialog box that is displayed. Click the Yes button to remove the selected program item.

When a program item is deleted, Windows does not actually remove the file associated with the program item from your hard disk. Only the reference to the file is deleted from the program group. If you want to actually delete a program file, you'll need to use the File Manager.

CHECK YOURSELF

1. Delete the program item called *Text Editor.*

2. True or false? When you delete an application item, the application file is removed from the disk.

ANSWERS

1. Open the group window where the Text Editor icon is stored, and click on the Text Editor icon (or use the arrow keys to highlight it). Choose the Delete command file from the File menu, and click Yes in the confirmation message box.

2. False.

▼ *Figure 3.22. Deleting a Program Item*

Moving and Copying Program Items

The easiest way to move and copy program items is to use the mouse. To move a program item to a new group, click on the icon, drag it to the new group, and release the mouse button. If you try to move an icon to a location outside of a program group, the pointer changes to a small circle with a slash through it.

The process of copying a program item is similar to the process of moving one, except that you must hold down the Control key while you drag the icon. After you've copied a program item, you can change its properties to create a custom version of the original.

CHECK YOURSELF

1. Copy the Control Panel icon in the Main program group to the Applications group.

2. What happens if you forget to hold the Control key down when you use the mouse to copy an icon from one group to another?

ANSWERS

1. First, open the Main window. Click on the Control Panel icon, hold the mouse button and the Control key down, and drag the icon to the Windows Applications group.

2. The icon is moved, instead of copied.

▼ *Figure 3.23. Moving a Program Item*

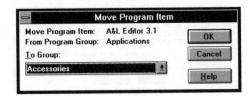

Using the Move and Copy Commands

The Move and Copy commands are typically used to move a program item from one window to another when you're working without a mouse.

To use these commands, first select and open the group from which the program item will be copied or moved. Next, select the object to be moved. (If you are using the keyboard, press one of the arrow keys.) Finally, open the File menu and choose either the Move or Copy command. These commands display a dialog box (Figure 3.23) that lets you select the destination group using the mouse or the up and down arrow keys.

CHECK YOURSELF

1. Move the Clipboard program item (located in the Main group) to the Accessories group.

2. Copy the moved Clipboard program item to the Main program group.

3. Delete the Clipboard program item from the Accessories group.

ANSWERS

1. Highlight the Clipboard icon in the Main window by clicking on it or selecting it with the arrow keys. Choose the Move command from the File menu. Press Alt+Down arrow to display the list of groups available in the To Group menu (Figure 3.24). Select the Accessories group. (The top of the Move Program Item dialog box displays the program item name and the source group window.) Click the OK button.

▼ *Figure 3.24. Selecting a Group*

2. Highlight the Clipboard icon in the Accessories window, and choose the Copy command from the File menu. Press Alt+Down arrow to display the list of groups available in the To Group menu. Select the Main group and click the OK button.

3. Highlight the Clipboard icon in the Accessories window, and choose the Delete command in the File menu.

Using the File Manager to Copy a Program Item

For the most part, we've been using the Program Manager exclusively to set up and manage program items and groups. You can, however, use both applications to help automate the process of adding new program items to a group.

To use both applications, you'll first need to arrange your desktop so that you can view both the Program Manager and the File Manager. Figure 3.25 shows one possible arrangement. Notice that both the File Manager's directory window and the Program Manager's group icons can easily be accessed. With this arrangement, you can copy programs and associated documents from the File Manager to a group in the Program Manager. When the files are copied, the Program Manager automatically sets up the properties for the files so that they can be launched as applications.

Here are the steps to follow:

1. Scroll through the File Manager's directory window to find the file you want to copy. The file can be a program file with extension EXE, COM, BAT, or PIF. In addition, you can copy a document that is associated with a program, such as a Paintbrush document file.

▼ *Figure 3.25. Arranging Applications to Copy a Program Item*

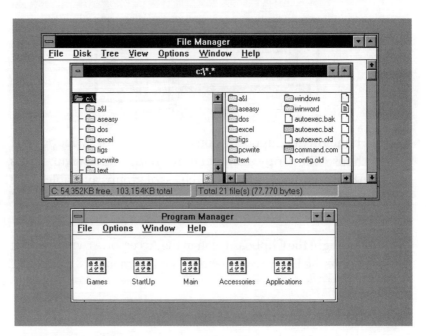

2. Select the desired file in the directory window and drag it to a group icon or window in the Program Manager. As the file is dragged, its icon is displayed as a file.

3. Windows automatically creates a program icon for the copied file.

4. You can then select the icon and make changes to the program item by using the Properties command.

If you copy a document file that is associated with an application, the Program Manager creates a program item for the file by including the name of the file in the Command Line text box along with the program's filename. For example, if you copy the file RIBBONS.BMP (a Paintbrush document) to a group, the Program Manager sets up a program item to launch Paintbrush and load in the associated file.

TIP

You can set up multiple files as program items by selecting multiple files in the File Manager's directory window and dragging them to the Program Manager.

Using Windows Setup to Add Program Items

If you have multiple program items that you need to set up, you'll find that the Windows Setup application comes in handy. The advantage of using Setup is that it will automatically search your hard disk to locate program files—both Windows and non-Windows applications—for you. Once you have located program files, you can select as many as you want and instruct Setup to create program items from them.

Here are the steps for using Setup to add program items:

1. Run the Windows Setup application. (The icon for this program is located in the Main group.)

2. When Setup appears, open the Options menu and choose the Set Up Applications option.

3. At this point, you can elect to have Setup search your entire disk for programs or you can select files from different directories. To search your entire disk, choose the "Search for applications" option; otherwise choose the option called "Ask you to specify an application."

4. Click the OK button and Setup will either locate the programs that are available for you or present you with a dialog box so that you can select your own program files to add as program items. If you have chosen the option to select your own program files, the Setup Applications dialog box presented in Figure 3.26 is displayed so that you can enter a program name and select the group where you want the program item to be set up.

▼ *Figure 3.26. The Setup Applications Dialog Box*

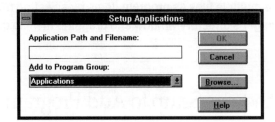

Changing a Program Item

After you create a program item, you may find that it doesn't do exactly what you want. If you want it to load a different document file or have a different title, for example, select the Properties command from the File menu. The trick to using this feature is to first select the program item icon you want to change, and then select Properties. As Figure 3.27 shows, this dialog box is the same as the dialog box displayed when you first create a program item. Again, notice that buttons are provided for locating a filename and a directory (Browse) and changing a program item's icon (Change Icon). You can also change the working directory and the shortcut key for a program item.

Exiting Windows

To exit windows from the Program Manager, select the Exit Windows command from the File menu. A warning dialog box appears to remind you that you are about to exit Windows. To exit, click the OK button.

If the Save Settings on Exit option in the Options menu is active, Windows will automatically save its current settings so that your desktop will look the same the next time you start Windows. For example, if you want the Accessories window to be open when Windows begins execution, then set everything up in the way you want it to appear, activate the Save Settings on Exit option, and then exit windows.

▼ *Figure 3.27. Changing a Program Item*

Exiting Windows

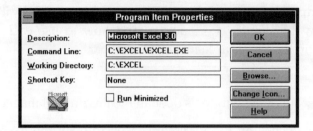

QUICK TASK SUMMARY

Task	Procedure
Start the Program Manager	Double-click the Program Manager icon
Run Program Manager as an icon	Use Minimize On Use (Options menu)
Open a group window	Double-click a group window icon
Create a group window	Use New (File menu)
Run an Application	Use the Run command (File menu); or
	Double-click a program icon
Minimize a running application	Click the application's minimize button
Create a program item	Select a group and use New (File menu)
Remove program item	Select item and use Delete (File menu); *or*
	Press Del key
Copy a program item to a group	Select item and use Copy command (File menu)
Move program item from a group	Select item and use Move command (File menu)
Change program item's properties	Select item and use Change Properties (File menu)
Assign shortcut key to a program	Select program and use Change Properties (File menu)
Tile or cascade group windows	Use Tile or Cascade (Window menu); *or*
	Use shortcut keys F5 and F6
Arrange icons	Use Arrange Icons (Window menu)
Exit Windows	Choose Exit Windows (File menu); *or* Double-click on Program manager's Control menu box.

PRACTICE WHAT YOU'VE LEARNED

In this chapter you learned about the Program Manager, why it's a key feature in the Windows 3.1 design, and how to use each option available in the Program Manager's menu bar.

1. Close all of the windows open in the Program Manager.

2. Double-click on the Accessories icon to open the Accessories window.

3. Click on the Notepad icon, and try to drag it into the Program Manager's window.

4. Click on the Notepad icon.

5. Click on the File item in the menu bar.

6. Click on the Move command.

7. Choose the option Main in the To Group box and click the OK button.

8. Open the Main window, and drag the Notepad icon from this window to the Accessories window.

9. Click on the Control Panel icon in the Main window, and select the Properties command from the File menu.

10. Select the Tile command from the Window menu.

11. Select the Main window as the active window, resize it using the mouse, and select the Arrange Icons command from the Window menu.

ANSWERS

1. The only window you should see displayed is the Program Manager window.

2. The Accessories window displays, and you see icons such as Write, Paintbrush, Terminal, and so on.

3. Windows won't let you drag a program item into a window that isn't a group window.

4. The icon is highlighted.

5. The File menu opens and displays commands such as New, Open, Move, Copy, and so on.

6. The Move Program Item dialog box displays.

7. The Notepad icon moves to the Main window.

8. The Notepad icon returns to the Accessories window.

9. The Program Item Properties dialog box displays, and the file name CONTROL.EXE is listed in the Command Line text box. This command executes when the Control Panel icon is selected.

10. The displayed windows, Main and Accessories, are tiled.

11. The icons are rearranged in the window.

Putting Windows to Work

After seeing how easy it is to use Windows, you're probably eager to put Windows to work. To get you started, this chapter takes you on a brief tour of a Windows application—Write. Along the way, you'll learn some useful techniques for working with Windows documents. After you read this chapter, you'll know how to:

▲ **Create a document with the Write application**

▲ **Create, open, and save documents**

▲ **Locate documents using the Open dialog box**

▲ **Perform basic document navigation and editing techniques**

▲ **Use the Clipboard to transfer data between documents**

▲ **Print a document**

▲ **Exit an application**

Working with Documents

We'll begin our discussion of windows documents by using the Write application. To start Write, open the Accessories group window and double-click on the Write icon.

Although we'll use Write to show you how to process your documents, the techniques presented here apply to most Windows applications—from spreadsheets to communications programs. For example, most Windows applications use the same basic set of commands for creating, opening, saving, and renaming document files.

Creating a New Document

When an application such as Write starts, the document window displays the window named "Untitled" to indicate that the document is new (see Figure 4.1). Once the document has been saved by assigning it a DOS filename, you can create a new document by choosing the New command from the File menu. (We'll explain how files are saved a little later.) Because Write only allows you to have one document open at a time, the New command will erase

▼ *Figure 4.1. The Write Application Window*

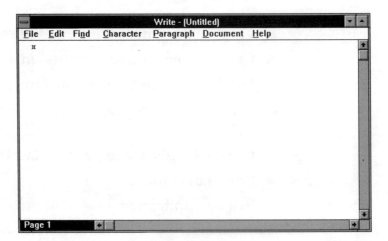

any document that is currently in memory. If you are using an application that allows you to have multiple document windows, such as Word for Windows, the New command will open a blank document window without removing any document currently in memory. Each document created in a Windows application is stored as a DOS file.

Working with Documents

TIP

Many Windows applications provide a menu called Window that allows you to select from the different documents that have been created or opened. If the application provides this menu, you'll know that the application supports multiple document windows.

Opening a Document

After a document file has been created and saved, you can open it at any time by using the File menu's Open command. This command is provided by every Windows application that uses documents. When you choose the Open command, you'll see a dialog box similar to the one shown in Figure 4.2. Notice that the main components of this dialog box are labeled.

The File Name text box is used to enter the name of the document file you wish to open. The name must be a valid DOS

▼ *Figure 4.2. The Open Dialog Box*

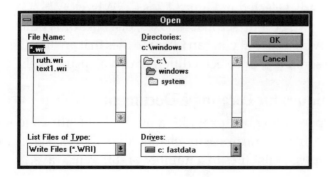

filename. That is, you can use eight characters to specify its name and three characters to specify its extension or file type. The file that you select must be of the correct type for the running application. For example, the Write application allows you to open files with the extension WRI (Write files), DOC (Microsoft Word for DOS files) or TXT (text files). If you try to open a file that was created by another type of application (such as Paintbrush), the file would be difficult to read in the Write document window.

TIP

Here's an easy way to determine which file types can be opened by an application: view the List Files of Type scrollable box in the Open dialog. For example, click on this box in Write's Open dialog box and you'll see these file types listed: Write (WRI), Word for DOS (DOC), and Text (TXT).

Directly below the File Name text box is a scrollable list box that shows you the list of files that are in the current directory. By default, this box lists all the files that have the main extension for the running application. For example, Write's Open dialog box lists only Write (WRI) files when it first appears. The Paintbrush application's Open dialog box, on the other hand, lists only BMP files. (We'll show you how to access other file types in the next section.)

The Directories selection box, located to the right of the File Name list box, indicates the directory that is currently active. This directory is represented by the open folder icon and it is also listed above the Directories selection box. For example, the directory that is currently selected in Figure 4.2 is C:\WINDOWS.

The two pop-up scrollable boxes, List Files of Type and Drives, are provided so that you can filter the files that are listed in the File Name scroll box or select a different drive, respectively.

Techniques for Locating a Document

The Open dialog box provides a number of features to help you locate a file. You can easily change disk drives, select different directories, or list files in a number of different ways.

Select a disk drive. Open the Drives pop-up scroll box by clicking on it or by pressing Alt+V to highlight it and then pressing the down arrow key to open it. Use the mouse or arrow keys to select a different hard or floppy disk drive.

Working with Documents

Select a different directory. Scroll through the list of directory folders in the Directories list box to find the one you want and double-click on the folder icon to select the directory. (If you are using the keyboard, highlight the directory by pressing the up or down arrow keys and then press Enter.) When the directory is opened, its full path will be displayed above the list box. The files in that directory will be listed to the right in the File Name list box. If you want to open a directory that is a subdirectory, you'll first need to open the parent directory to locate the subdirectory.

List all files in the current directory. Enter the DOS wildcard specification *.* in the File Name text box or select the All Files (*.*) option in the List Files of Type selection box and then choose the OK button.

List selected file types in the current directory. To limit the types of files in a directory listing, you can either use the List Files of Type selector or you can specify a filter in the File Name text box. For example, to list only files with the extension .DOC in the Write application's Open dialog box, select the option Word for DOS Files (DOC) in the List Files of Type selection box or type in the filter *.DOC in the File Name text box.

TIP

You can also specify multiple filter conditions in the File Name text box by separating each filter with a semicolon. For example, to view files with the extensions WRI, TXT, and DOC, enter this text in the File Name box: *.WRI;*.TXT;*.DOC.

Converting Documents

Some Windows applications will convert files for you if they are not directly supported by the application. For example, if you are using Microsoft Word and you attempt to open a file that is not of the standard Word format (DOC), the application will display a dialog box like the one shown in Figure 4.3 so that you can tell the application how the file should be converted. When the file is opened, the application automatically converts the file for you.

CHECK YOURSELF

1. Using Write, open a file, enter some text into the file, and then choose the Open command again to open a second file. What happens?

2. What filter should be entered in the Open dialog box to display all files in the current directory?

3. When the Open dialog box is displayed, how can you tell which directory is selected as the current directory?

ANSWERS

1. Write will display a warning dialog box that asks whether you want to save the changes to the first file before you open the next file.

2. *.*

3. The current directory's path is listed directly above the Directories scroll box.

▼ *Figure 4.3. Converting a File*

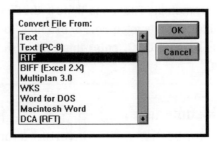

Entering Text in a Document Window

Entering Text in a Document Window

In Chapter 2 we covered the basic techniques for selecting, moving, minimizing, maximizing, and scrolling through document windows. We'll now show you how to use the Write application to enter and edit text in a document window. Keep in mind that the techniques explained in this chapter can be used with many other Windows applications.

Assume that you want to write a letter to your congressperson, opposing a proposed federal tax on high-fiber cereals. In the Untitled document window, start typing your letter. Notice that the blinking cursor (also called the *insertion point*) remains to the right of the last character typed. If you keep typing when the vertical cursor reaches the right-hand edge, Write wraps the text to start on the next line. To remove the character immediately to the left of the bar cursor, press the Backspace key. To remove the character to the right of the cursor, press the Delete key.

Adding or deleting text in the window is a snap; just position the cursor at the desired location using the arrow keys or the mouse. If you place the mouse cursor within the text area, the cursor changes from an arrow to a pointer that resembles a capital letter I. Move this pointer to the desired location and press the left mouse button once; the blinking cursor will move immediately to that location.

After you've entered a few lines of text, your document window will look something like the one shown in Figure 4.4. Assume at this point that you need to go back to the top of the letter to add the name and address. Move the blinking cursor to the beginning of the text and press the Enter key several times to create new lines ahead of the original text. Place the I-beam pointer cursor at the top line, using the mouse or the arrow keys, and type the name and address.

▼ *Figure 4.4. Entering Text in a Window*

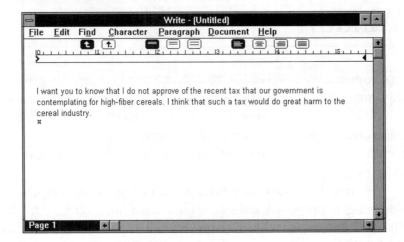

CHECK YOURSELF

1. Position the text cursor at the beginning of a line. What happens to the cursor when you press the following navigation keys?
   (a) Ctrl+Right arrow
   (b) Ctrl+Left arrow
   (c) End
   (d) Home
   (e) Ctrl+End
   (f) Ctrl+Home

2. Position the text cursor at the beginning of a line again. What happens to the cursor when you press the following text-selection keys?
   (a) Shift+Page Down
   (b) Shift+Page Up
   (c) Shift+End
   (d) Ctrl+Shift+End
   (e) Ctrl+Shift+Right arrow

3. Mark a word in your document and press the Delete key to delete the word. Then, press Alt+Backspace. What happens?

4. Change the font type of your document to Helvetica 12 point.

5. Change your document to display double-spaced lines.

6. Change the text line that begins with Dear... to display in bold.

ANSWERS

1. (a) Moves right one word.
   (b) Moves left one word.
   (c) Moves to the end of the line.
   (d) Moves to the beginning of the line.
   (e) Moves to the end of the document.
   (f) Moves to the beginning of the document.

2. (a) Selects text down one window.
   (b) Selects text up one window
   (c) Selects text to the end of a line.
   (d) Selects text from the current cursor position to the end of the document.
   (e) Selects the next word.

3. The deleted word is replaced. The Alt+Backspace keys perform an undo operation.

4. (a) Highlight the entire document by placing the cursor at the beginning and pressing Ctrl+Shift+End.
   (b) Select the Fonts command in the Character menu.
   (c) In the Fonts dialog box shown in Figure 4.5, select Helvetica as the Font, and the number 12 as the Size.
   (d) Click the OK button.

▼ *Figure 4.5. Changing Fonts*

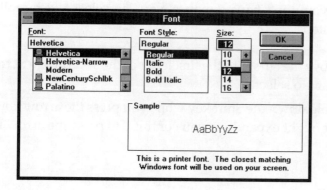

5. (a) Highlight the entire document by placing the cursor at the beginning and pressing Ctrl+Shift+End.
   (b) Open the Paragraph menu and select the Double Space option.

6. (a) Highlight this line with the mouse or keyboard.
   (b) Open the Character menu and select the Bold option. The shortcut for performing this operation is to Ctrl+B.

Editing a Document

You'll probably spending quite a bit of time editing documents that you create. Fortunately, Windows documents are easy to edit because Windows applications share a common set of editing techniques, which we'll explore next.

Selecting Text

Before you can perform an operation such as deleting or moving a line of text or changing a formatting option, you'll need to first select the text. To select text with the mouse, move the cursor to the beginning of the text to be selected, press and hold down the left mouse button, and drag the mouse until all of the text to be selected is highlighted. This technique is called *marking a block* of text. Next, release the mouse button. (The text stays highlighted.) Figure 4.6 shows a line of text that has been highlighted with the mouse.

If you don't have a mouse, you can select text by following these steps:

1. Move the cursor to the first letter of the section of text that you want to select.

2. Hold down the Shift key while you press the arrow keys. The highlight expands as you continue to press the arrow keys.

▼ *Figure 4.6. Marking a Line of Text*

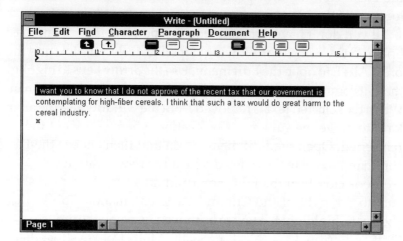

TIP

Some applications provide mouse and keyboard shortcuts so that you can easily select sections of a document. For example, in both Write and Word for DOS, you can select a word by double-clicking on it. To select a complete sentence, hold down the Ctrl key and click once on the sentence.

Moving and Copying Text

Imagine that you want to move the first sentence in a document to another location. You can do so in several ways. The obvious way is to delete the text using the Backspace key and then retype the text in the new location. The faster way is to select the text to be moved, and then use the Cut and Paste commands to move the marked block of text

After the text is selected, move the pointer to the menu bar, open the Edit menu, and choose the Cut command to tell Write to cut out this text and place it into the Clipboard. The Clipboard is a temporary storage area that Windows uses to hold data (either text or graphics) that has been cut from a document. After your text has been cut, move the mouse cursor to the location where you want to insert the text, and then click the left mouse button to move the

I-beam pointer to that spot. Open the Edit menu again, and choose the Paste command to paste the previously deleted text at the location of the I-beam pointer.

If you don't have a mouse, you can perform the cut and paste operation by using the following steps. First select the text and then press Alt+E to open the Edit menu. Use the arrow keys to highlight the Cut command, and press the Enter key to choose this command. When the selected text is removed from the window, use the arrow keys to move the cursor to the location where you want the text reinserted. Open the Edit menu again and then choose the Paste command to paste the deleted text at the new location.

Look closely at the Edit menu and notice the keyboard shortcuts to the right of the Cut and Paste commands. To use these shortcuts, highlight the text to be moved by using the mouse or the Shift and arrow keys. Next, press the Shift+Del keys together to perform the Cut. Move the cursor to the desired position and press Shift+Ins to paste the text.

Removing Text

You can use either of two methods to remove text from a document. If you only need to remove a few characters, position the cursor next to the characters you want to delete. Then, press the Backspace key to remove each character to the left of the insertion point or press the Del key to remove a character to the right of the insertion point.

To remove a block of text, such as a line or a paragraph, first select the text and then press Del or Backspace, or choose the Cut command from the Edit menu. If you delete the text by pressing the Del or Backspace key, the removed text will not be placed in the Clipboard.

CHECK YOURSELF

1. Press the Ctrl key and click on a line of text. What happens?

2. Double-click on a word. What happens?

3. Mark text, copy it by using the Copy command in the Edit menu, and then paste it with the Paste command. What happens?

4. Click the mouse at the beginning of your document, hold down the Shift key, move the mouse pointer down three lines, and press the mouse button. What happens?

ANSWERS

1. The current line is selected.

2. The word is selected.

3. The Copy command copies the selected text to the Clipboard, and the Paste command pastes a second copy into your document, starting at the position of the cursor.

4. The first three lines are selected. The Shift key serves as an anchor so that you can select multiple lines using the mouse without having to reposition the cursor.

Transferring Data with the Clipboard

As you've just seen, the Clipboard makes it easy to move text from one location in a document to another location. Because the Clipboard stores data that has been cut from an application until the data has been replaced by another cut operation, you can easily use the Clipboard to transfer data from one application to another. To show how this works, we'll copy text in a Write document and paste the text into a Cardfile document.

Figure 4.7 shows the selected text in a Write document that will be copied. After the Copy command is chosen from the Edit menu, the selected text is copied to the Clipboard. You can then easily examine the contents of the Clipboard by running the Clipboard Viewer application. (The icon for this application is stored in the Main group.)

Figure 4.8 shows the Clipboard Viewer window after our text has been copied. Notice that the text is formatted the same as it was in the Write document. To transfer this data to a Cardfile docu-

▼ *Figure 4.7. Marking a Block of Text*

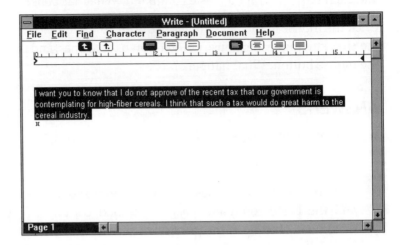

ment, start the Cardfile application (its icon is stored in the Accessories group), and choose the Paste command from the Edit menu. Figure 4.9 shows the final result.

Undoing an Editing Operation

Most applications like Write provide an Undo command in the Edit menu so that you can easily undo the most recent editing operation. For example, if you accidently delete a line of text in

▼ *Figure 4.8. Text Copied to the Clipboard*

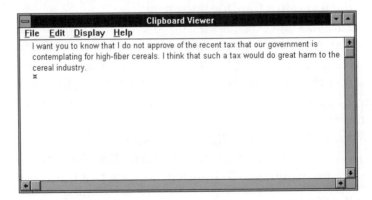

▼ Figure 4.9. Pasting Text in a Cardfile

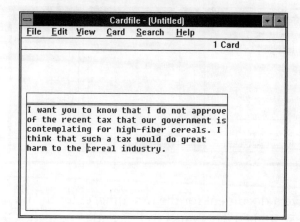

your document, choose the Undo command and the line of text will reappear. Keep in mind that in most applications, the Undo command can only be used to undo the most recent editing change.

TIP

You can also use the Undo command to cancel a formatting change made to a document. After you complete a formatting operation, such as changing a font style or the line spacing, the Undo Formatting command will appear in the Edit menu.

Saving a Document

After you finish typing and editing a document, you can save it by choosing the Save command in the File menu. If the document you are working with has not been saved yet, you'll see the Save As dialog box shown in Figure 4.10. Notice that this dialog box looks very similar to the Open dialog box used to open a file. The options for saving a file are similar to those for opening a file because you can save the file in a different directory and/or disk drive, save the file as a different file type, and save the file using a different name.

▼ *Figure 4.10. Saving a File*

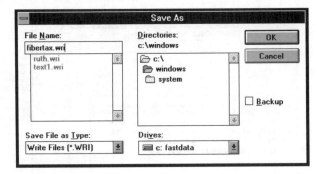

To save a document for the first time, enter the filename you want to use in the File Name text box and choose the OK button. The application will save the document using its standard format. For example, a Write document is saved as a WRI file, while a Paintbrush document would be saved as a BMP file by default.

TIP

If you try to save a document using a filename that already exists in the current directory, the application will display a warning message so that you don't accidentally write over an existing file.

Saving a Document in a Different Directory

To store a document in a different directory from the one currently selected, simply type in a full name (including the DOS path information) in the File Name text box. For example, assume you want to save your letter in the file FIBERTAX.WRI in the directory C:\MISC. (Recall that WRI is the extension for files created by the Write program.) First, type the text C:\MISC\FIBERTAX.WRI into the File Name text box and then choose the OK button.

You can also select a directory for saving a document by using the Directories list box. To select a different directory, scroll through the box to locate the desired directory and then double-click on the directory to open it. If you then enter a filename in the File Name text box, the file will be saved in the directory you just opened.

Saving a Document with a Different Name

To save a document you are editing with a different name, choose the Save As command from the File menu. In the Save As dialog box, enter the new name for the document and then choose the OK button.

Saving a Document Using a Different File Type

The File Save As dialog provides the Save File as Type option so that you can save a document using a different file type. As an example, in Write's Save As dialog box, options are provided for saving a document as Write (WRI), Word for DOS (DOC), Word for DOS/Text Only (DOC), and Text (TXT). Choose the format needed for your document before you save it.

TIP

To save a document as a text file, choose one of the text options listed in the Save File as Type selection box. This option allows you to export your document so that it can be read by another application.

Making a Backup Copy

You can tell an application such as Write to make a backup copy of your document whenever you save it. If you select the Backup check box, Write makes two files for you whenever you save a file. The working file has the extension WRI, and the backup file has the extension BKP.

CHECK YOURSELF

1. What default file format does Write use to save your file?

2. Save the text file you've created by selecting the Backup check box. Which two files are created?

ANSWERS

1. The Write format, with the file extension WRI.

2. FIBERTAX.WRI and FIBERTAX.BKP.

Printing Your Document

To print a document, select the File option from the menu mar and then choose the Print option to invoke another dialog box (Figure 4.11). In our particular example, use the Tab key until the dashed square surrounds the OK button, and then press the Enter key. (With the mouse, simply click on the OK button.)

If you want to print multiple copies of your document, enter a number other than 1 in the Copies text box. The Print dialog box also lets you specify a range of pages to print. To use this feature, select the From option button and then type values into the From and To text boxes. For example, to print pages 2 through 7 of a document, type 2 into the From text box and type 7 into the To text box.

To use a printer different from the currently active printer, or to change the setup of your printer, select the Print Setup command from the File menu. The Print Setup dialog box displays (Figure 4.12) with a list of the available printers. After choosing the Specific Printers option button, you can scroll through the list of printers that have been installed for your computer to select a different one. You can also change the orientation of your paper, the paper size, and so on by using this dialog box.

▼ *Figure 4.11. Printing a File*

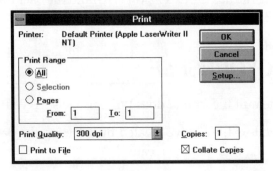

▼ *Figure 4.12. Selecting a Printer*

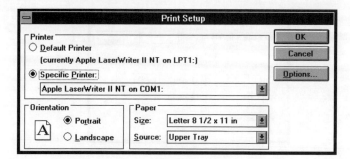

CHECK YOURSELF

1. Turn off your printer and then use the Print command. What happens?

2. How can you stop the printing of a document after Write starts printing?

3. Change the format of your document to print with 2" margins on the left, right, top, and bottom.

ANSWERS

1. Windows displays a warning message box to indicate that the printer isn't connected.

2. When a document is being printed, a dialog box displays. To cancel your print job, select the Cancel button in this dialog box.

3. (a) Select the Page Layout command from the Document menu to display the Page Layout dialog box (Figure 4.13).
   (b) Enter the number 2 in the text boxes marked Left, Right, Top, and Bottom.
   (c) Choose the OK button.
   (d) Choose the Print command to print your document.

▼ *Figure 4.13. The Page Layout Dialog Box*

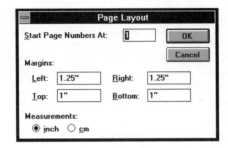

Exiting an Application

You can exit an application, such as Write, by choosing the Exit command from the File menu or by double-clicking on the Control menu box at the top-left corner of the application window. If you've made changes to your document, a dialog box displays to ask if you want to save your document before exiting. As an example, Figure 4.14 shows the warning dialog box that is displayed if you try to exit Write without first saving the document you are editing. In such a case, choose the Yes button if you want to save your most recent editing changes.

CHECK YOURSELF

1. Make a few editing changes to your document and then select the Exit command. What happens if you select the Cancel button?

2. Which keyboard shortcut can be used to exit from Write?

3. True or false? After exiting Write, you'll be returned to the Control Panel.

ANSWERS

1. Write returns you to your document.

2. Alt+X.

3. False. Windows returns you to the Program Manager.

▼ *Figure 4.14. Exiting Write*

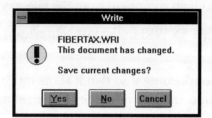

QUICK TASK SUMMARY

Task	*Procedure*
Create a new document	Choose New (File menu)
Open an existing document	Choose Open (File menu)
View all files in a directory	Use the filter *.* in the Open dialog box
Enter text in a document	Position the insertion point (cursor) and enter the text
Move to the top of a document	Press Ctrl+Home
Move to the end of a document	Press Ctrl+End
Select a word	Double-click on the word
Select all text in a document	Press Ctrl+Home and then Ctrl+Shift+End
Copy text to the Clipboard	Select the text and choose Copy (Edit menu)
Paste text from the Clipboard	Position insertion cursor and choose Paste (Edit menu)
Save a document with the same name	Choose Save (File menu)
Save a document with a new name	Choose Save As command (File menu)
Print a document	Choose Print command (File menu)

PRACTICE WHAT YOU'VE LEARNED

You've now been introduced to the main techniques for processing documents with Windows applications. Use these exercises to practice using the document processing techniques explored in this chapter.

1.   Open Write by double-clicking on the Write icon.

2.   Choose the Open command from the File menu.

3.   Enter FIBERTAX.WRI in the File Name text box. Click the OK button.

4.   Change your document so that it starts on page 5. Choose the Page Layout command from the Document menu.

5.   Enter the number 5 in the Start Page Numbers At text box. Click the OK button.

6.   Scroll to the middle of the document, position the cursor on a line, and press Ctrl+Enter.

7.   Highlight the inserted dotted line and press Delete.

8.   Choose the Ruler On command from the Document menu.

9.   Mark your document by moving the cursor to the top and pressing Ctrl+ Shift+End.

10.   Click on the centered-alignment icon located above the ruler. This icon is the third one from the right.

11.   Click on the double-space icon in the ruler bar. This icon is the fifth one from the right.

ANSWERS

1.   The Write application starts and displays a window that has the title bar Write- - (Untitled).

2.   The Open dialog box appears.

3.   The Open dialog box disappears, the file FIBERTAX.WRI displays in Write's window, and the title bar changes to Write - FIBERTAX.WRI.

4.   The Page Layout dialog box displays.

5.   The Page Layout dialog box disappears. The page number indicator in the left corner of the Write window changes to read "Page 5."

6. A dotted line is inserted above the cursor to indicate that a page break has been inserted.

7. The inserted page break is removed.

8. A ruler is added to the top of the document displayed in Write's window.

9. The entire document is highlighted.

10. The document is center aligned.

11. The document is double spaced.

5

Using the Control Panel

If you've been wondering how you can customize the Windows environment to suit your own needs, then you've come to the right place. In this chapter, you'll learn how to use the Control Panel to perform such setup operations as:

▲ Selecting and creating custom colors

▲ Setting the system time and date

▲ Setting up a screen saver

▲ Changing international settings

▲ Configuring the keyboard and the mouse

▲ Installing icons and fonts

▲ Selecting and configuring printers, ports, and networks

Overview of the Control Panel

You've probably heard the old joke about three people in one room having four separate opinions; the same principle applies to software users! No matter how many colors and basic configuration features a software product provides, users will want more. Fortunately, Windows provides a powerful and flexible Control Panel that allows you to easily customize your own desktop. Figure 5.1 shows how the Control Panel window looks when invoked, and Figure 5.2 lists the subtasks that you can run from the Control Panel. Table 5.1 provides a short description for each of these subtasks.

▼ **Table 5.1. Control Panel Options**

Option	Description
Colors	Customizes the colors for the different parts of the Windows environment
Date/Time	Updates the system date and time
Desktop	Customizes the appearance and the operation of the desktop
Drivers	Install, remove, and configure drivers for optional devices such as video players and sound cards
Fonts	Selects or deletes fonts to be used in the Windows environment or with your printer
International	Customizes country-related parameters, such as currency symbol, date and time formats, and so on
Keyboard	Adjusts the keyboard auto repeat rate
Mouse	Adjusts the mouse parameters
Network	Changes the parameters associated with a PC network (only works if you've set up Windows to run on a network)
Ports	Sets the parameters associated with each I/O port
Printers	Updates/adds/deletes the installation information associated with a printer
Sound	Enables or disables the warning tone
386 Enhanced	Adjusts the percentage of time devoted to foreground/background tasks, and controls how these tasks share peripheral devices (only available when running Windows in 386 enhanced mode)

▼ *Figure 5.1. The Control Panel Window*

Overview of the Control Panel

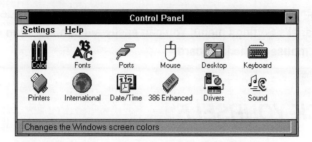

Starting the Control Panel

Before you can customize your Windows environment, you need to learn how to start the Control Panel. Because this tool is a Windows application, you can start it by opening the Main group window and double-clicking on the Control Panel icon. If you don't have a mouse installed, highlight the icon and press the Enter key.

When the Control Panel window appears, it displays a set of icons that you'll use to change Windows settings. If you're running Windows in standard mode, you'll see 11 icons. If you're running the 386 Enhanced mode, 12 icons are provided. (The extra icon controls the 386 Enhanced settings.) You'll also see one extra icon if you're running Windows on a network. This extra icon, called Network, allows you to change network settings.

▼ *Figure 5.2. The Control Panel Options*

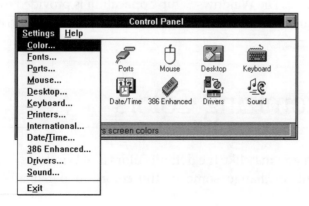

TIP

Keep in mind that the icons correspond to the commands provided in the Control Panel's Settings menu. You can easily set configuration options using the mouse or the keyboard.

CHECK YOURSELF

Start the Control Panel by double-clicking on the Control Panel icon.

1. Double-click on one of the configuration icons, such as Color. What happens?

2. Get help information for the Control Panel.

3. Which command is used to exit the Control Panel?

4. True or false? The Control Panel is the only application available for changing hardware settings.

ANSWERS

1. A dialog box displays with the name of the setting option, so that you can change the configuration options. For example, if you double-click on the Color icon, the Color dialog box displays.

2. Click on the Help menu item or press Alt+H.

3. The Exit command in the Settings menu.

4. False. The Windows Setup application is provided to set up hardware such as the monitor, the keyboard, and so on.

Customizing Colors

Although you may like the default colors that Windows uses, you may want to change some of the colors to personalize your desktop. Fortunately, Windows provides an easy-to-use color tool that allows you to interactively customize your colors.

Before using the tool, you'll need to know the basics about the color system Windows uses. Windows assigns a color to every type of display item–such as a window title bar, menu text, window text, button, and so on–that you see on the screen. The set of colors that define how each item should be displayed is called a *color scheme*.

After Windows is installed, a color scheme called Windows Default is used. Windows also provides other color schemes that you can select or modify to suit your needs. You can also create your own color scheme by selecting colors from a palette for each Windows display item. If you want to go one step further, you can also define your own custom colors.

Selecting a Color Scheme

Before selecting or changing a color scheme, you'll need to start the Color tool. In the Control Panel window, double-click on the Color icon or open the Settings menu and choose Color.

Figure 5.3 shows the window that appears. The top of the window contains a pull-down scroll box called Color Schemes. Notice that the default color scheme is selected, Windows Default.

▼ *Figure 5.3. The Color Dialog Box*

Click on the down arrow in the scroll box (or press Alt+Down arrow), to expand the box and view the list of color schemes that Windows provides (Figure 5.4). Use the scroll bar with the mouse to find the color scheme you want, and choose the name to see it demonstrated in the Windows minienvironment. Choose the OK button to select the color scheme.

To view the options with the keyboard, press the down arrow key. Each time you press this key, the next available color scheme is demonstrated in the minienvironment, and the color scheme's name appears in the one-line scroll box. After viewing the available options, you can work your way back up the list using the up arrow key until you return to the default scheme. If you prefer one of the other color schemes, leave it visible in the minienvironment and use the Tab key to select the OK button. Press the Enter key to choose the OK button and return to the Control Panel.

TIP

If you have previously made a change to the current color scheme and have not saved those changes, the Color Schemes box will be empty.

▼ *Figure 5.4. Selecting a Color Scheme*

CHECK YOURSELF

Start at the Color window by double-clicking the Color icon.

1. Click on the Color Schemes pull-down box. What is the name of the color scheme provided for monochrome systems?

2. What is the name of the default color scheme?

ANSWERS

1. Monochrome.

2. Windows Default.

Modifying a Color Scheme

To modify an existing color scheme, choose the Color Palette window button by using the mouse, the Tab and the Enter keys, or by pressing Alt+P. The window expands to the right to show a group of multicolored boxes at the top right (Basic Colors), and a group of blank boxes below them (Custom Colors) (Figure 5.5). If you expand the Screen Element scroll box (using the mouse, Alt+E,

▼ *Figure 5.5. Selecting Colors for a Scheme*

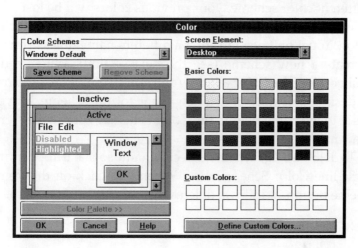

or the Tab key and Alt+Down Arrow), a list of selectable Windows display items is provided. Choose an item to be modified by clicking it, or by highlighting it with the up/down arrow keys and then pressing Alt+Up Arrow to close the list box.

Next, choose the desired color from the palette by clicking on it with the mouse, or by using the Tab key to select the Basic Color group. (When this group is selected, the current color, will be highlighted with an outlined box.) If you're using the keyboard only, use the arrow keys to move the dotted box to the desired color and then press the space bar. The item viewable in the Screen Element box changes to the selected color. Repeat these steps until you finish selecting colors for each display item.

TIP

Always double check the colors you select for overlapping display items such as the window title bar and the title bar text. If two overlapping display items are set to the same color, you won't be able to tell them apart. Whenever you select a different color, examine the minienvironment on the left to make sure the item you have changed is still visible.

Saving and Removing a Color Scheme

If you have made changes to a color scheme, you'll want to save them. Windows will continue to use the colors you have selected even if you don't save the color scheme; however, if you later select a different color scheme, your previous colors will be lost.

To save a modified color scheme, choose the Save Scheme button. You won't need to enter a different name unless you want to create a new scheme (see the next section). When you are finished, close the Color window and you'll see your new colors on the desktop. Next, type in a new name for the scheme. Move the cursor to the name field in the Color Schemes window and create a new name for your version.

To delete a color scheme, select its name so that it appears in the single-line Color Schemes box. When you click on the Remove Scheme button, Windows deletes this color scheme for you.

TIP

When a scheme is modified, created, or deleted, Windows makes a change to the CONTROL.INI file. This file stores the definitions for all of the color schemes. If you remove one of the standard Windows color schemes, its definition will in turn be removed from the CONTROL.INI file. If you decide later that you want to use it, you'll need to either reinstall Windows or else create the color scheme using the Color tool.

TIP

If you are using a color scheme on one computer and you want to use these same colors on another system, you can easily set them up without using the Color tool. Copy the color definitions from the CONTROL.INI file used with the system whose colors you want to access, and insert these color definitions in the CONTROL.INI file used with the other system.

Creating Your Own Color Scheme

You can follow the procedure just presented for modifying a color scheme; however, when you select the Save Scheme button, make sure that you enter a new name for the color scheme. After the color scheme has been saved, its name will appear in the Color Schemes list box.

Creating Custom Colors

What if you don't like the set of colors in the default palette? If your PC has an EGA or higher-resolution graphics display adapter, you can activate the Define Custom Colors button to create your own colors. When you select this option, the window shown in Figure 5.6 is displayed. Notice that a "bombsight" appears somewhere in the large multicolored square at the top-left of the window. You can move this indicator by locating the mouse cursor at a different spot within the rectangle and clicking the left mouse button. When this

▼ *Figure 5.6. Creating a Custom Color*

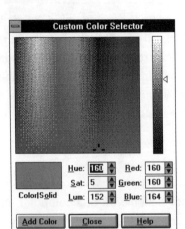

happens, the numbers in the boxes immediately below the multi-colored box change to the values that represent the color you just selected.

You can also move the color mix indicator by activating the up and down scroll buttons with the mouse, or by tabbing over to the color attribute box and changing the number in the box. The numbers for Red, Green, and Blue range from 0 to 255, where 255 indicates maximum brightness. If all three colors are set to 255, you get bright white. If all three colors are set to 0, you get pure black. Intermediate mixes produce various colors.

Notice that when you modify the numbers, the colors in a small box to the left of the controls change to show the new settings. The part on the left side marked "Color" shows the current adjustment, and the part on the right marked "Solid" indicates the closest pure color that your screen can display.

After you've selected a color combination, click on an empty box in the Custom Colors section of the window and click on the Add Color button to transfer this setting to the selected box. Choose the Close button to close this window and return to the previous Color Palette window. You can now set any of the Windows display items to be a particular custom color by repeating the process for selecting the basic colors in the palette.

CHECK YOURSELF

Display the Color dialog box.

1. Display the palette so that you can select your own colors.

2. How many basic colors are provided for creating a color scheme? How many custom colors can be created?

3. Create a new color scheme. What happens when you choose the OK button in the Color dialog box?

4. Create a new custom color and then try to delete it. What happens?

5. What is the difference between a color scheme and a custom color?

ANSWERS

1. Select the Color Palette button.

2. Forty-eight basic colors and 16 custom colors.

3. First, choose the screen element whose color you want to change by using the Screen Element drop-down box. Select a color by clicking on one of the boxes in the Basic Colors group. Repeat this process for each screen element. After you choose the OK button, you can view the selected colors without saving them or exiting the Color dialog box.

4. Select the Define Custom Colors button, and click on the square color grid to select a color. To change the brightness or intensity of the color, click and slide the triangular slider bar to the right of the color grid. When the color is correct, select the Add Color button. You can't remove a custom color; you can only replace it with another color. You can, however, set a custom color to white so that it appears to be blank.

5. A color scheme consists of the set of colors used to display the various Windows interface components. A custom color is an individual color that you can create using color mixes.

Setting the Date and Time

When you choose the icon marked Date/Time, a window similar to the one shown in Figure 5.7 appears. This window allows you to modify the system time and date (the time and date maintained by your PC). Keep in mind that these settings are used by DOS and the File Manager to record when files are created or modified and therefore they should be checked and correctly set.

Suppose the "minutes" portion of the time display is a couple of minutes slow. Use the Tab key or the mouse cursor to move the highlight to the minutes field on the display. Enter the correct value for this field, or use the up and down buttons next to the time display to increase or decrease the number in the field. Repeat the same technique with the other numeric fields in the window until the time and the date are correct. Next, use the Tab+Enter keys or the mouse to choose either the OK or the Cancel button. Either action returns you to the Control Panel window.

TIP

You can also change the display format for the date and time by using the International dialog box. To open this dialog box, double-click on the International icon.

CHECK YOURSELF

1. True or false? Any changes you make to the date and time affect your computer's clock.

2. True or false? You can use the Date & Time dialog box to set an alarm.

3. How do you change only the month portion of the date?

ANSWERS

1. True.

▼ *Figure 5.7. Setting the Date and Time*

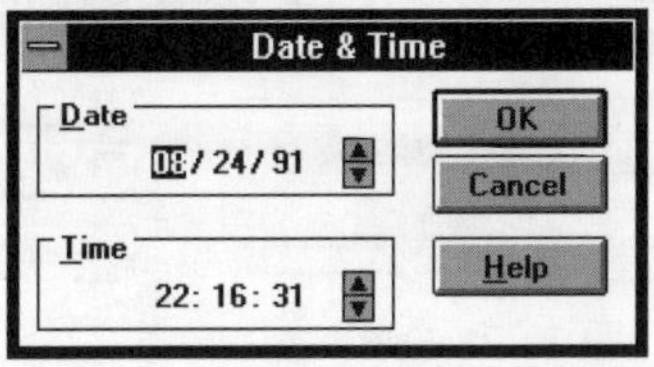

2. False. The Calendar application is used to set an alarm.

3. Highlight the month component by double-clicking on it with the mouse, and then click on the up or down arrows to change the month number.

Setting the Desktop

The Desktop tool allows you to customize the appearance of Windows to a great extent. You can set up a custom background picture for your desktop, turn on a grid to help you align windows and icons, change the spacing used for icons, set up a useful screen saver, and more.

When the Desktop icon is chosen, the dialog box shown in Figure 5.8 is displayed. Notice that six groups of options are provided: Pattern, Screen Saver, Wallpaper, Icons, Cursor Blink Rate, and Sizing Grid. In this section. we'll show you how to use each of these options to customize your desktop.

Selecting a Desktop Pattern

The first option in the Desktop dialog box (starting from the top-left corner of the window) is called Pattern. Use this option to select a background pattern for the desktop; you can either select an existing pattern or you can create one of your own. Select the option using the Tab key or the pointer. If you use the keyboard, press Alt+Down Arrow to expand the scroll box. Use the up and

---

▼ *Figure 5.8. The Desktop Dialog Box*

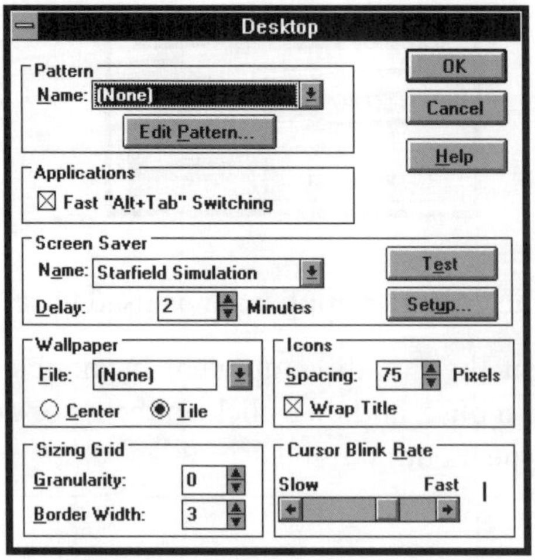

down arrow keys to scroll through the various options, and then press Alt+Up Arrow to choose the selection.

Using the mouse, scroll up or down with the scroll bar and then click on an item to choose it. Next, use the Tab and Enter keys or the mouse to select and choose the OK button for the Desktop window. Notice that the background display area (which is the Windows desktop) changes from the default pattern to the pattern you selected.

Creating Your Own Desktop Pattern

If you're not happy with the patterns provided with Windows and you have a mouse, you can easily modify an existing pattern or create your own by choosing the Edit Pattern button. When you choose this button, another window appears over the Desktop window (Figure 5.9). If you didn't select a pattern to edit (the name field showed None), Windows will beep and expect you to enter a name for the pattern. (Make one up if you're creating a new pattern rather than modifying an existing one.)

Next, click on the large blank square in the middle of the window and watch it change from gray to black. This box represents a grid of 8 by 8 squares that can each be changed from gray

▼ *Figure 5.9. Editing a Desktop Pattern*

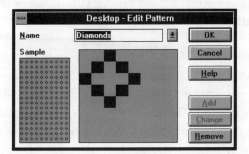

to black, and back to gray again, by clicking on the particular square. The elongated box on the left, marked Sample, shows how the pattern looks when it's replicated many times on the desktop. Try playing around with various patterns until you get the hang of how this feature works. You can save the pattern by choosing either the Change or Add button. (Choose Change to modify an existing pattern or choose Add to save a new pattern. If you use Add, you must make sure that you specify a new name for the pattern in the Name text box.) To quit without saving your work, choose Cancel. Choose the OK button to exit from this window.

CHECK YOURSELF

1. Select the Name drop-down box in the Edit Pattern dialog box. Which patterns are provided with Windows?

2. True or false? If you create a new pattern and select it, the pattern will be used by Windows even after you exit and start Windows again.

3. After you create a pattern and select it, select the Remove button in the Edit Pattern dialog box. What happens?

ANSWERS

1. The patterns are 50% Gray, Boxes, Critters, Diamonds, Paisley, Pattern, Quilt, Scottie, Spinner, Thatches, Tulip, Waffle, and Weave.

2. True.

3. A message box displays asking you to verify the deletion of the pattern.

Unfortunately, when you select a pattern for the desktop, the new pattern may make your icons or other screen objects hard to read. As an example of this problem, activate the Cardfile application from the Accessories group, and then reduce it to an icon by clicking on the Minimize box at the top-right corner of the screen. If you have selected a pattern for the Desktop, note that it's virtually impossible to read the legend under the Cardfile icon. For this reason, test your patterns to make sure they're not too "busy."

Using a Screen Saver

The next option in the Desktop dialog box is the Screen Saver. This feature has been added to Windows 3.1 to allow you to give your screen a rest when your computer is idle.

To select one of the Windows-supplied screen savers, click on the down arrow in the Screen Saver Name box. A list of screen saver files, which have the extension .SCR, are displayed. Select the desired screen saver and then use the Delay box to set a time delay for your screen saver. The number you select corresponds to the amount of time (in minutes) you want to pass before the screen saver is activated. For example, if you select two minutes, your computer must be idle for two minutes before the screen saver will start. After the screen saver has been selected, choose the OK button.

TIP

If you want to test a screen saver, first select the screen saver and then choose the Test button in the Desktop dialog box. To stop the screen saver and return to the dialog box, simply move the mouse or press any key on the keyboard.

Changing a Screen Saver

After using one of the screen savers, you may want to make changes to it so that you can personalize it. Some of the screen savers can be easily customized by selecting the screen saver and then choosing the Setup button. A dialog box will be displayed that provides options for the specific screen saver you are using. For example, if you have selected the Marquee screen saver, you'll see the dialog box shown in Figure 5.10 when the Setup button is chosen. Notice that options are provided for changing the text, text position, background color, speed, and so on. After you change the settings, you can easily test the screen saver by choosing the OK button to return to the Desktop dialog box and then choosing the screen saver Test button.

Protecting Your Computer with a Password

You may be doing work with your computer that you don't want anyone else to see or access. In such a case, you'll want to set up a password for a screen saver so that you can leave your computer unattended without having to turn it off. If other people try to access your computer by interrupting the screen saver, Windows displays a dialog box asking them for a password.

To set up this password protection, select a screen saver in the Desktop dialog box and choose the Setup button. In the Setup dialog box, select the Password Protected check box, and choose the Set Password button. You'll then see the Change Password dialog box shown in Figure 5.11, which is used to enter a new

▼ *Figure 5.10. Setting Up a Screen Saver*

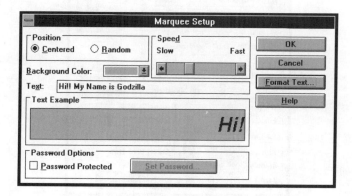

Setting the Desktop

▼ *Figure 5.11. Setting a Password for a Screen Saver*

password or change a password for a screen saver. If you are entering a new password, type the password in the New Password text box. You'll also need to type this same password in the Retype New Password text box. After entering the password, choose the OK button in both the Setup dialog box and the Desktop dialog box.

Using Wallpaper

You can use the Wallpaper option to select a bitmap picture as the desktop background. Let's explore how this is done.

Bitmaps tend to be large files that contain color information about each individual *pixel* (dots that make up the picture) on the screen. These files are typically created with the Paint application (discussed in greater detail in Chapter 10), but can also be created using special programs that bring in pictures from scanners or video cameras.

▼ *Figure 5.12. Selecting a Desktop Pattern*

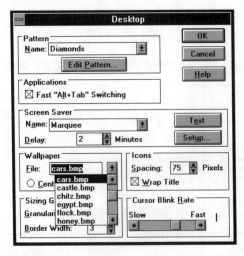

Unlike the pattern option, which limits you to an 8 by 8 grid, the Wallpaper option allows you to fill the entire screen with only one image. Open the File scroll box in the Wallpaper section to see a list of BMP files provided by Windows (Figure 5.12). If you select one of these files and choose the OK button in the Desktop dialog box, the pattern appears as the desktop background screen.

Many of the bitmap files provided by Windows are fairly large in size, so leave the options in the Wallpaper area set to Center. Figure 5.13 presents a sample of some of the wallpaper images. If you decide to create a picture later using Windows Paint, you can display it on the desktop by following these steps:

1. Move the file to the same directory where the Windows files are located.

2. Select the filename in the Wallpaper scroll box.

3. Choose the OK button.

Setting the Desktop

▼ *Figure 5.13. Bitmap Patterns*

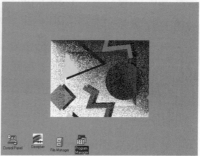

If your bitmap file is small, display it several times by activating the Tile option, rather than the Center option.

Unfortunately, wallpaper can take up a substantial portion of your computer's system memory. This may perceptibly degrade the performance of Windows if you have a modest amount of system memory. It may also make Windows slower at startup because Windows will need to move a copy of the file from the disk into memory. If the selected bitmap file is too large, or if there isn't enough memory available to contain it, Windows will not display the file at all. If you have selected a pattern and a wallpaper, the pattern may be visible around the edges of the desktop if the wallpaper bitmap is smaller than the entire desktop.

CHECK YOURSELF

1. True or false? Files created by Paint to be used as wallpaper screens must be saved with the extension .BMP.

2. Select (None) for the File name in the Desktop dialog box. What happens?

3. Select the Chess wallpaper pattern. Does it fill the entire screen when the Center option is selected?

4. Use both a wallpaper pattern and a basic pattern. What happens?

ANSWERS

1. True.

2. The wallpaper pattern is removed.

3. Yes.

4. The wallpaper covers up the pattern.

Controlling Icon Spacing

At the right side of the Desktop dialog box, about half way down, notice a section for controlling Icon spacing. Windows defaults this setting to a value that adequately spaces icons with typical descriptions. Unfortunately, some icons need more space than others because they might have long labels.

By increasing the number for icon spacing, you can tell Windows to move the icons farther apart when it builds a window. The number in the box refers to pixels, which are the smallest units (dots) on the screen. For example, a typical VGA display is 640 pixels wide and 480 pixels high.

Setting Border Widths

The bottom-left section of the Desktop, called Sizing Grid, allows you to change the way that windows are placed on the screen, and to adjust the thickness of the window borders. When Windows starts for the first time, it sets the grid size to zero, which means that you can leave a window or an icon in any location on the screen. If you set the number in the Granularity box to a nonzero value, Windows defines a grid on which to align all windows and icons. The larger the number, the coarser the grid.

These grid lines are invisible; you only see the effect of the granularity setting. For example, set the value in the Granularity box to the maximum of 49, and choose the OK button to keep the value. Try moving the Main window by a small amount. Notice that the window seems to "jump" to a new location when you release the mouse button.

The Border Width box allows you to define the thickness of the window border that you use to resize a window. Allowable values range from 1 to 49, but you will probably find anything larger than 10 to be rather extravagant. To experiment with this setting, use the Tab key to select the box and then enter a desired value (or use the pointer and the up/down arrow boxes). When you've set a value, choose the OK button to save the setting.

CHECK YOURSELF

1. What is the default setting for the Border Width option?

2. Can you see the frame of a window with Border Width set to 1?

3. What is the largest value that can be used to set the Granularity?

ANSWERS

1. 3.

2. Yes.

3. 49.

Setting the Cursor

The last (bottom) option on the right side of the Desktop dialog box is Cursor Blink Rate. Some people are bothered by fast-blinking objects; others have a hard time finding the cursor if it isn't blinking rapidly. This option allows you to select a comfortable blink rate.

The rate of blinking speeds up when you move the square to the right, and slows down when you move it to the left. Observe the screen closely: Immediately to the right of the scroll bar is a vertical cursor that blinks at the selected rate.

Selecting Fonts

If you have a high-resolution monitor, such as an EGA or VGA, Windows can display various character styles (fonts) on the screen at the same time. You can easily add new font files by double-clicking on the Fonts icon, or by selecting the Fonts option from the Settings menu. The upper part of the Fonts dialog box (Figure 5.14) contains a scroll box listing the fonts provided by Windows. Move through the list using the mouse (or the up and down arrow keys) and notice that the contents of the lower box (labeled Sample) changes to show how the particular character style looks. Notice also that two buttons, Remove and Add, are provided for removing and adding font files, respectively.

These different fonts may not mean a great deal to you if you own a daisy-wheel printer or a simple dot-matrix printer, but they

▼ *Figure 5.14. The Fonts Dialog Box*

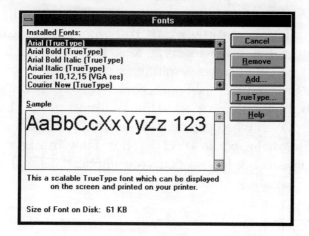

are quite useful if you own a high-capability device, such as a laser or ink-jet printer.

CHECK YOURSELF

Display the Fonts dialog box. What fonts are shown in the Installed Fonts list?

ANSWER

Examples of fonts include Arial, Courier, Modern, Roman, Times New Roman.

Using TrueType Fonts

Windows 3.1 provides a new type of characters called *TrueType* fonts. Because these fonts are easily scalable to any size, they look good on your screen and they can be resized and updated quickly. TrueType fonts appear on the screen exactly as they will look when printed. This true "what you see is what you get (wysiwyg)" feature allows you to accurately view a document before printing it.

When Windows was installed, an option was provided for selecting the True Type fonts. The TrueType fonts that have been installed are listed in the Fonts dialog box. You can easily tell if a font is TrueType because the word "TrueType" appears to the right of the font name. If the TrueType fonts have not been installed, Windows will use a lower-resolution screen font.

If the Enable TrueType Fonts check box has not been selected in the TrueType dialog box, these fonts will not appear. This dialog box is displayed when you choose the TrueType button. You can also use this dialog box to select the Show Only TrueType Fonts in Applications check box so that your applications will only list TrueType fonts.

Adding Fonts

A number of companies create and sell fonts for use with Windows and various printers. Sometimes the fonts come with the printer or can be purchased as font cartridges that are plugged into the printer. If you need to install additional fonts, select the Fonts tool and then choose the Add button. The Add Fonts dialog box (Figure 5.15) appears.

To see how this feature works, let's step through the process of adding a font file. From the Fonts dialog box, choose the Add button. In the List of Fonts list box, select the name of the font file. You can also select a drive or directory (where additional fonts are

▼ *Figure 5.15. Adding a Font*

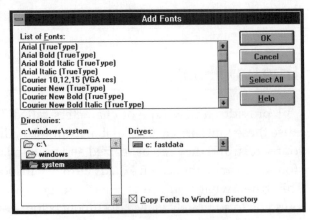

stored) by using the dialog box. Once you've selected the correct filename, choose the OK button to install the font file.

To access fonts directly from some other directory or disk, without having to copy them into the Windows SYSTEM directory, select the Use Fonts from Selected Directory check box.

TIP

Here's a keyboard shortcut for marking multiple font files so that they can be added: Hold down the Control key and click the mouse on each font file that you want to add. After you've highlighted the desired font files, choose the OK button.

You can also use the Add Fonts dialog box to install font files stored on a diskette. Place the diskette with your fonts in drive A, and select the a: item in the Drives list box. The dialog box lists all of the available font files.

CHECK YOURSELF

1. Verify that a font has been properly installed.

2. True or false? Only font files with the extension FON can be installed.

ANSWERS

1. Return to the Fonts dialog box, select the font in the Installed Fonts list box, and make sure the font displays correctly in the Sample box.

2. False. TrueType fonts use the extension TTF.

Removing Font Files

If you think you might not need some of the fonts listed in the Installed Fonts list, you can remove them by highlighting them and choosing the Remove button. Because each font file installed takes up additional memory, it is a good idea to remove fonts if you don't plan to use them. When a font is removed using the Control Panel, the font file is not actually deleted from your hard disk.

As an example, imagine that your Windows files are in the directory C:\WINDOWS and that Windows installed your font files in a subdirectory that it created called SYSTEM. (You can check that the font files are in that subdirectory before starting Windows by entering

```
CD C:\WINDOWS\SYSTEM
```

and then typing DIR *.FON. You'll see a list of the Windows font files, which have the extension .FON.)

To remove a font, select one of the less-useful fonts for deletion, and write its name on a piece of paper. (The Arial font is used by many Windows applications, so don't delete it or you may encounter some unusual problems.) Choose the Remove button. When the dialog box appears, confirm that you want to remove the font.

CHECK YOURSELF

Highlight the Times font and select the Remove button. What happens?

ANSWER

A warning dialog box displays, asking you to confirm that you want to delete the selected font.

Selecting TrueType Fonts

Windows gives you the option of turning TrueType fonts on or off at any time. For the most part, you'll want to use these fonts because they are designed to work well with Windows. However, if you are using other scalable fonts, such as Postscript fonts, and you don't want to use up additional memory for the TrueType fonts, you can turn them off.

To turn TrueType fonts on or off, choose the Fonts icon to display the Fonts dialog box. Next, choose the TrueType button in this dialog box to access the TrueType dialog box. and select or deselect the Enable TrueType Fonts check box. Before your change will take effect, you'll need to restart Windows.

Selecting Fonts

International Settings

You can use this configuration option to customize certain display defaults that tend to be language/culture dependent. Figure 5.16 illustrates how the default International dialog box looks. The first four boxes—Country, Language, Keyboard Layout, and Measurement—allow you to specify the default country, language, keyboard layout, and basis of measurements. You won't need these four settings unless you plan to use Windows in a foreign country. If you select a different country and language, Windows requests that you insert a particular diskette in the A: drive so that it can read the information associated with that installation option.

The fifth box in the International dialog box allows you to select a different list separator. The default value is the comma, but this can easily be replaced with any other character (for example, the hyphen or the vertical bar). Unless you need to change this to get around

▼ *Figure 5.16. The International Dialog Box*

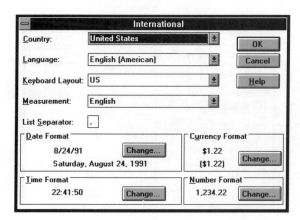

an unusual problem, leave this option unchanged. The important point is that the option is available should you need to use it.

Setting the Date Format

When you choose the Change button in the Date Format box, the dialog box shown in Figure 5.17 appears. Use the three options along the top of the dialog box to specify month/day/year, day/month/year, or year/month/day as the template for the short date format. The Separator box allows you to replace the slash character, which is normally used to separate the date fields, with any other valid character. (Some practical alternatives are the hyphen and the underscore.)

You can use the three other options in the Short Date Format group to select leading zeros for the day and month numbers when they are each single digits, and to identify whether only the two last digits should be displayed for the year. If either the Day or Month boxes contain an X, the leading zero appears for single-digit days or months. If the X is present for the Century option, all four digits are displayed for the year field of the Short Date Format.

The other group provided with the International Date dialog box is called Long Date Format. Its three option buttons—MDY, DMY, and YMD—allow you to choose the displayed order for the date in the same way you selected the Short Date Format.

▼ *Figure 5.17. Setting the Date Format*

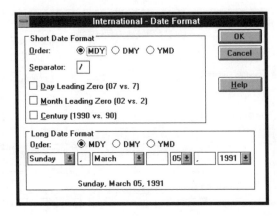

You can use the drop-down scroll boxes to choose abbreviations for the day of the week and the date. To make a selection, expand the scroll box by clicking on it with the mouse or using the Tab key and Alt+Down Arrow.

International Settings

Once you've made your selection, close the menu by clicking on the arrow box immediately above the up scroll arrow box or by pressing Alt+Up Arrow. The small square data boxes between drop-down menus allow you to define custom separators between each field in the Long Date Format. The first and last boxes contain commas because this is the standard separator used in the United States.

Experiment with various symbol—such as slashes and asterisks—to achieve unusual effects. To move from one data field to another, either click on the field that you want or use the Tab key to move the highlight there. The changes that you make to the Long Date Format are immediately reflected in the sample date at the bottom of the box. When you're satisfied with your changes, choose the OK button to save them.

CHECK YOURSELF

1. Display a short date in the format 11-02-59.

2. Display the date as 11-02-1959.

3. What is the main difference between the Short Date Format and the Long Date Format?

ANSWERS

1. Select Order: MDY and Separator: -.

2. Select Century (1990 vs. 90).

3. The Short Date Format represents a date numerically, and the Long Date Format represents a date in a completely spelled-out format.

▼ *Figure 5.18. Setting the Time Format*

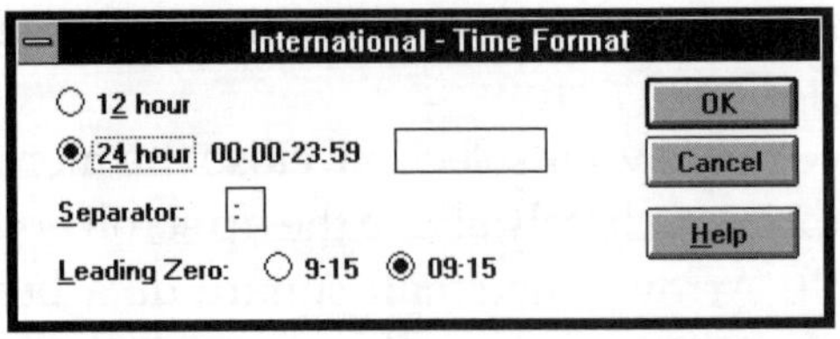

```
┌──────────────────────────────────────────────┐
│ ▬         International - Time Format          │
├──────────────────────────────────────────────┤
│  ○ 1̲2 hour                          ┌──────┐   │
│  ◉ 2̲4 hour  00:00-23:59  ┌────────┐ │  OK  │   │
│                          └────────┘ └──────┘   │
│  S̲eparator:   [:]                   ┌──────┐   │
│                                     │Cancel│   │
│  L̲eading Zero:  ○ 9:15  ◉ 09:15     └──────┘   │
│                                     ┌──────┐   │
│                                     │ H̲elp │   │
│                                     └──────┘   │
└──────────────────────────────────────────────┘
```

Setting the Time Format

The next feature in the International dialog box allows you to customize the time format. When you choose the Change button in the Time Format section, the dialog box shown in Figure 5.18 appears. You can select a 12-hour format or a 24-hour format. You can change the contents of these boxes to a new description of up to 8 characters in length.

The box labeled Separator allows you to change the character that separates the various time fields. If you position the cursor to the right of the colon and press the backspace key, you eliminate the separator altogether and get military time. Unfortunately, when you remove the colon between the hours and the minutes, you also remove the separator between the minutes and the seconds, so you end up with a five- or six-digit display for the time.

The last option allows you to select or delete a leading zero on the Hours field. When you've made your selections, choose the OK button to keep the changes.

Setting the Currency and Number Format

The final two features of the International window are of limited value to most U.S. users. The International Currency Format (Figure 5.19) lets you define how to show information associated with money fields. You can place the currency symbol in several different places, and show negative numbers by various permutations of the currency symbol and either a hyphen or parentheses.

The other feature, International Number Format (Figure 5.20), allows you to customize the separator between the hundreds and

▼ *Figure 5.19. Setting the Currency Format*

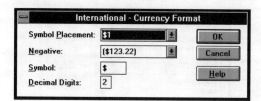

thousands digits, the decimal separator and the number of digits displayed to the right of the units digit. (In Europe, many countries use a comma to separate the whole units from the fractional part.) The main intent of these options is to provide standard information for future applications (such as accounting packages) that will run under Windows 3.1 and future releases. After entering your changes, remember to choose the OK button.

Setting the Keyboard

The Keyboard option in the Control Panel displays a simple dialog box (Figure 5.21) that allows you to set a keyboard speed delay that defines the time interval between when a key is pressed and an action occurs, and the rate at which a key repeats when it's held down (the *repeat* rate). To set these features, two slider bars are provided: Keyboard Speed and Repeat Rate.

To increase or decrease the keyboard delay, use the mouse or the arrow keys to move the slide box to a desired speed setting. Then Tab (or click, or press Alt+T) to the test area and hold down a letter key to check the response rate.

▼ *Figure 5.20. Setting the Number Format*

▼ *Figure 5.21. The Keyboard Dialog Box*

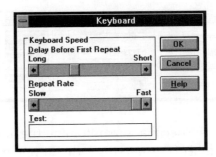

To change the response rate, move the slider bar in the Repeat Rate box toward Fast or Slow. Again, you'll want to check your settings using the Test box.

When you're comfortable with both setting, choose the OK button to save your changes.

Setting the Mouse

You can select the Mouse option (Figure 5.22) to customize the speed at which the mouse cursor moves across the screen, and the speed with which you have to click the left button to count as a double-click. When you move the scroll box for the Mouse Tracking Speed to the right, notice that the mouse appears "twitchier." When you move the box to the left, mouse travel appears slower and smoother.

TIP

This section covers only the techniques for setting your mouse. If you are using some other type of pointing device, Windows will provide different options to help you set up the pointing device.

If you move the Double Click Speed scroll box to the right, you need to click the button faster for Windows to recognize it as a

▼ *Figure 5.22. The Mouse Dialog Box*

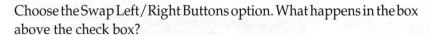

double-click. Moving the scroll box to the left allows you to take your time between clicks. To allow you to experiment with the click speed, Windows provides a Test box immediately below the speed selector. If you move the cursor to the test area and double-click fast enough, the box changes from white to black. Double-clicking again at the proper speed changes the color back. This adjustment is rather personal and important because some users are speed demons and other like to do things at a slower pace.

The next option available is the Swap Left/Right Buttons check box. If you select this option, the functions of the left and right mouse buttons are switched. This feature enables left-handed users to use the physical right button on the mouse to click or double-click on objects. If you choose this option, it goes into effect immediately, so you have to use the physical right button to click the OK button to save the changes. Of course, if you change your mind at a later time, you can always choose the Mouse tool again and use the Swap option to change back to the default button operation.

CHECK YOURSELF

Choose the Swap Left/Right Buttons option. What happens in the box above the check box?

ANSWER

The L is now on the right side.

Setting Network Options

The icon for this option appears only if you told Windows during installation that your PC is connected to a network. When you activate the Network feature, a dialog box provides the necessary information for your particular network. You can use this dialog box to specify information about logging on and off the network (including passwords) and the protocol for sending messages to other users on the network.

Setting Communication Ports

The Ports option allows you adjust the settings for a particular serial communications port. *Serial ports* are information paths between computers where only one wire carries the information in each direction (as compared to a parallel port, where data is usually transmitted over eight data lines at the same time). Serial ports are typically used for hooking up modems, mice, and printers. You will often hear the term *RS-232 port* used to refer to a serial port because this is the name of the standard that specifies the voltage and wiring characteristics of these ports.

When you select the Ports option, several icons identify the possible output ports (Figure 5.23). When you select the port to be updated, the Ports Settings dialog box appears (Figure 5.24). The drop-down scroll box called Baud Rate indicates the speed at which your data is sent and received by this particular port.

▼ *Figure 5.23. The Ports Dialog Box*

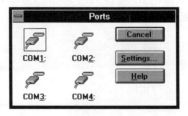

▼ *Figure 5.24. Changing Port Settings*

*Setting
Communication
Ports*

The standards for serial ports define certain fixed speeds for these transfers (such as 300 baud, 1200 baud, and 2400 baud). You must find out what baud rate is expected by the device on the other end of the wire. The communications speed for most printers and modems is specified in the owner's manual. The common settings for baud rates are 9600 for printers and 300, 1200, and 2400 for modems.

The next scroll box in the dialog box allows you to identify the number of bits of data sent out in one group. (The sending computer has to pause between groups in order to give the receiving equipment a chance to look at the incoming data and to do something with it.) Most equipment today expects either seven or eight bits of data at a time, but this can be verified by referring to the owner's manual.

The Parity box allows you to select the error-detection method used by the devices. When each group of data bits is sent, the serial port can send another bit to indicate the parity of the sum of the data bits. In other words, the serial port hardware can add the 1s and 0s for a group, and then insert a 1 or a 0 at the end to make the sum of all of the bits in the group either odd or even. If you select the None option, no parity bit is calculated. The Mark option forces the parity bit to a 1, and the Space option forces it to a 0. The use of parity can be very important when your computer is operating in an electrically noisy environment (such as a manufacturing area with many induction motors or fluorescent lights).

The Stop Bits box allows you to specify the minimum pause between data groups. This is typically either 1 or 1.5 bits. (Again, check the manual of the other machine for this information.)

The Flow Control box allows you to select data metering between the hardware units. The serial hardware specification identifies additional wires that can be run between the computers to request that the sender pause for a while. The receiving unit can also send a software code on the data wire back to the sender to instruct the sender to pause. This software code is typically used with modems (because the communications between modems consists of unique tones that signify 1s and 0s for the sender and the receiver), and is known as Xon/Xoff. Of course, if you are using a serial protocol to send information between two PCs in the same area, use the hardware flow control (rather than the software code) to allow the PCs to send pure data without wasting time checking the data stream for the Xon/Xoff codes.

CHECK YOURSELF

1. True or false? The standard Microsoft Mouse connects to a serial port.

2. Open the Ports Settings dialog box for Com1. Which default settings are listed?

ANSWERS

1. True.

2. Baud Rate—9600; Data Bits—8; Parity—None; Stop Bits—1; Flow Control—Xon/Xoff.

Installing Printers

When you select the Printers option, you see the same dialog box that was presented for printer installation when you installed Windows. (The Windows installation program invoked the Control Panel Printers application so that you could tell Windows which printers were available.)

TIP

Installing a new printer is actually a multistep process. The details for installing and setting up different types of printers are presented in Chapter 7. The information here covers only the basic features of the Printers dialog box.

When you choose the Printers configuration icon, a rather complicated dialog box appears (Figure 5.25). As indicated, this dialog box allows you to install, setup, and remove printers. If you have added one or more new printers to your computer system, use the Add button to select the additional printers from the list of printers that Windows supports. After you select a printer, you'll need to choose the Install button (Figure 5.26). A dialog box asks you to insert a specific Windows diskette in drive A so that Windows can obtain the printer driver file.

Insert the diskette and choose the OK button. When the dialog box disappears, choose the Connect button to select the output port for the new printer (Figure 5.27). Use the scroll box to select the output port. (One of the options even allows you to send the data to a file, instead of a port.) Next choose the Setup button to move on to selecting printer details (Figure 5.28).

Use the Setup dialog box to select between various printers that share the same print driver, and to define the paper size, graphics resolution, and so on for the particular printer. (The information in the Setup window varies depending upon the type of printer selected.) After you've made the desired changes, choose the OK button to save them.

▼ *Figure 5.25. The Printers Dialog Box*

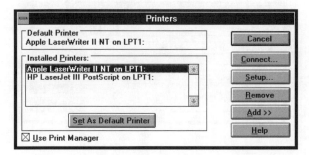

▼ *Figure 5.26. Installing a Printer*

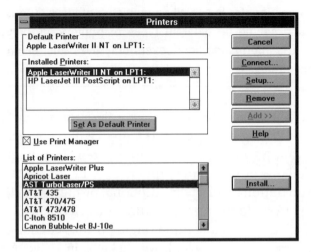

▼ *Figure 5.27. The Connections Dialog Box*

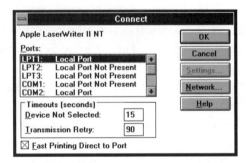

▼ *Figure 5.28. Selecting Options for a Printer*

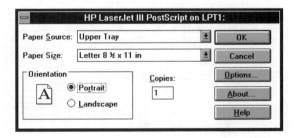

CHECK YOURSELF

True or false? When the Printers dialog box displays, the active printer is highlighted.

ANSWER

True.

Removing an Installed Printer

Return to Figure 5.26 and notice that the Printers dialog box can also be used to remove the printer highlighted in the dialog box. When you're finished with the configuration window, close the dialog box to save your configuration changes. When you return to the main Printers dialog box, select one of the printers in the Installed Printers list, and then choose the Set As Default Printer button to make this printer the active system printer. The other printers in the list are changed to inactive because Windows allows only one active printer per printer port at a time.

Windows also allows network users to install network printers by choosing the Network button in the Connect dialog box. If you're not connected to a network, you can try to select the Network button, but you'll get an error message if you don't have a network driver installed and ready to go. Windows will then display a Printers-Network Connections dialog box because it figures you might just want to change the path to the server.

Setting Sound

This option opens a simple dialog box (Figure 5.29) where you can assign sounds to system and application events. For example, you can play special sounds whenever Windows starts, exits, or displays a message. You can also use the Sound dialog to enable or

▼ *Figure 5.29. The Sound Dialog Box*

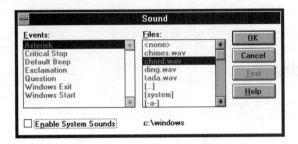

disable the computer beep that Windows uses to tell you that an error has occurred.

In order to fully use the sound feature, you'll need to have a sound card installed in your computer. If your system does not have a sound card, you will not be able to access any of the features in the Sound dialog box except the Enable System Sounds check box.

To enable or disable the system beep, use the Enable System Sounds check box. (If the X is present in the check box, Windows beeps when you do something wrong. If the box is empty, the sound is turned off.) Choose the OK button to save any change.

Assigning Sounds to Events

If your computer has a sound card installed, you can assign a sound to an event by following these steps:

1. Select an event, such as Windows Exit or Windows Start, in the Event list.

2. Select the sound file in the Files list.

   You can continue this process for each event you want to assign a sound to. If you want to disable the sound for an event, select the event and then select the <none> option in the Files list.

Windows stores sounds in special files having the extension .WAV. You can test a sound at any time by selecting the file and choosing the Test button.

Setting up Drivers

Windows 3.1 provides a new feature so that you can install, configure and remove special drivers for devices such as video controllers, MIDI, and sound cards. To access this feature, choose the Drivers icon in the Control Panel window. Figure 5.30 shows the dialog box that is displayed.

The Drivers dialog box lists the drivers that are currently installed. To add a driver, choose the Add button. A second dialog box will be displayed so that you can select a new driver file. This dialog box lists the drivers that Windows knows about. If the driver you want to install is not listed, select the Unlisted or Updated Driver option and choose the OK button. Windows will then ask you to enter either a disk or specify a pathname so that it can find the driver.

After a new driver has been installed, you may need to configure it. Select the driver in the Drivers dialog box and choose the Setup button. Windows will then display a unique dialog box so that you can select the appropriate settings for your driver.

Setting 386 Enhanced Mode Options

The 386 Enhanced icon appears only when Windows is running in 386 enhanced mode. When it's chosen, you can select options to

▼ *Figure 5.30. The Drivers Dialog Box*

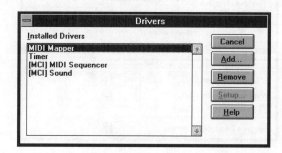

control how Windows applications compete for peripheral devices by accessing I/O ports, and how system resources should be allocated for Windows and non-Windows applications.

Accessing Devices

The first option in the 386 Enhanced dialog as shown in Figure 5.31 allows you to define how Windows should react if several programs try to access the same I/O hardware at the same time. (This will usually happen only if non-Windows applications access a port at the same time when Windows tries to access it.) The three options for each port are: Always Warn, Never Warn, and Idle.

Always Warn means that whenever Windows detects a conflict, a warning dialog box appears to allow you to decide what to do.

The Never Warn option is the "What, me worry?" one of the bunch; you should only select this option if you know that a conflict will never arise because you only use 100-percent Windows 3.1-compatible applications. The Idle option tells Windows to wait for the number of seconds specified in the box to the right of the option before trying to use that particular port again. No warning will be issued if you select the Idle option because it will just keep trying until it succeeds.

To set up your I/O devices, you must first select the serial port that is connected to a hardware device, such as a modem or a printer. Next, select the desired setting for that port–Always Warn, Never Warn, or Idle–and choose the OK button.

▼ *Figure 5.31. Setting 386 Enhanced Mode Options*

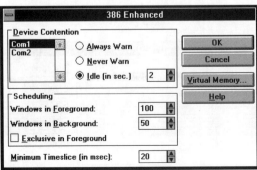

Scheduling Your Applications

The other options in the 386 Enhanced dialog box are provided to help you set up Windows so that it can better run multiple Windows and non-Windows applications at the same time. This technique of running multiple applications is called *multitasking*.

Overall, the Scheduling options allow you to identify what percentage of the total execution time should be consumed by Windows when it runs in foreground and in background. Unless you plan to run a non-Windows task in the background (such as your own custom serial port program), leave the Windows in Foreground option at 100%. If you want Windows to be suspended while you run a non-Windows program, you may want to reduce the Windows in Background percentage to something very small. The Exclusive in Foreground option indicates that only Windows tasks should run when Windows is in the foreground.

The Minimum Timeslice option identifies how long a span of time will be allowed for either a non-Windows task or for all active Windows tasks. The larger the number, the higher the apparent system throughput (less interruptions), but the response time to your actions (as the user) might become slower (the interface may appear "jerky"). The default value of 20 milliseconds is probably a good compromise, but you may wish to experiment with different values to optimize system operation for your typical mix of programs. As always, choose the OK button to save the changes when you're finished.

Setting the Swap File

The Virtual Memory button in the 386 Enhanced dialog box allows you to specify settings for the swap file. In the 386 Enhanced mode, Windows uses a swap file on your hard disk to move data from your computer's memory when the memory is full. When the data is later needed, it is restored from the swap file. The swap file actually serves as an extension of your memory and helps create a virtual memory system.

Windows supports two types of swap files for the 386 Enhanced mode: permanent and temporary. As its name implies, the permanent swap file is allocated on your hard disk as a permanent storage area. You can easily specify the size of this file and its size remains constant. The temporary swap file, on the other hand, is allocated by Windows when it needs more virtual memory. For this type of file, you specify the maximum number of bytes you want Windows to use to write data to the swap file.

To view or change the swap file settings, choose the Virtual Memory button in the 386 Enhanced dialog box. The first dialog box that is displayed lists the current virtual memory settings for your system. including the swap file's drive name size, and type.

Figure 5.32 shows the Virtual memory dialog box that is displayed if you choose the Change Button. Notice that the first group in the dialog box, Current Settings, show you how the swap file is currently set up.

To change the disk drive where the swap file is stored, use the Drives selector. The swap file type is selected from the Type box. Here you'll find three options: Permanent, Temporary, and None. The text box at the bottom of the dialog, which is labeled Approximate Size if you are selecting a permanent swap file or Size otherwise, is used to specify the size of the swap file in megabytes (KB).

If you change any of the Swap file settings and click the OK button, Windows will display a warning dialog so that you can restart Windows. In order for the new settings to take effect, you must restart Windows.

▼ *Figure 5.32. Setting Virtual Memory*

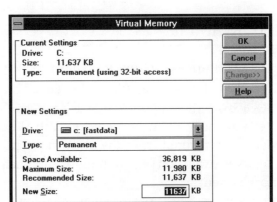

QUICK TASK SUMMARY

Task	Procedure
Start the Control Panel	Double-click on Control Panel icon
Select new color scheme	Use Color tool and select option in Color Schemes box
Change color of an item	Select item and choose a new color
Change date or time	Use Date/Time tool
Select a screen saver	Use Desktop tool and select screen saver in the Screen Saver Name box
Select a desktop pattern	Use Desktop tool
Change icon spacing	Use Desktop tool, and enter new spacing value
View/Install font	Use Font tool
Remove font	Use Font tool, select font, choose Remove button
Turn on TrueType fonts	Use Font tool, select TrueType button
Change keyboard setting	Use Keyboard tool
Change mouse setting	Use Mouse tool
Set up a communication port	Use Ports tool, select port, change settings
Install a printer	Use Printers tool
Select a printer as default	Use Printers tool, select printer, select the Set As Default Printer button
Change 386 options	Use 386 Enhanced Mode tool
Exit Control Panel	Choose Exit (File menu); or Double-click on Control Panel's Control menu box

PRACTICE WHAT YOU'VE LEARNED

In this chapter, you've been exposed to the configuration options available under the Control Panel. As you can see, Windows is a complex and flexible system that needs to know a great deal about the available hardware and software in order to run at peak efficiency. Use these exercises to further explore the features of the Control Panel.

1. Start the Control Panel by double-clicking on the Control Panel icon in the Main group window.

2. Double-click on the Desktop icon.

3. Click on the Name pull-down box, and select the Diamonds pattern.

4. Click on the Edit Pattern button.

5. Click the OK button.

6. Click the OK button in the Desktop dialog box.

7. Double-click on the Mouse icon in the Control Panel menu.

8. Slide the scroll box in the Mouse Tracking Speed option toward the Fast indicator (to the right).

9. Click the OK button.

10. Slide the mouse around on your desktop.

11. Double-click on the Ports icon.

12. Double-click on the Com1 icon.

13. Click on the Baud Rate pull-down box.

14. Leave the baud rate unchanged, and click the Cancel button.

15. Exit the Control Panel by selecting the Exit command from the Settings menu.

ANSWERS

1. The Control Panel window displays with its associated icons. Some of these icons include Color, Fonts, Ports, Mouse, and Desktop.

2. The Desktop dialog box displays.

3. The text in the Name box changes from (None) to Diamonds.

4. The Desktop - Edit Pattern dialog box displays. This dialog presents an example of the Diamonds pattern.

5. Control returns to the Desktop dialog box.

6. The background screen changes from the default pattern to the Diamonds pattern.

7. The Mouse dialog box appears.

8. The scroll box moves to the right.

9. The dialog box disappears.

10. The response time for the mouse is faster.

11. The Ports dialog box displays.

12. The Settings dialog box displays.

13. The list of available baud rates displays.

14. The Settings dialog box disappears.

15. Control returns to the Program Manager.

Managing Your Files and Disks

This chapter explains the basics of DOS file management, and shows you how to use the Windows File Manager to simplify the way you can manage your files and disk resources. We'll begin by taking a brief look at DOS directories, and then we'll move on to explore the powerful File Manager features. In this chapter, you'll learn:

- ▲ How files and directories are stored and accessed under DOS
- ▲ How to start and use the File Manager
- ▲ How to copy, delete, and search for files
- ▲ How to create, delete, and rename directories
- ▲ How to copy and move directories
- ▲ How to print files
- ▲ How to format and copy diskettes

DOS Directory Basics

If you're an experienced DOS user and you know how to create and use directories, skip this section and move directly to the next section, where we'll cover the File Manager. If you're a relatively new DOS user, you'll want to read this section. In order to understand why DOS does certain things, you must first understand some basics about your computer. We'll start with a simple explanation about how disk drives work.

You can think of a blank disk (especially a hard disk) as a huge warehouse full of identical shoe boxes. You can store all kinds of information in these shoe boxes, but you will quickly lose track of the information unless you have a method for organizing it. DOS provides special disk partitions called *directories* that allow you to group your files. You can issue commands to create directories and copy files into new directories that you create. DOS is called a *hierarchical directory system* because it allows you to place one directory (subdirectory) inside of another, creating a directory system called a *tree structure.*

Figure 6.1 presents an example of a tree directory system. The *root directory* is the very top of the tree. This directory is the only directory present when a disk is first formatted.

You can use DOS commands (such as MKDIR) to create subdirectories. (Later in this chapter, we'll show you how to create and delete subdirectories using the File Manager). For example, Figure 6.1 shows a subdirectory called WINDOWS immediately below the root directory (\), and a directory called SYSTEM that is connected to the WINDOWS subdirectory. Thus, the root directory

▼ *Figure 6.1. A Sample Tree Directory*

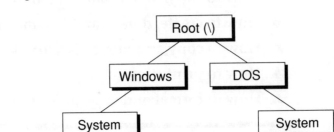

(\) is considered to be the *parent* of the WINDOWS directory, and the WINDOWS directory is the parent of the SYSTEM directory.

Notice that the root directory is also the parent of another directory called DOS (a good place to keep most of the DOS files). Within practical limits (which keep growing with subsequent versions of DOS), you can have as many subdirectories as you wish, and can connect as many subdirectories as you want to a single directory.

DOS Directory Basics

Directory Requirements

Let's return to our simple directory model, shown in Figure 6.1. The root directory is identified as C:\. The WINDOWS subdirectory is C:\WINDOWS, and the system directory is C:\WINDOWS \SYSTEM. Notice that the separator character between the subdirectory names is the backslash. (If you use a normal slash, which leans in the opposite direction, DOS gets very confused.)

Another limitation imposed by DOS is that each directory can only have one parent. Thus, in our previous example, it would be possible to create a subdirectory from the DOS directory called SYSTEM. This directory would be identified as C:\DOS\SYSTEM, and would be completely independent of the subdirectory under WINDOWS, which would be identified as C:\WINDOWS\SYSTEM.

When you create directories and place files in them, try to limit the number of files you put into any one directory. A large directory slows DOS down because DOS must search through more files. If you think your directories are becoming too large, reorganize them by using more subdirectories. (Again, you don't have to do this in DOS. We'll show you how to create directories and copy files into directories later in this chapter.)

CHECK YOURSELF

1. Refer to Figure 6.2 to answer the following questions:
   (a) How many subdirectories are present?
   (b) How many parent directories contain subdirectories?

▼ *Figure 6.2. A Directory Tree Example*

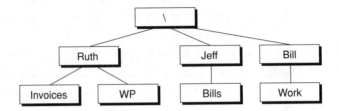

(c) Specify the path to access a file in the subdirectory INVOICES.
(d) Specify the path to access a file in the subdirectory BILLS.

2. Go to the DOS prompt and execute the TREE command. What happens?

ANSWERS

1. (a) 7
   (b) 4
   (c) \RUTH\INVOICES
   (d) \JEFF\BILLS

2. DOS lists all of the subdirectories available in your system.

Introducing the File Manager

Now that you've had an opportunity to review the basics of disk organization under DOS, let's explore the File Manager—the tool Windows provides for managing files and directories. The File Manager performs most of the major file and directory management operations that can be performed by DOS, including:

▲ Copying, moving, deleting, and renaming files
▲ Viewing files in selected directories
▲ Viewing directories
▲ Searching for files

▲ Selecting directories

▲ Creating, deleting, and renaming directories

▲ Copying and moving entire directories

▲ Running programs

▲ Associating files with an application

▲ Printing text files

▲ Formatting and copying diskettes

▲ Selecting drives

▲ Connecting to a network file server

**Introducing the
File Manager**

Starting File Manager

The easiest way to start the File Manager is to double-click on the File Manager icon, located in the Main group window.

If you don't have a mouse, open the Window menu in the Program Manager by pressing Alt+W and select the number for the Main window. After this window appears, use the arrow keys to highlight the File Manager icon and press the Enter key.

You can also start the File Manager from the Program Manager by following these steps:

1. Choose the Run command from the File menu.

2. Enter the program name, WINFILE, in the Command Line text box.

3. Choose the OK button.

Starting File Manager Automatically

You can set up Windows so that the File Manager will automatically appear whenever Windows starts. To customize Windows in this manner, you'll need to change one of the initialization files, SYSTEM.INI:

1. Bring up the file SYSTEM.INI in a text editor such as Notepad.

2. Change the Shell command so that it reads:

    ```
    Shell=WINFILE.EXE
    ```

    (By default, this command is set as Shell=PROGMAN.EXE to direct Windows to run the Program Manager when Windows starts.)

3. Save the file, exit Windows, and then restart Windows to have this change take effect.

The File Manager will then be used as the startup application instead of the Program Manager.

TIP

As an alternative to changing SYSTEM.INI, you can copy the File Manager icon from the Main group to the StartUp group by pressing the Ctrl key and dragging the icon to make Windows run the File Manager at startup. If you use this technique, keep in mind that the File Manager shell will not actually replace the Program Manager shell. Instead, Windows will run the File Manager as a minimized icon, making it easy to access the File Manager at any time during a Windows session.

A Quick Look at the File Manager

Figure 6.3 shows how the File Manager window looks when it starts up. Notice that the main components have been labeled. The File Manager actually has two separate parts: the File Manager window (containing the typical Windows menu bar), and the directory window (which displays the contents of the current drive).

The File Manager window provides the set of file-management commands that you can use to manage the contents of your disks. To access these commands, select the menu items, such as File, Disk, Tree, View, and so on. The main file and directory maintenance commands are located in the File menu.

The directory window provides a great deal of information at a glance. When it first appears, it is divided into two parts. The left

▼ *Figure 6.3. The File Manager*

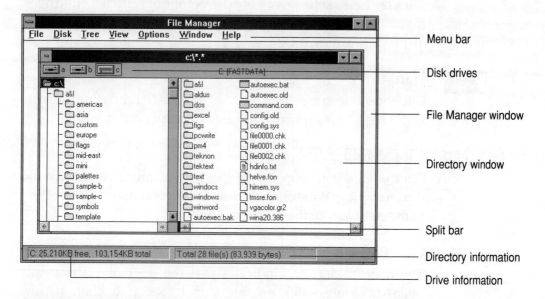

half displays the directory tree for the current drive and the right half displays the contents of the current directory. This dual view, called the *tree and directory* view, is very useful for helping you locate and select directories and then viewing the files in the selected directory.

Here are some of the important features of directory windows:

▲ Directories and the files stored in directories can be viewed at the same time

▲ Multiple directory windows can be displayed

▲ Directory windows function as document windows and can be moved, resized, and minimized to icons

▲ Directory windows can be viewed in three different ways: Tree and Directory view, Tree Only view, and Directory Only view

The File Manager Icons

The directory window uses a number of different icons to represent disk drives, files, directories, and programs.

Diskette drive

Click on the diskette drive icon to select one of your diskette drives. If you don't have a diskette in the selected drive, Windows will display a warning message.

 Hard drive

Click on this icon to select your hard drive. After choosing this icon, you'll see a new directory window for your hard disk.

Closed folder

Click on this icon to open a directory. If you are using the tree and directory view, Windows will display the contents of this directory in the right half of the directory window.

Open folder

The open folder icon indicates that the directory is currently opened. Double-click on this icon to see if it contains any subdirectories. If the directory's subdirectories are currently displayed in the tree view and you double-click on this icon, the subdirectories will be collapsed.

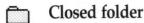 **Program icon**

This icon represents a program file (any file having the extension BAT, COM, EXE, or PIF). Double-click on this icon to start a program.

Document file icon

This icon represents a DOS file that has not been associated with any Windows or DOS application. Double-click on this icon and a warning message appears because Windows will not know which application to launch for the file.

Associated file icon

This icon represents a file that has been associated with a program. Click on this icon and Windows will start the program associated with the file and open the file.

Up arrow icon

Click this icon to move up one level in the directory tree.

Minimized directory window icon

This icon represents a directory window that has been minimized to an icon. Click on this icon to open its associated directory window.

Selecting a Drive

The drive icons appear on the line immediately below the title bar of a directory window. The icons that represent your diskette drives are listed first, followed by the hard disk icons. When a drive is selected, its icon is outlined with a rectangle. For example in Figure 6.3, the system has three drives A, B, and C. Drives A and B are the diskette drives and drive C is the hard drive, which is currently selected.

To choose a different drive as the active one, click once on the drive's icon. From the keyboard, use the Tab key to highlight one of the drive icons and then press the right or left arrow keys to place the selection frame (rectangle) around the desired drive. When the drive is highlighted, press the Enter key. You can also select a drive by pressing the Ctrl key and the first letter of the drive. For example, to select drive A, press Ctrl+A.

When a new drive is selected, the directory window changes to display the files and directories for the drive, starting with the active directory. (The active directory is the directory that was previously selected when the drive was in use.)

TIP

If you double-click on a drive icon, you can open a new directory window and the previously opened directory window will still be available for viewing. This technique is useful for quickly opening multiple directory windows. In fact, you can double-click on the drive that is currently in use to open a second window (copy) for the active directory.

CHECK YOURSELF

Start at the File Manager by double-clicking on the File Manager icon.

1. How many disk drives does your system have?

2. What's the difference between a floppy drive icon and a hard disk icon?

3. Open the File menu. What are the available commands?

4. Open the menus in the File Manager. Where is the Format Disk command located?

5. What information displays in the status bar at the bottom of the File Manager window?

ANSWERS

1. Count the icons that appear under the directory window below the title bar.

2. A floppy disk icon has a door that looks like a floppy disk faceplate.

3. Click on the File menu item, or press Alt+F. The commands are Open, Move, Copy, Delete, Rename, Properties, Run, Print, Associate, Create Directory, Search, Select Files, and Exit.

4. In the Disk menu.

5. The letter of the current drive and the amount of free disk space available, the size of the selected drive, the number of files in the selected directory, and the size of the selected directory.

Using the Directory Window

The directory window in Figure 6.4 shows a directory structure with the directory C:\EXCEL and numerous subdirectories. The title bar of the window displays the full pathname for the directory that has been selected. Each subdirectory is represented with a file

▼ *Figure 6.4. Viewing Directories and Subdirectories*

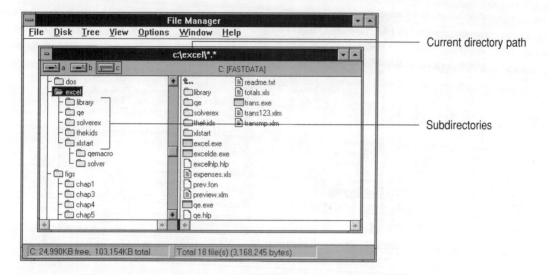

Current directory path

Subdirectories

folder icon. Notice that the subdirectory icons for the EXCEL and FIGS subdirectories contain branches for other directory icons. This representation indicates that these two directories contain subdirectories.

TIP

If you use the Indicate Expandable Branches option from the Tree menu, directories that contain subdirectories will be displayed as a file folder with a (+). You'll also find a minus sign (-) on some directory icons. This symbol indicates that a directory has been expanded. If you double-click on the icon, the subdirectory branches extended from that icon are collapsed.

Figure 6.5 shows what happens if you click on the WINDOWS subdirectory and then choose the Expand Branch command from the Tree menu. As you can see, the WINDOWS subdirectory has one subdirectory, called SYSTEM. (If you had chosen the Expand All command from the Tree menu rather than Expand Branch, then both the WINDOWS and SYSTEM directories would have been expanded to show the next level of subdirectories.)

▼ *Figure 6.5. Expanding the Windows Subdirectory*

Viewing Options

So far, the directory windows that we've presented have displayed information in a dual tree and directory window format. Although this configuration is the one you'll find most useful, you can select from two other methods for displaying your files and directories: Tree Only and Directory Only. Choose either of these viewing options from the View menu. The View menu provides a number of other options for displaying your directories and files, such as viewing files by size, date, type, and so on. We'll explore these options later in this chapter.

Tree Only

Displays only the directory tree structure for the selected disk drive. This viewing option is useful for quickly examining the structure of a disk drive.

Directory Only

Displays only the content of the selected directory. This viewing option is useful if you are only interested in examining or selecting the files in a directory and you don't need to see the directory tree.

Splitting the Directory Window

If you are using the Tree and Directory view option, you can easily control how the right and left parts of a directory window are displayed. At the bottom of the directory window you'll find a split bar that you can slide to the right or left with the mouse to change the sizes of the tree and directory portions of the window. You can also move the split bar by choosing the Split command from the View menu. When this command is chosen, the split bar is highlighted, allowing you to move it with the mouse or the right and left arrow keys. Either click the mouse or press the Enter key to anchor the split bar.

Navigating the Directory Tree

In using the directory tree to locate and view your directories, you should learn about a few commands that you'll find useful. Each of these commands can be selected from the Tree menu or by using shortcut keys.

Expand One Level

This command allows you to view the first level of subdirectories in the selected directory. For example, if you select the root directory and then choose this command, you'll see the first level of subdirectories that are inside the root directory (see Figure 6.6). You can also perform this operation by double-clicking on a directory icon or highlighting the icon and pressing the + key.

Expand Branch

This command allows you to view all of the directories beneath the selected directory. To use the keyboard shortcut for this command, select the directory you wish to expand and press the * key.

Expand All

This command allows you to view every subdirectory on a disk drive. If you have many directories and subdirectories, this command may take a moment to execute. The keyboard shortcut is Ctrl+*.

▼ *Figure 6.6 Viewing the First Level of Subdirectories*

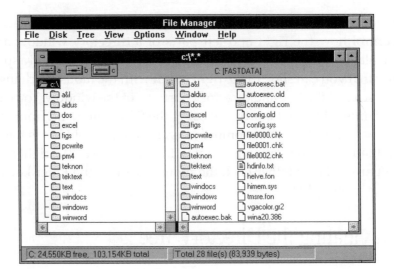

Collapse Branch

To eliminate a directory's subdirectories from a tree view, select the directory and then choose this command. If you want to collapse all the directories on a drive, select the root directory before using this command. You can also collapse a directory tree branch by double-clicking on an expanded directory or highlighting the directory and pressing the - key.

TIP

If you want to quickly examine every directory on a drive, follow these steps:

1. Choose the Expand All command to view the full directory tree.

2. Press the Home key to select the root directory.

3. Keep pressing the down arrow key to view the contents of each directory in the left side of the directory window.

Viewing a Directory

*Viewing a
Directory*

Now that you've seen the basic features of the File Manager, let's examine how the contents of directories are displayed. You can view the list of files and subdirectories in a directory by clicking on the directory icon when the Tree and Directory option is chosen. For example, Figure 6.7 illustrates what you see if you open the WINDOWS directory. Notice that the first two entries are the up arrow and the SYSTEM subdirectory. Windows provides a consistent location for subdirectories by placing the subdirectory icons at the beginning of the listing, so you don't have to search through a directory to find a particular subdirectory.

To use the keyboard to open a directory, press the up or down arrow key to select the desired directory. When a directory is selected, its files will be displayed automatically.

As Figure 6.7 shows, the title of the window represents the full pathname for the selected directory, including the drive and subdirectories. A filename pattern after the directory name indicates the types of files that appear in the directory window. The default pattern is *.*, which indicates that all files will be displayed.

▼ **Figure 6.7. Opening the Windows Subdirectory**

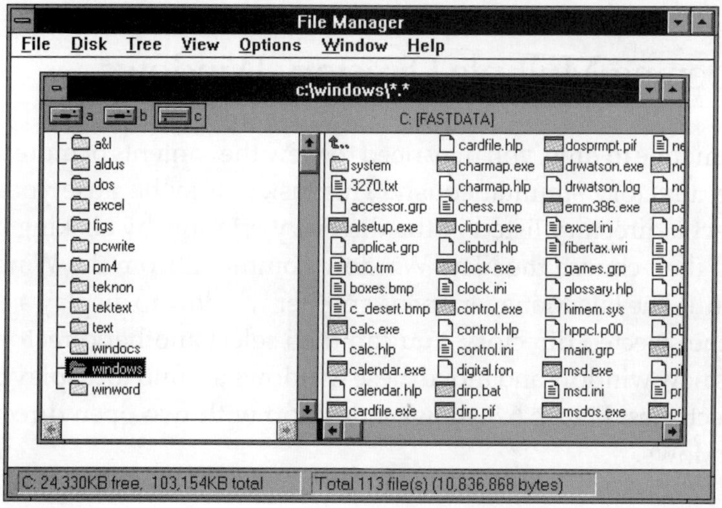

CHECK YOURSELF

1. What is the full directory path for the directory window shown in Figure 6.7?

2. What is the file pattern shown in Figure 6.7?

3. What information displays in the status bar at the bottom of the window?

4. True or false? The directory window allows you to display the directory structure of one drive at a time.

5. Double-click on the title bar of a directory window. What happens?

ANSWERS

1. C:\WINDOWS.

2. *.* (all files).

3. The number of files selected, the number of bytes in the selected files, the total number of files listed in the window, and the size of the directory in bytes.

4. True.

5. The window expands to its full size.

Opening Multiple Directory Windows

From time to time, you may need to view the contents of more than one directory simultaneously. This task is easy because you can select a directory listed in the directory window by clicking on it and then choose the New Window command from the Window menu. The File Manager opens another window to display a copy of the selected directory. You can then select another directory in this new window and move these windows around to display both directories. Figure 6.8 shows a desktop with two open directory windows.

▼ *Figure 6.8. Viewing Multiple Directory Windows*

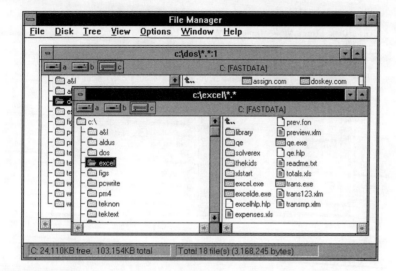

TIP

Here's another method for opening an additional directory window. Hold down the Shift key and double-click on a directory icon. When another directory window is opened for the same directory, notice that a number is displayed in the directory window title bar to indicate that multiple windows are opened for the same directory.

Remember that the directory windows operate in the same way as other scrollable windows. That is, you can scroll, shrink, enlarge, and move the directory windows by using the mouse or the keyboard. For example, you can enlarge a directory window so that it covers the desktop by clicking the Maximize button in the upper-right corner, or you can scroll the window by sliding the horizontal or vertical scroll bar.

If you plan to use multiple directories but you don't want to see them all open simultaneously, minimize a directory window to reduce it to an icon. Whenever you need to view the directory, click on the icon. If the File Manager becomes cluttered with icons, choose the Arrange Icons command from the Window menu to better arrange your work area.

▼ *Figure 6.9. Displaying Windows in a Cascade Format*

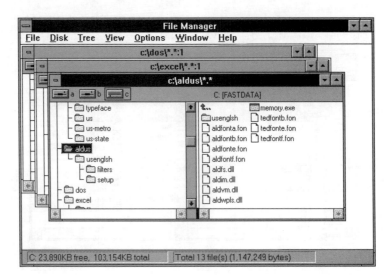

TIP

If you have multiple directory windows open and are having difficulty viewing information in your work area, choose the Cascade command from the Window menu. This command displays your directory windows in the format shown in Figure 6.9.

Navigation Shortcuts

You can use the mouse to easily access all of the File Manager commands and perform navigation-related tasks in the directory windows. If you use the keyboard, a number of shortcuts will help you navigate and perform basic commands. Table 6.1 lists the keyboard shortcuts for the File Manager.

CHECK YOURSELF

Make sure that the Tree and Directory option has been chosen from the View menu before performing these self-checks.

1. Open a directory so that its contents display in a directory window. Click in the right side of the split window and press Ctrl+/. What information displays in the bottom status bar?

2. Highlight a directory and press the Enter key. What happens?

3. If multiple directory windows are displayed, which key combination is available for switching between the windows?

4. True or false? You can move to a directory listed in a directory window by typing the first letter of the directory's name.

Navigation Shortcuts

ANSWERS

1. The number of bytes required to store all of the files, and the number of files in the selected directory.

2. The directory tree in the left side of the split window will expand the directory if it has subdirectories. If the directory does not have subdirectories, nothing will happen.

3. Ctrl+F6.

4. True.

▼ *Table 6.1. Shortcut Keys for Navigating in the File Manager*

Key	Description
Shift+F4	Tiles directory windows
F5	Issues the Refresh command
Shift+F5	Cascades directory windows
Enter	Issues the Open command
F7	Issues the Move command
F8	Issues the Copy command
Delete	Issues the Delete command
Alt+Enter	Issues the Properties command
-	Collapses a directory tree branch
+	Expands a directory tree branch
*	Expands entire branch of directory

Continued

▼ *Table 6.1. Shortcut Keys for Navigating in the File Manager (continued)*

Key	*Description*
Ctrl+*	Expands all directories
X	Moves to directory or file with first letter X
Ctrl+X	Selects and activate disk drive with first letter X
Right arrow	Moves to first subdirectory of selected directory
Left arrow	Moves to directory in previous directory level
Ctrl+Up arrow	Moves to previous directory in same level
Ctrl+Down arrow	Moves to next directory in same level
Page Up	Moves to first directory in the directory window
Page Down	Moves to last directory in the directory window
Home or \	Moves to root directory or the beginning of the list of files
End	Moves to the last directory or the end of a list of files
Up Arrow	Moves to file or directory above selected one
Down Arrow	Moves to file or directory below the selected one
Ctrl+/	Selects all files in window
Ctrl+\	Deselects all files in window

Determining File and Directory Information

If you examine the File Manager example shown in Figure 6.10 you'll notice that the nondirectory files are sorted alphabetically by name. In addition, directories are listed before files. This is fine if you just want to find a specific file, but what if you want to know how big a file is, determine the attributes of a file, or view all files having the same extension in one group? Fortunately, the File Manager provides a number of options to help you view files and directories. You can perform these major tasks:

▲ List files and directories in alphabetical order

▲ List files categorized by their extensions

▼ *Figure 6.10. Viewing Directory Entries in Default Order*

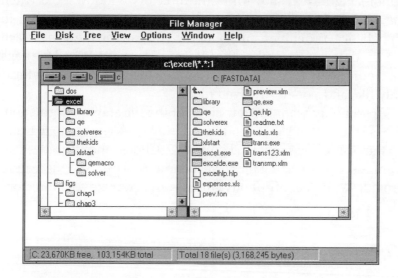

**Determining File
and Directory
Information**

▲ Sort files by their size or their last modification date

▲ List files and directories with all of their attributes displayed

▲ List hidden and system files and directories

▲ List only selected file types

Finding the Size of a File

You can find a file's size by looking at the status bar at the bottom of the File Manager window. When you scroll down the file list using the up and down arrow keys, the highlighted bar moves to the next file on the list. When each new file is highlighted, the status bar indicates that file's size. You can also highlight a file by clicking once on its name. Don't double-click on a filename, however, otherwise the File Manager will attempt to launch an application for you.

Viewing File Information

Another way to get more information about files is to choose the All File Details command from the View menu. Notice that the previous default was Name (a checkmark appeared next to the option). Figure 6.11 shows how the directory window looks when the All File Details option is active. The files are still sorted in alphabetical order by name, but now you can see the size of each file, the date and time when the file was last modified, and file flags that indicate whether the file is a Hidden file, a System file, a Read only file, and /or an Archived file.

If you only want to view some of the file status information, choose the Partial Details command from the View menu to bring up the dialog box shown in Figure 6.12. Choose the attributes you want to see by selecting the corresponding check box. This feature provides a number of options to help you customize your directory display.

TIP

Any file viewing settings that you change will affect every new directory window that you open. However, once a new window is opened, you can change its settings without these settings affecting the windows that were previously opened.

▼ *Figure 6.11. Viewing with All File Details*

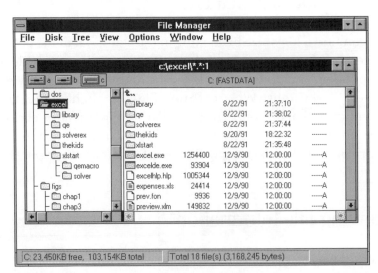

▼ *Figure 6.12. Selecting Directory Viewing Options*

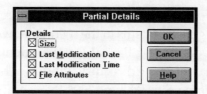

CHECK YOURSELF

Start at the directory window. Make sure that one of your hard disk drives is selected by clicking on a drive icon.

1. Open one of the directories listed in the directory tree. What happens?

2. Configure the directory window so that all of the file attributes display.

3. Choose the Partial Details command from the View menu. What happens?

4. Click on the File Attributes check box (or press Alt+F) to deselect this option. Then, choose the OK button. Which attributes display?

ANSWERS

1. Click on a directory icon. A directory window with the same name as the selected directory opens, and the set of files displays for that directory.

2. Choose the All File Details option from the View menu. Each file is listed with its attributes, such as size, date, and time.

3. The Partial Details dialog box displays, and all of the check boxes are selected.

4. Only the attributes for file size, date, and time display.

Viewing Files by Categories

Return to the View menu, where we'll explore several more options. The third group of items in the menu that we just discussed (Name, All File Details, and Partial Details) identify the level of information displayed in the directory window. The next group of options (Sort By Name, Sort By Type, Sort By Size, and Sort By Date) identify how your files are arranged in the directory window.

The first option in the fourth group, Sort By Name, displays the files in alphabetical order based on the filename to the left of the extension. (This is the default setting.) The second option, Sort By Type, arranges the files in alphabetical order based on the file extension, such as DOC or EXE. This feature is especially useful if you are trying to find a file such as a program in a directory that contains numerous files.

The third option, Sort By Size, displays files in order of decreasing size. The fourth option, Sort By Date, sorts files for display using the date when the files were last modified; the most recently modified files display first.

Excluding Files in a Directory Listing

You can tell the File Manager which files you want to view by using the By File Type command in the View menu. With this feature, you can limit the number of files that display in a window. For example, you can use this option to list only the directories or files with the extension EXE .

The By File Type command opens the dialog box shown in Figure 6.13. Notice that you can select categories of files such as directories, programs, documents, and other files.

To view only directories, deselect all of the check boxes in the File Type group except the Directories option. To view files that have a program icon, select only the Programs option. These files consist of all files with the extensions EXE, COM, BAT, or PIF. You can select the Documents option, on the other hand, to view all files that serve as document files for applications. (A Word for Windows or Write document file would fit in this category.) Any file type that you have associated with an application when you set up windows or

▼ *Figure 6.13. Selecting Files for Viewing*

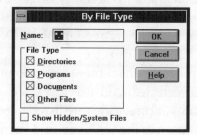

when you used the Associate command from the File Manager would be listed. To view all files that don't belong to the other directories, programs, and documents, select the Other Files category.

Using a Filter

You can also specify that only a particular group of files should display by filling in the filter information in the Name text box at the top of the By File Type dialog box. To specify a filter, use the two standard DOS wildcards: ? and *. The ? wildcard represents a single character, and the * wildcard represents a series of characters. For example, if you want to display all files with the BMP extension (recall that BMP files are created by Windows Paint and can be used as the Desktop Wallpaper), type the five characters *.BMP in the text box. To view BMP files whose name fields start with the letter C, type the six characters C*.BMP into the box at the top of the window.

The By File Type dialog box contains one additional check box: the Show Hidden/System Files option. This option allows you to view the names, sizes and other information associated with files that are normally hidden from the user.

Selecting Files and Directories

Before you can use the File Manager to perform file and directory operations (such as copying, deleting, moving and renaming files), you need to know how to select these operations. You've already seen how to click on a single directory or file to select it from a directory window. With the keyboard, you can use the arrow keys and the other direction keys (Page Up, Page Down, Home, and End) to highlight a file or a directory.

To perform some file management operations, such as copying files or deleting directories, you need to select multiple files or directories. If the files or directories are listed together, click on the first file or directory, press the Shift key, and then click the last file in the group. The File Manager highlights the group of files for you. You can use the keyboard to highlight the first item, press and hold down the Shift key, and then press the up or down arrow to select the rest of the files in the group.

TIP

The selection techniques just described apply to the right side of the split directory window only when the window is in the Tree and Directory view setting. The techniques can also be used in any window that is viewed with the Directory Only setting.

How can you select files that aren't listed together? Using the mouse, click on the first item, and then press the Ctrl key and click on each additional item. Each time you click on an item, it becomes highlighted. If you select an item that you don't want, simply click on it again.

To select nongrouped files with the keyboard, first select the right side of the directory window and then press Shift+F8 to activate the selection frame (Figure 6.14). Notice that the selection frame looks like the outline of a rectangle. Move the selection frame around with the arrow keys, and press the spacebar to select an item. When you're done selecting files or directories, press Shift+F8 again.

TIP

Here's a shortcut for selecting all of the files in a directory window: press Ctrl+/. To deselect a group of selected files, press Ctrl+\ .

▼ *Figure 6.14. Using the Selection Feature*

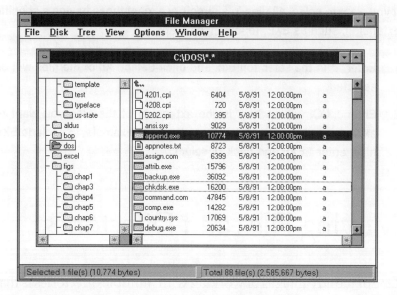

Using the Select Files Dialog Box

In addition to selecting files and directories with the mouse and keyboard, you can select files by using the Select Files dialog box. To open the selector, choose the Select Files command from the File menu. Figure 6.15 shows the dialog box that displays.

To select one or more files in the current directory window, enter the specification for the file(s) you want to select in the File(s) text box. Then, click the Select button. For example, if you enter *.PIF and click Select, all the files with extension PIF will be selected. After you have selected your files, make sure you click the Close button.

▼ *Figure 6.15. Selecting Files*

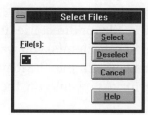

TIP

If you want to select all files in a directory except those having a specific extension, such as EXE, follow these steps:

1. Enter *.* in the selection box and click Select. All of the files will be selected.

2. Enter *.XXX (where XXX is the extension of the files you want to exclude) and click the Deselect button. For example, to exclude EXE files, enter *.EXE and click Deselect.

Moving Files and Directories

One of the advantages of working with multiple directories is that you can maintain temporary or extra copies of files in different directories. For example, if you're using a word processor (such as Word for Windows) to create document files that you're storing in a directory named \WORD\DOCS, you can keep extra copies of the files in another directory named \WORD\DOCS \BACKUP.

The process of moving and copying files or directories from one directory to another is quite easy with the File Manager, especially because you don't have to memorize any cryptic DOS commands. Let's examine the move operation first, and then we'll show you how to copy files and directories.

When you move a file from one directory to another on the same disk drive, an image of the file is moved to the destination directory, while the original image is deleted from the source directory. When you move a directory, on the other hand, the File Manager physically places that directory into the destination directory, so all of the files and subdirectories associated with that directory are also moved.

To move one or more files or directories using the mouse, open the directory that contains the item(s) you want to move. You must also know where you want to move the item, and make sure that this destination directory is visible on the desktop. (If you've

opened many directory windows, remember that you can minimize a directory window and represent it as an icon.) When both
the source and the destination directories are in plain view, click on
the item you want to move and drag it to the destination directory.
This action brings up the Confirm Mouse Operation dialog box
(Figure 6.16). Click the Yes button to complete the operation.

**Moving Files
and Directories**

TIP

The easiest way to move and copy files or directories is to use the Tree and
Directory view option and follow these steps:

1. View your disk drive in the tree format on the left side of the split
    screen.

2. Scroll through the directory tree until you locate the directory that
    contains the file or subdirectory you want to move or copy.

3. Click on the directory and its contents will be displayed on the right-
    hand side of the window.

4. Scroll through the directory tree until you locate the directory where
    you want the items to be copied or moved.

5. Select the file or directory you want to move or copy and drag it to the
    directory icon on the left-hand side of the window.

When moving files or directories, keep in mind that you can
also move multiple files or directories at the same time. Hold the
Ctrl key down and click on each item you want to move until
they're all highlighted. Next, release the Ctrl key and drag the

▼ *Figure 6.16. Confirming the Move Operation*

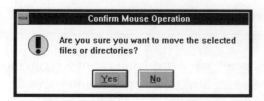

group of selected items to the destination directory. As you drag the items to move them, multiple icons will be displayed to represent each item that you are moving.

TIP

When dragging files to a new directory window, make sure the files are placed in an open area of the window and not on top of a file folder icon. If you drag the highlighted items on top of a file folder, the files are placed into the directory represented by the icon, and not into the directory represented by the directory window.

Using the Move Command

As an alternative to using the mouse to move a file or directory, the File Manager provides the Move command in the File menu. To use this feature, select the items you want to move and choose the Move command. The dialog box shown in Figure 6.17 asks you to specify a destination directory. The From text box lists the files or directories that you have selected to be moved. Type the name of the destination directory, including a complete pathname into the To text box. For example, if you want to move files to the directory C:\WORD\DOCS\BACKUP, type C:\WORD\DOCS\BACKUP in the To box. Choose the OK button to finish the operation.

TIP

Using the Move command, you can move a group of related files by using a wildcard specification. For example, if you want to move all of the PIF files in the directory C:\WINDOWS to another directory, enter this speci-fication in the From text box:

```
C:\WINDOWS\*.PIF
```

Up to this point, we've explained how you can move files and directories between directories on the same drive. In some cases, you'll also want to move them between drives. For example, you

▼ *Figure 6.17. Moving a File with the Move Command*

**Moving Files
and Directories**

```
┌──────────────────── Move ────────────────────┐
│ Current directory: C:\DOS           ┌──────────┐ │
│                                     │    OK    │ │
│ From:   append.exe                  └──────────┘ │
│                                     ┌──────────┐ │
│ To:                                 │  Cancel  │ │
│                                     └──────────┘ │
│                                     ┌──────────┐ │
│                                     │   Help   │ │
│                                     └──────────┘ │
└───────────────────────────────────────────────┘
```

might want to move a document file on drive C to a diskette in drive A to make a backup copy. Moving items between drives with the mouse is essentially the same as moving items on the same drive. The only difference is that you must hold down the Alt key when dragging the item.

CHECK YOURSELF

Start at a directory window for one of the hard disks installed on your system.

1. Move a file from one directory to a new directory.

2. Move a file from one directory to a new directory so that the file has a new name in the destination directory.

ANSWERS

1. (a) Make sure that the window or icon for the destination directory is in view.
   (b) Select the file to be moved by clicking on it.
   (c) Drag the file to the destination directory window or icon.
   (d) Click the Yes button in the Confirm Mouse Operation dialog box.
   (e) Examine the source directory to make sure the file has been moved.

2. (a) Select the file to be moved by clicking on it.
   (b) Press Alt+F to open the File menu, and then choose the Move command.
   (c) Enter the destination directory and the new filename.
   (d) Choose the OK button.

Copying Files and Directories

The process of copying a file or directory is different than moving one because the File Manager makes a duplicate of the selected file or directory in the destination directory without affecting the original version. To copy a file on the same drive, first open the source directory so that the file is visible. Make sure that the destination directory icon is also visible in the File Manager window. Hold down the Ctrl key, and then click and drag the item you want into the destination directory. Release the mouse button and the Ctrl key. When the Confirm Mouse Operation dialog box appears (Figure 6.18), click on the Yes button.

The File Manager allows you to copy multiple files or directories at once. Again, you must first select all of the files or directories to be copied. Recall that to select a group of files that appear together in the directory listing, you click on the first one and then press the Shift key while clicking on the last file in the group. (You can also click on the last file and Shift+click on the first file.) To select several files that don't appear together in the directory window, click on the first one and hold down the Ctrl key while you click on the other files.

Another useful operation is copying a file from one drive to another. To do this, simply drag the selected items to the destination directory without holding down the Ctrl key.

TIP

When you use the mouse, the process of copying files is so similar to moving files that you might have trouble remembering if you are performing a copy or move operation. For a visual aid, The File Manager displays a file icon with a + symbol when it is being dragged to a new directory to indicate that it is being copied.

Using the Copy Command

Using the keyboard, you can copy files by following the basic procedure we described for moving files. First, highlight the files

▼ *Figure 6.18. Confirming a Copy Operation*

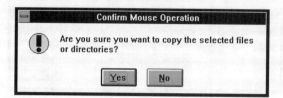

or directories to be copied, and then choose the Copy command from the File menu. When you see the dialog box shown in Figure 6.19, type the complete pathname of the destination directory into the To text box, and choose the OK button.

TIP

To copy a file to a directory and change the file's name, simply enter a destination path and new filename in the To text box. For example, to copy the file BUDGET.DOC in the directory \WORD to the directory \WORD\DOCS and give it the new name OLDBDG1.DOC, type the text \WORD\DOCS \OLDBDG1.DOC into the To box.

Deleting Files

Deleting a file is quite easy, but remember: once you delete a file, it will be inaccessible unless you use a separate file undelete utility (not included in Windows) to recover it. To delete a file, click on the file name to highlight it, and press the Del key. The File Manager

▼ *Figure 6.19. Copy a File with the Copy Command*

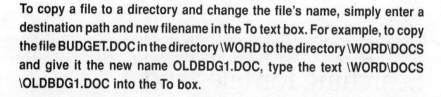

▼ *Figure 6.20. Deleting a File*

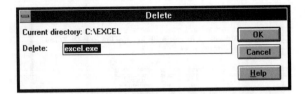

displays the Delete dialog box (Figure 6.20), so that you can review or change the name of the file that has been selected. After you choose the OK button, you'll see the Confirm File Delete warning box shown in Figure 6.21, asking you to confirm the delete operation. When you click the Yes button, the file is deleted. If you marked multiple files for deletion, and you are sure that you want to delete all of the files, choose the Yes To All button so that you won't have to view a warning dialog for each file before it is deleted.

Searching for Files and Directories

If your hard disk contains numerous files and subdirectories, you already know how difficult it can be to locate a file or directory. Fortunately, if you know the name of the file or the directory, you can easily locate it using the File Manager's Search command, available from the File menu.

Before choosing this command, you must decide where you want Windows to start its search. By default, searching begins with

▼ *Figure 6.21. Confirming the Delete Operation*

the directory highlighted in the directory window (the active directory). If the selected directory contains subdirectories, these subdirectories are also searched. Figure 6.22 shows the dialog box that appears when the Search command is chosen. Notice that the active directory is listed in the Start From text box. Change this directory name if you want to start the search from a different directory. Next, enter the desired filename in the Search For text box and click the OK button to start the search.

You can also use the DOS wildcard symbols * and ? to specify a filename. For example, imagine that you have created a Windows Write file that starts with the three letters JOE, but you can't remember the rest of the filename. Write files have the WRI extension, so you can enter JOE*.WRI in the Search For text box.

Searching for Files and Directories

TIP

If you don't remember where a file is located, enter only the name of your drive and root directory in the Start From text box. For example, if you enter C:\, Windows will start the search from the root directory of drive C. Then, select the Search All Subdirectories check box. Be prepared to wait for a while because a complete disk search can take several minutes.

The results of a search are shown as icons in a Search Results document window (Figure 6.23). Each icon provides the full path for the file. You can access these icons just as you would access the file icons in a directory window. That is, you can open, delete, rename, move, or copy any of them. When you're done using this window, double-click on its Control menu box to close it, or press Alt+F4.

▼ *Figure 6.22. Searching for a File*

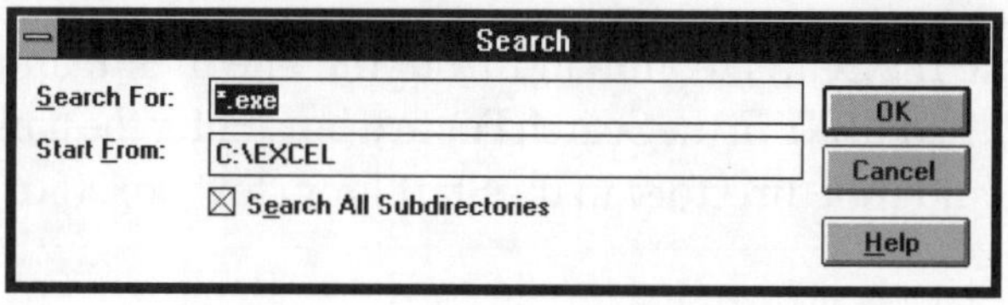

Search
Search For: *.exe
Start From: C:\EXCEL
☒ Search All Subdirectories
OK
Cancel
Help

▼ *Figure 6.23. Displaying the Results of a Search*

```
┌─────────────────────────────────────────────────────────────────────┐
│ ─                          File Manager                         ▼  ▲ │
│ File  Disk  Tree  View  Options  Window  Help                        │
│ ┌─────────────────────────────────────────────────────────────────┐ │
│ │ ─                          c:\excel\*.*                     ▼  ▲ │ │
│ │ ┌──┐a ┌──┐b ┌──┐c              C: [FASTDATA]                      │ │
│ │ │ ─              Search Results: C:\excel\*.exe          ▼  ▲   │ │
│ │ │ ▒ c:\excel\excel.exe                                          │ │
│ │ │ ▒ c:\excel\excelde.exe                                        │ │
│ │ │ ▒ c:\excel\qe.exe                                             │ │
│ │ │ ▒ c:\excel\trans.exe                                          │ │
│ │ │                                                               │ │
│ │ │                                                               │ │
│ │ │                                                               │ │
│ │ │                                                               │ │
│ │ │                                                               │ │
│ ├──────────────────────┬────────────────────────────────────────┤ │
│ │ 4 file(s) found       │ Total 18 file(s) (3,168,245 bytes)      │ │
│ └─────────────────────────────────────────────────────────────────┘ │
└─────────────────────────────────────────────────────────────────────┘
```

TIP

Instead of closing the Search Results window after a search, you may want to minimize it to an icon so that you can view it later. This technique is especially useful if you have performed a search that locates two or more files that have the same name. If you keep the Search Results window minimized, you can later open the window and examine the duplicate file names to determine which file you actually want.

CHECK YOURSELF

Start at a directory window for one of the hard disks installed on your system. Search for all of the program (EXE) files in all of the directories of your hard disk.

ANSWER

Choose the Search command from the File menu, and type the search text *.EXE in the Search For text box. Enter the name of your drive and root directory in the Start From text box. (For example, enter C:\.) Select the Search All Subdirectories check box, and then click the OK button.

Searching for Files and Directories

Creating and Deleting Directories

The File Manager makes it extremely easy to create and delete directories. To create a directory, use the directory window and select the directory that will be the parent of (be located immediately above) the new directory. When the parent directory is highlighted, choose the Create Directory command from the File menu. A dialog box appears (Figure 6.24) to show the current directory name and to ask you for the name of the new subdirectory. Type the new name (no more than eight characters in length) in the Name text box and choose the OK button. The new directory is now created and ready to store files.

If you're unfamiliar with the rules for naming DOS files and directories, keep in mind that you can use only eight characters in a name. You may use any characters you want, except a period, comma, forward slash (/), backslash (\), vertical bar (|), semicolon, colon, quotation marks, or brackets ([]).

You can delete a directory just as easily as you can create one. With the File Manager, you don't need to delete the files within the subdirectory before removing the actual directory. You should, however, make certain that you aren't deleting files you'll need later.

To delete a directory, select the directory icon in the directory window. Next, choose the Delete command from the File menu or press the Del key. A dialog box (Figure 6.25) identifies the current

▼ *Figure 6.24. Creating a Directory*

Create Directory
Current directory: C:\
Name: TEXT
OK
Cancel
Help

▼ *Figure 6.25. Deleting a Directory*

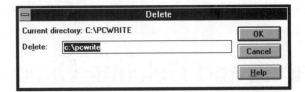

directory and lets you approve or cancel the delete operation. After choosing the OK button, a second dialog box (Figure 6.26) asks you to confirm the directory deletion. If you choose the Yes button, the File Manager will list each file in the directory before deleting the file. If you are certain you want to remove all of the files in the directory, choose the Yes To All button to bypass the warning prompts.

Renaming Files and Directories

The more files and directories you add to your system, the more likely it will be that you'll have to rename older files and directories occasionally. The File Manager allows you to rename a file or directory at any time by using the Rename command in the File menu.

To rename a file, click on the filename in a directory window and choose the Rename command. A dialog box is displayed to show you the current directory name and to ask you to provide a new filename. Enter the new filename in the To text box and choose the OK button.

▼ *Figure 6.26. Confirming a Directory Deletion*

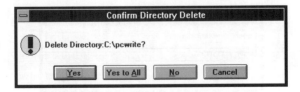

To rename a directory, select the directory and choose the Rename command. Enter the new directory name in the To text box (remember that you can use only eight characters) and choose the OK button.

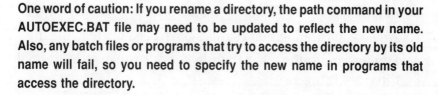

Renaming Files and Directories

TIP

One word of caution: If you rename a directory, the path command in your AUTOEXEC.BAT file may need to be updated to reflect the new name. Also, any batch files or programs that try to access the directory by its old name will fail, so you need to specify the new name in programs that access the directory.

CHECK YOURSELF

Start at a directory window for one of the hard disks installed on your system.

1. Rename a file.

2. Rename a directory.

ANSWERS

1. (a) Open a directory to locate the file you want to rename.
   (b) Click on the file to highlight it.
   (c) Choose the Rename command from the File menu.
   (d) Type the new name for the file into the To text box.
   (e) Click the OK button.
   (f) Check the directory where the file was stored to make sure the file has been renamed.

2. (a) Locate the directory that you want to rename by using the directory window, and click on the directory to highlight it.
   (b) Choose the Rename command from the File menu.
   (c) Type the new name for the directory into the To text box.
   (d) Click the OK button.

Changing File Attributes

We mentioned earlier that all DOS files have special attributes. The four attributes are:

▲ Read Only, indicating that the file can only be viewed and not modified

▲ Archive, indicating that changes have been made to the file

▲ Hidden, indicating that the file is not displayed in normal directory listings

▲ System, indicating that the file is a special DOS system file

Each file stored in a directory can be assigned any combination of these attributes. For example, a file can be read-only and hidden. The File Manager allows you to change a file's attribute by choosing the Properties command from the File menu. To use this feature, highlight a file and choose Properties. When the dialog box shown in Figure 6.27 appears, notice that check boxes are provided for each of the four attribute types. Select the attribute options you want, and click the OK button.

TIP

You can also change the attributes of a directory. For example, if you choose the read-only attribute for a directory, you won't be able to change the contents of the directory by copying files to it or moving files from it.

▼ *Figure 6.27. Changing File Attributes*

Properties for wchap2.rtf		
File Name:	wchap2.rtf	
Size:	76,872 bytes	
Last Change:	8/23/91 16:52:20	
Path:	c:\text	

OK

Cancel

Help

Attributes
☐ Read Only   ☐ Hidden
☒ Archive   ☐ System

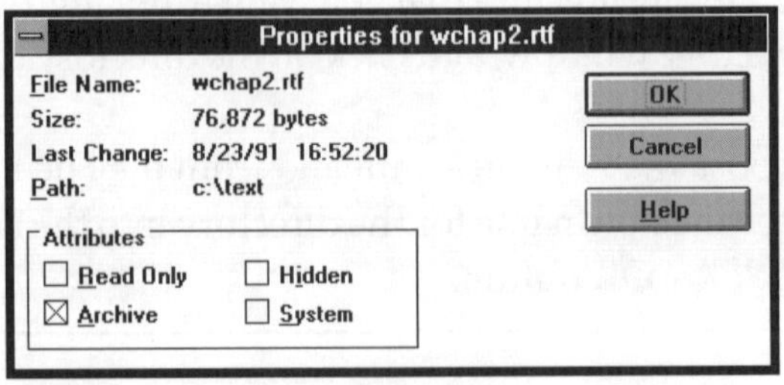

Launching Applications

Launching
Applications

The File Manager allows you to launch applications from its environment. This means you can use the directory windows to locate and then start an application. (You don't need to exit to the Program Manager to run the application.) The easiest way to start an application is to double-click on an icon displayed as a rectangle with a blue stripe. If the icon represents a Windows application, such as Write or Notepad, the application is launched in its own window. If the application is a DOS program, on the other hand, it's executed in the DOS full-screen area.

If you attempt to double-click on an icon that is not a program or a document file that has been associated with a program, you'll see the warning dialog displayed in Figure 6.28. Before you can launch an application by choosing one of its documents, you'll need to associate the document with the application. The techniques for associating documents with applications are discussed in the next section.

If you're using the keyboard, launch an application by choosing the Run command from the File menu. As Figure 6.29 shows, this command displays a dialog box that you can use to enter the application's name. If the application is not in the directory currently selected, include the full directory path for the application so that the File Manager can locate it.

TIP

You can launch an application and have the application load in a file even if the file has not been associated with the application. To do this, select the document icon with the mouse and drag it on top of an application icon. For example, if you have a text file named NOTES.001 and you want to view the file with the Notepad application, simply drag the icon for the file on top of the icon for NOTEPAD.EXE. Windows will then display a message box asking if you want to start the application using the file you've selected as the initial file.

▼ *Figure 6.28. File Execution Warning Dialog*

Associating Files with Applications

When you run an application, the first task you often need to perform is to open a file. Fortunately, the File Manager allows you to associate files with applications so that it will know which application to launch when you double-click on a file's icon. You'll find that this feature can save you a lot of time.

How are files associated with applications? The File Manager uses the file extensions to determine which group of files should be associated with an application. For example, all files with the extension WRI are associated with the Write application and all files with the BMP extension are associated with Paintbrush. When Windows is installed, it automatically sets up associations for some of your application documents. If you take a look at some of the files in the WINDOWS directory, you'll see that they are represented as associated file icons. You can view and change these associations at any time and you can also associate other files with applications.

Determining File Associations

To determine which application an associated file icon has been assigned to, select the icon and then choose the Associate com-

▼ *Figure 6.29. Using the Run Command*

```
┌─────────────────────── Run ───────────────────────┐
│ ─                                                   │
│ Current Directory: c:\pcwrite          ┌────────┐   │
│ Command Line:                          │   OK   │   │
│ ┌─────────────────────────────────┐    └────────┘   │
│ │ inword.exe                      │    ┌────────┐   │
│ └─────────────────────────────────┘    │ Cancel │   │
│                                         └────────┘   │
│ ☐ Run Minimized                        ┌────────┐   │
│                                         │  Help  │   │
│                                         └────────┘   │
└─────────────────────────────────────────────────────┘
```

▼ *Figure 6.30. Associating a File with an Application*

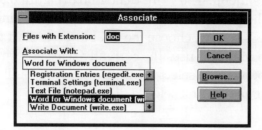

mand in the File menu. This command displays the dialog box shown in Figure 6.30. If the None option is selected, all files with the extension listed in the Files with Extension text box will not be associated with any application.

Defining and Removing Associations

To associate files that have a common extension to an application, select one of the files in the directory window and choose the Associate command. Double-check that the extension listed in the Files with Extension text box is correct and then select the appropriate application in the Associate With scroll box. For example, if you are associating files with extension .DOC to the application Word for Windows, type the extension DOC in the Files with Extension text box and select the Word for Windows document option in the scroll box.

To remove an association, select a file having the extension you want to remove an association for and then choose the Associate command. Next, choose the None option and click the OK button.

Printing Files

The File Manager provides a Print command in the File menu so that you can print either ASCII text files or files that are associated with applications. If you use the feature to print an associated file, such as a Word document, the File Manager will use the application (for instance, Word) to print the file.

To print a file, select the file and choose the Print command from the File menu. The Print dialog box (Figure 6.31) appears, displaying the name of the file you selected in the Print text box. If the filename is correct, choose the OK button to start printing the file. The File Manager uses the currently selected printer to print the file. If you want to select a different printer, you'll need to use the Control Panel to first select a different printer.

TIP

You can also print a text file or a file that has been associated with an application by selecting the file with the mouse and dragging it to the minimized Print Manager icon. To use this feature, make sure that you have previously started the Print Manager and minimized it to an icon.

Working with Networks

If your computer system is connected to a network, the File Manager will provide special features to help you access network drives. Because networks operate differently, the File Manager provides different commands and dialog boxes for connecting to networks and viewing network drives—depending on the type of network you are using. You access network commands and options from the Disk menu.

Connecting to a Network Drive

To connect to a network drive, open the Disk menu and look for a command such as Net Connections or Connect Net Drive. If one of these commands is not listed, your computer will not be able to access the network. The network connection command displays a dialog box so that you can enter necessary connection information, such as:

1. The path required to access the network.

2. The drive you wish to select.

▼ *Figure 6.31. Printing a File*

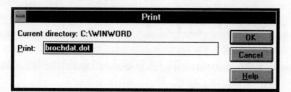

3. An optional password.

When you are finished entering your information, choose the Connect button. Once you are connected, you can access the network drive. If you want to connect to other network drives, stay in the Network Drive Connections dialog box and enter the information for another network drive and choose the Connect button.

If you no longer need to use a network drive that you are connected to, use the Network Drive Connections dialog box, select the drive, and choose the Disconnect button. When you are finished with the dialog box, choose the Close button.

Viewing Network Drives

Display the Network Drive Connections dialog box and see if it has a Browse button. If this button is available, you can select it to view the list of drives on your network. This feature is useful because you can locate a network drive without having to first connect to it.

When the Browse button is chosen, a dialog box will be displayed with the list of network drives. Examine the list and select the drive that you want. You can connect to this drive by using the Network Drive Connections dialog box.

Performing Disk Maintenance

So far, we've discussed all of the basic file and directory-related operations that the File Manager performs. Let's now look at two important disk-related operations—copying and formatting disks. To start these operations, use the Disk menu.

Copying Disks

Follow these steps to copy a disk:

1. Place the disk you want to copy into one of your diskette drives. This disk is called the *source disk.*

2. Click on the drive icon for the source disk. Recall that the drive icons display in the directory window. If a disk is not in the drive represented by the selected icon, you'll receive a warning dialog box.

3. Choose the Copy Disk command from the Disk menu to display the dialog box shown in Figure 6.32.

4. Choose the correct source and destination disk drives using the Source In and Destination In boxes. Then, click the OK button. When the Confirm Copy Disk warning box (Figure 6.33) appears, click the Yes button to continue the operation. Keep in mind that the original data in the destination disk will be erased.

5. The File Manager will then present a message box asking you to enter both the source and destination disks. Make sure that these disks are inserted and then choose the OK button.

6. The disk will then be copied.

TIP

If your computer only has one diskette drive installed, the File Manager will provide you with special instructions for inserting and removing the source and destination diskettes.

▼ *Figure 6.32. Copying a Disk*

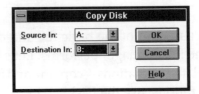

▼ *Figure 6.33. Confirming a Disk Copy Operation*

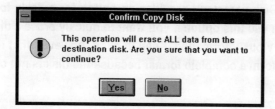

Formatting Disks

As you know, disks must be formatted before they can be used. When you format a disk, all of the data stored on the disk (if there is any) is removed. The format operation maps a disk into components, called *sectors*, so that DOS can read the disk and store information on it.

To format a disk with the File Manager, place the disk into one of your diskette drives, and select the Format Disk command from the Disk menu. When the Format Disk dialog box appears (Figure 6.34), select the drive name for the disk you want to format. The Disk In option consists of a pull-down box that lists the available diskette drives. Click on the arrow to the right of this box, or press Alt+Down arrow. Select the correct diskette name.

You'll also need to specify the storage size of the disk using the Capacity box. Select an option such as 1.2 MB or 360 KB. If you want to provide a label for the disk or format the disk as a system disk, select these options in the Options group.

▼ *Figure 6.34. Formatting a Disk*

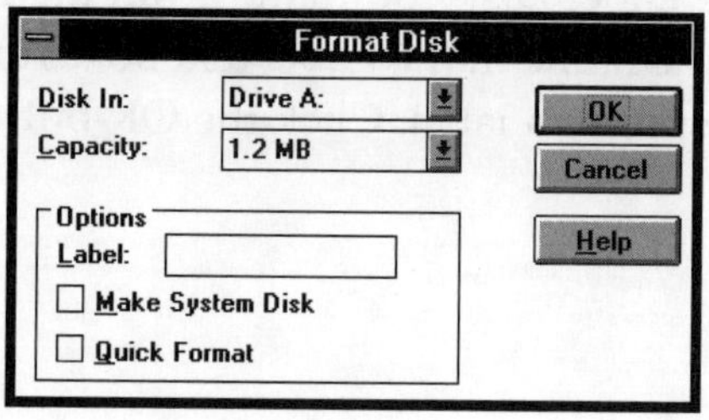

TIP

The Format Disk command provides an option for quickly formatting a disk. You can use this option if you want to quickly erase a diskette that has been previously formatted. Keep in mind, however, that this feature does not perform a complete format because the disk is not checked for bad sectors.

Before the format operation starts, Windows displays the Confirm Format Disk warning box to remind you that the data on the disk you plan to format will be lost. To proceed, click the Yes button.

When your disk has been formatted, a dialog box displays, asking if you want to format another disk.

Making a System Disk

In addition to formatting a disk, you can initialize a disk so that it can be used as a boot disk for other computer systems. When a disk is initialized in this manner, the File Manager copies special DOS system-level files to the disk.

To initialize a system disk, insert the disk in one of the diskette drives, select the disk icon, and choose the Make System Disk command from the Disk menu. Follow the prompts that are presented to complete the operation.

Labeling a Disk

To create or change a disk's label, insert the disk in one of the available diskette drives and click the appropriate drive icon. Then, choose the Label Disk command from the Disk menu and enter or change the name in the Label text box. You can use up to 11 characters to specify a label. Click the OK button to select the new label.

Customizing the File Manager

Customizing the File Manager

Before we leave the File Manager, there are a few customization and setup features we need to discuss. These features allow you to change how the File Manager displays information and how it responds to the file and directory management commands that you perform.

Changing the Display Font

By default, the File Manager displays the names of files and directories in 8 point Arial font (assuming you are using TrueType display fonts). If you want to change this font or its size, choose the Font command from the Options menu. This command displays the dialog box shown in Figure 6.35. Notice that options are provided for selecting a different font as well as changing the font style (bold, italic, etc.) and the font size. As you select different options, the Sample box will show you how the font will be displayed. If you want file and directory names to be displayed in all uppercase, deselect the Lowercase check box. Choose the OK button to save your changes.

Changing Confirmation Options

Each time you perform a file or directory operation such as copying or moving files, the File Manager provides a confirmation

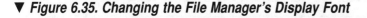

▼ *Figure 6.35. Changing the File Manager's Display Font*

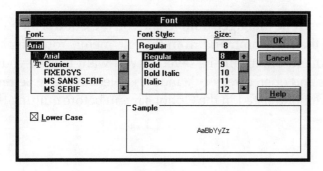

message box. You can selectively disable this feature by choosing the Confirmation command from the Options menu. As Figure 6.36 shows, this command allows you to change the settings for five options: File Delete, Directory Delete, File Replace, Mouse Action, and Diskette Commands. By default, all of these options are selected. if you deselect one or more of them, the File Manager will no longer display a confirmation box when the corresponding command is performed. For example, if you disable the Diskette Commands option, you won't see a warning message before you format or copy a diskette.

TIP

The Mouse Action option controls the display of warning messages whenever a file is moved or copied by dragging it with the mouse.

Minimizing the File Manager

If you are using the File Manager to launch applications and you find that it gets in the way and clutters your screen, select the Minimize On Use command from the Options menu so that the File Manager will be reduced to an icon whenever an application is launched. To later bring up the File Manager, double-click on its minimized icon.

Quitting the File Manager

To quit the File Manager, double-click on the Control menu box or choose the Exit command from the File menu. Your display settings will automatically be saved. If you want to save your view settings and open directory windows, select the Save Settings On Exit command listed in the Options menu before quitting the File Manager.

▼ *Figure 6.36. Changing Confirmation Options*

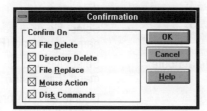

Quitting the File Manager

TIP

If you plan to use the File Manager again, you may want to minimize it to an icon to get it out of the way instead of quitting. This will allow you to access it much quicker if you need it later. Remember that when you first start the File Manager, it takes a moment to load because it must read your disk drive and build the directory tree.

QUICK TASK SUMMARY

Task	Procedure
Start File Manager	Double-click File Manager icon
Display files in a directory	Click on directory folder icon
Display files on a disk drive	Click on drive icon; *or* Press Ctrl and letter of drive
Open a new directory window	Use the New Window command (Window menu)
Select one file in a directory window	Click once on the file icon
Select all files in a directory window	Press Ctrl+/
Move a file	Click and drag file from one directory to another; *or* Select file and use Move command (File menu)
Copy a file	Press Ctrl key, click and drag file from one directory to another; *or* Select file and use Copy command (File menu)
Delete a file	Select file and press Del key
Search for a file or directory	Use the Search command (File menu)

Task	*Procedure*
Create a directory	Use the Create Directory command (File menu)
Rename a file or directory	Select file or directory and use Rename command (File menu)
View or change a file attribute	Select file and use Properties command (File menu)
Launch an application	Double-click on program icon or associated file icon
Print a file	Select file and use Print command (File menu)
Copy or Format a disk	Use Copy or Format command (Disk menu)
Change File Manager's display font	Use Font command (Options menu)
Quit File Manager	Use Exit command (File menu)

PRACTICE WHAT YOU'VE LEARNED

In this chapter, you've been introduced to Windows file management using the File Manager. In the next chapter, we'll cover the basics of setting up printers and using the Print Manager to help you print files from Windows. Use the following exercises to gain more experience using the File Manager.

1. Start the File Manager and select one of the hard disks listed in the directory window. (If you have only one hard drive, it will already be selected.)

2. Select a floppy disk (diskette) drive.

3. Choose the Indicate Expandable Branches command from the Tree menu and click on a file folder that has a + symbol.

4. Double-click on a file folder that has a + symbol.

5. Choose the Run command from the File menu.

6. Rename a file using the Rename command in the File menu.

7. Delete a file.

8. Search for a group of files, such as *.EXE, using the Search command.

9. Change the attributes of a file.

10. Format a diskette using the Format Diskette command from the Disk menu.

ANSWERS

1. The window displays the main directory paths for the selected hard disk.

2. The directory paths for the selected floppy disk drive display. If the selected drive is empty, File Manager asks you to insert a diskette.

3. The subdirectories for that directory display.

4. The directory tree branch for that folder (directory) expands to show you the directory's subdirectories.

5. A dialog box displays so that you can enter the name of a program to run.

6. The file's name changes, and the directory window lists the new filename.

7. The file disappears and its name is no longer listed in the directory window.

8. The located files display in a special Search Results window. You can select a file and open, rename, or delete it.

9. The file is listed in a directory window with its new attributes. To view the attributes, choose the File Details command from the View menu.

10. You're asked to place a diskette in a floppy drive. A dialog box warns you that this operation will erase the data on your diskette.

Printing with Windows

By now you probably realize why you can be very productive with Windows: you can access different applications without exiting one to start another. If you own an 80386-compatible PC, you can even run non-Windows applications in the background while a different application runs in the foreground. This means you can print files while you perform other tasks.

This chapter will show you how to get the most out of Windows printing features. After you complete the chapter, you'll know how to:

▲ **Install, set up, and remove printers**

▲ **Change the default printer**

▲ **Select options for a printer**

▲ **Use the Print Manager to view and control print files**

▲ **Use multiple printers**

▲ **Print to a file**

The Problem with Printing

Imagine that you're a consultant who performs studies for multiple customers. Your job requires you to prepare reports (including graphs, pie charts, and other illustrations) as well as memos and proposals. Your reports are printed on paper that contains preprinted information. The memos and proposals are printed on your letterhead; both types of documents are processed through your laser printer. You also have an accounting program that prints continuous-form checks using tractor-fed paper.

You have to finish a large report (including several Paintbrush pictures) and pay a group of bills today. You instruct each of your Windows applications to send output to the printer. And then you wait.

Unfortunately, all of your applications want access to the printer at the same time. This situation calls for the help of the Print Manager, an electronic traffic cop that controls which job goes out to which resource. Print Manager allows you to adjust the priority of print jobs and control the order in which they'll be printed. You can also pause and restart print queues, and activate and deactivate each of the printers on your system.

We'll show you how to use the Print Manager in this chapter, but first we'll explain how printers are installed and configured so that they can be accessed by Windows applications.

Installing and Setting up Printers

Before you can use a printer with a Windows application, such as Write or Paintbrush, you'll need to make sure that the printer has been properly installed and set up. Fortunately, all of the printer and installation tasks can easily be performed from the Control Panel. We covered some of the basics for using the Control Panel to install and remove printers in Chapter 5. In this chapter, we'll explain the installation and setup procedures in much greater detail.

TIP

Each printer that you use with Windows must have its own printer driver file. Windows provides driver files for most of the standard dot matrix, laser, and other types of popular printers. If you are using a printer that is not currently supported by Windows, contact the manufacturer of your printer to see if they can provide you with a Windows printer driver file.

The steps that you'll need to follow to install and set up your printer include:

1. Install (copy) the printer driver for your printer. You'll need the Windows installation disks for this step.

2. Set up the printer by selecting a printer port and choosing port settings.

3. Select custom printer settings such as paper size, print quality mode, and paper orientation.

4. Select the default (active) printer for your system.

Installing a Printer Driver

To start the installation process, run the Control Panel application and double-click on the Printers icon or choose the Printers command from the Settings menu. The Printers dialog box will appear. You use this dialog box to install printer drivers and to configure printers for the Windows environment. As Figure 7.1 shows, the available printers are listed in the List of Printers scroll box. Scroll through the list, select the printer you want to install by clicking on it, and then choose the Install button.

Unless the printer driver file for the printer you've selected has already been installed on your hard disk, Windows will display a dialog box that asks you to insert one of the Windows installation disks. Windows may also ask you to insert other diskettes to install necessary font files for the printer.

▼ *Figure 7.1. Viewing the List of Available Printers*

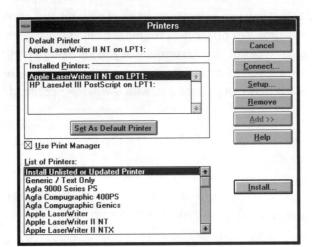

TIP

If you have previously installed a printer driver file for your printer and you now want to update the printer driver file, follow these steps:

1. **Select the Install Unlisted or Updated printer option in the List of Printers box and choose the Install button.**

2. **When the Install Driver dialog shown in Figure 7.2 is displayed, specify a drive and pathname for the new driver file.**

3. **Insert the diskette that contains the new driver file in one of your drives and choose the OK button.**

Keep in mind that the same driver file may be used to support different printers. For example, Windows uses a general Postscript driver file to support Postscript laser printers such as the Apple LaserWriter NT or the Postscript version of the HP LaserJet III.

Installation Troubles

If you can't find the driver file for your printer, don't despair; you still have a few options:

▼ *Figure 7.2. Installing a Printer*

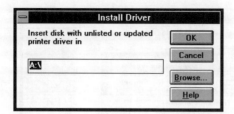

1. Read your printer's documentation to see if your printer is compatible with one of the Windows-supported printers. For example, many dot matrix printers are Epson compatible and many laser printers are HP LaserJet compatible. You may need to change the hardware settings of your printer so that it is compatible with a Windows-supported printer.

2. Contact the manufacturer of your printer to see if a Windows printer driver is available. If you are in a rush, you may be able to download the driver from the vendor's bulletin board or a network such as CompuServe.

3. Contact Microsoft to obtain the latest set of printer driver files.

4. Set up the printer as a generic text-only printer by selecting the Generic/Text Only printer driver. Although this driver does not support graphics output, it may get you going until you can obtain a proper driver for your printer.

Configuring a Printer

After you have installed the driver file, you're ready to configure the printer. This is essentially a two-step process. First, you'll need to connect your printer by selecting a printer port, and then you'll need to select printing options for your printer. Both of these tasks are performed using the Printers dialog box.

Selecting a Printer Port

To connect your printer, first select the printer in the Installed Printers list box and then choose the Connect button. Figure 7.3

▼ *Figure 7.3. Connecting a Printer*

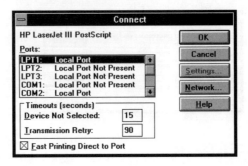

shows the Connect dialog box that is displayed. Notice that all of the printer ports are listed in the Ports list box. The label "Local Port" is listed next to the ports that your computer system has available. If a port is listed with the "Local Port Not Present" label, you shouldn't select the port because it is not available on your computer.

In most cases, you'll want to use either the parallel ports LPT1: or LPT2:, or the serial ports COM1: or COM2:. By default, Windows selects the first parallel port, LPT1: for your printer. If your printer is connected to a different port, scroll through the list to find the correct port, click on it to select it, and then choose the OK button.

If your printer is connected to a serial port, you may also need to set the communication settings for the port. To do this, click the serial port, and then choose the Settings button. Use the dialog box shown in Figure 7.4 to change the communication settings, such as the baud rate, data bits, and parity.

▼ *Figure 7.4. Changing Serial Port Settings*

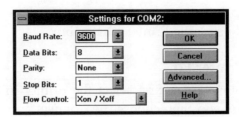

TIP

You can use the Connect dialog box to assign a printer to a file. (Select the FILE: option listed in the Ports scroll box.) This feature allows you to send your output to a file instead of to a printer. If you set up the default printer in this manner, each time you print a file from an application Windows will provide a dialog box so that you can provide the name of the file where you want your output sent.

Setting the Timeout Options

Whatever type of port you select, parallel or serial, Windows allows you to specify the amount of time that an application should wait before sending you a transmission error. Each time you print a file, Windows starts checking to see if the default printer is online and ready to print. The Device Not Selected value in the Timeouts box specifies the timeout delay in seconds. Although the default is only 15 seconds, you'll find that this setting will work for most printers.

The other setting, Transmission Retry, determines the amount of time Windows waits for a printer to start printing after first sending it data. The default value for this setting is 45 seconds.

You can change either of these values by highlighting the number in the text box and then entering a new number. If you are having a problem getting Windows to send data to a printer, you may want to experiment with these settings.

Using the Print Options

After you select a printer port, you'll be ready to select printing options for your printer. From the Printers dialog box, choose the Setup button. You'll then see a custom dialog box for your printer driver. Figure 7.5 and 7.6 show two different printer option dialog boxes: one is for an Epson printer and the other is for an HP LaserJet Postscript printer.

Because each type of printer driver has its own unique setup dialog box, we can't cover all of the options here. You will find, however, that most of the options for your printer are easy to determine and set up. In most cases, the basic options—such as

▼ *Figure 7.5. Setup Options for Epson Printer*

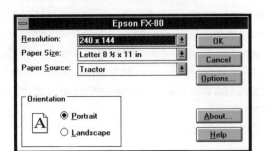

paper size, paper source, and orientation—are listed in the first dialog box. If you want to set other options, choose the Options button. If you are having trouble understanding or setting an option, choose the dialog box's Help button to get specific help information for your printer driver.

Selecting the Default Printer

Now that you've installed and configured your printer, you can put the printer into service by selecting the printer in the Installed Printers dialog box and then choosing the Set As Default Printer button. Your printer will then be listed in the Default Printer box. When you run a Windows application and choose the Print command, Windows will send your output to the default printer.

▼ *Figure 7.6. Setup Options for PostScript HP LaserJet Printer*

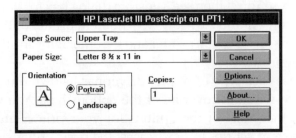

TIP

You can still print a file using one of your installed printers even if the printer has not been selected as the default printer from the Control Panel. Many applications, such as Write, provide a command called Printer Setup that allows you to select a different printer as the default. This command also allows you to change print options for the printer—such as page size, page orientation, number of copies to print, and so on.

Using a Network Printer

If you are running a network and you wish to print to one of the printers on the network, you'll need to follow these steps to connect to the network printer:

1. Display the Printers dialog box by running the Control Panel and choosing the Printers setting.

2. Choose the Connect button.

3. In the Connections dialog box, choose the Network button to display the Network Connections dialog box. (Keep in mind that the features listed in this dialog box will vary depending on which network you are using.)

4. Locate the Network Path box and enter the network name for the printer.

5. Open the Port box and choose the port for your printer.

6. In the Password box, enter a password if one is required.

7. Choose the Connect button.

Removing an Installed Printer

If you have a printer installed that you no longer need, you can easily remove it by selecting the printer in the Printers dialog box and choosing the Remove button. You'll then be asked to verify that you want to remove the printer. Choose the Yes button to proceed. Windows will delete the printer driver file for the printer *only if* no other printer requires the driver.

Introducing the Print Manager

If you've ever used a basic DOS word processor, you know that you often can't edit a file or exit the program while a file is printing. Fortunately, Windows applications are much more flexible. When you choose the Print command from an application, a temporary file is created on your disk and the information created by the application is sent to this file. The file is then closed, and the Print Manager takes over and prints it. This process is illustrated in Figure 7.7. If several files are created, Print Manager sends the first file to the printer while holding the other temporary files in reserve. When the first file is finished, Print Manager deletes it and

▼ *Figure 7.7. The Process of Printing a File*

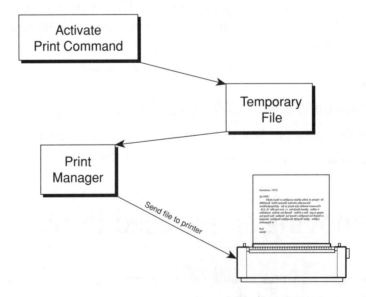

begins to print the next file in the print queue (the list of files that are waiting to be printed).

You can also use the Print Manager to change the priorities of all pending jobs in the print queue. (Once the Print Manager begins to print a job, that job has the highest priority in the queue.)

Selecting Print Manager

You can turn the Print Manager on or off from the Control Panel. To select it, start the Control Panel and double-click on the Printers icon. When the Printers dialog box (Figure 7.8) appears, select the check box at the bottom of the dialog box, called Use Print Manager. After you select the Print Manager, it automatically manages your print jobs. You can choose a number of options that control how the Print Manager operates. To access these features, you need to run the Print Manager application.

Starting Print Manager

The Print Manager application operates quietly in the background. You can open the Print Manager application at any time to check the status of your print jobs by double-clicking on its icon in the Main group window. Figure 7.9 shows the Print Manager window, which contains a menu bar with the View, Options, and Help menus. The next item below the menu bar is a message box that displays information about the currently active printer. This area also contains the Pause, Resume, and Delete buttons that allow

▼ *Figure 7.8. Selecting the Print Manager*

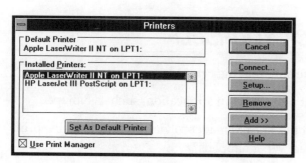

▼ *Figure 7.9. The Print Manager Window*

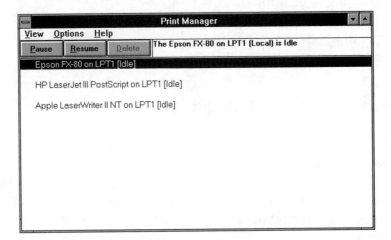

you to control the currently selected printer queue. The printer queue information line indicates the current activity of the selected queue. The remainder of the window displays the files in each of the active queues.

We'll begin by considering the most common case: only one printer is connected to the system. In this case, the message box contains information about the default (only) printer. If you open the Print Manager window in the Main program group when no files are being printed, the box identifies the default printer and states that the status of the printer is idle. If you click on the Pause button, the word Pause appears on the second line of the message box, and the printer queue information line changes to show that the queue is stopped. Clicking on the Resume window button cancels the Pause operation. Unless there are entries in the queue, the Delete button is not active.

CHECK YOURSELF

1. Make sure that the Print Manager is selected.

2. Print a file from an application, such as Notepad.

3. Start the Print Manager to view the status of the print jobs in the queue. What happens?

4. Pause your print job.

5. Continue printing.

ANSWERS

1. Start the Control Panel and double-click on the Printers icon. Select the Use Print Manager check box in the Printers dialog box. Click the OK button and exit the Control Panel.

2. Open the application by double-clicking on its icon, then load a file and choose the Print command from the File menu.

3. You see the name of the installed printer and the file you have just started printing from your application. If multiple files were being printed, you would also see a list of each file and the time and date when it was being processed by the Print Manager.

4. Click the Pause button.

5. Click the Resume button.

Working with the Queue

If the queue has several entries and you want to delete an entry, move the pointer to the item to be removed and click on it once to highlight it. Next, click on the Delete button to remove the entry from the queue.

If you want to move a print job to the rear of the queue, click on the item to be moved, drag it to the bottom of the queue list, and release the mouse button. You can use the same principle to move a print job ahead of other print jobs: click on the item to be advanced, drag it toward the front of the queue, and release the mouse button. Notice that you can only rearrange the order of items that are waiting to be printed. The top item in a queue is currently being printed, and other print jobs can't be moved in front of it.

Using Multiple Printers

If you have multiple printers, things get a bit more complicated. Imagine that you've already queued several jobs to the laser printer on LPT1:, but you want to send a quick Notepad memo to a dot-matrix printer connected to LPT2:. Assuming that you've installed the printers correctly, take the following steps:

1. Select the Printer Setup option from the File menu in the Notepad.
2. Click on the line containing the information for the dot-matrix printer.
3. Choose the OK button to confirm your selection.
4. Choose the Print command from the File menu.

The memo in Notepad is sent to the alternate printer that you selected (rather than the primary laser printer). Open the Print Manager window and notice that an additional entry has been created to show the status of the other printer. If you want to stop or resume this new queue, click on the file in the queue. The information in the message box, and in the printer queue information line, changes to display information about the dot-matrix printer. The Pause and Resume buttons now affect the operation of the newly selected queue.

The Options Menu

The Options menu allows you to control certain attributes of the Print Manager. You can use the first three entries in the menu to define the priority for the Print Manager as Low, Medium, or High.

As we mentioned in previous chapters, many microprocessors in PCs (especially the 80386 and 80486 chips) are capable of sharing the available execution time among several tasks. The first three entries in the Options menu tell Windows about the relative importance of the print operation. For example, if your printer is slow, you prefer to use most of the computer's processing time for the current foreground task, and you're in no hurry to get the printout, you can choose Low Priority. If you want to bias computer time usage toward the foreground task, but you're willing to sacrifice some execution time for increased printing speed, choose the Medium Priority setting. If you need the printout above all else, choose High Priority to make certain that the printer is never waiting for information from the PC.

The Options Menu

CHECK YOURSELF

1. Use an application (such as Write) and start printing two files.

2. What is the default printing speed?

3. Set the printing speed so that the files are printed as slowly as possible.

4. What is the advantage of using the priority options?

ANSWERS

1. (a) Start the application.
    (b) Open a file and print it using the Print command.
    (c) Open another file and send it to the print queue using Print.

2. Start the Print manager and open the Options menu. A checkmark appears next to the Medium Priority option to indicate that this setting is the default.

3. Choose the Low Priority option.

4. You can allocate more or less time to the printer so that your computer can perform other tasks.

Print Manager Messages

The next set of options—Alert Always, Flash if Inactive, and Ignore if Inactive—control how the Print Manager reacts when certain unusual events occur. For example, if your printer runs out of paper or the ink ribbon runs out, your PC receives a message from the printer that identifies the problem. Windows processes the information and takes one of three actions. If you choose the Alert Always option, Windows displays a message box on the screen when the event is detected. (The message box won't display with a non-Windows application.)

When you choose the second option, Flash if Inactive, your computer beeps once, and then flashes either the Print Manager icon or the title bar of the Print Manager window until the Print Manager becomes the active task. This option is handy when you're printing while performing another operation (such as editing a different file). When you hear the beep and see the icon blink, you know that the printer needs attention, and when you reach a convenient stopping point, you can enlarge the icon or bring the window forward to read the message. The Flash if Inactive option is the default when Windows is installed.

The third option is Ignore if Inactive. If you choose this option and a problem arises while printing, and the Print Manager window is either an icon or not the active window, Windows won't make an attempt to get your attention. It's not a good idea to select this mode unless your activity is time-critical. For example, if you're using your modem to communicate with a computer network and the printer runs out of paper, you may want to ignore the messages from Print Manager until you're done with your Terminal session.

Using a Network

The Options menu also provides a feature for controlling a network. This option is only available if you've properly installed a network driver. If you choose this option, an additional menu opens to allow you to inhibit automatic update of the network status, and to enable the printing of network jobs directly to the network. The first option minimizes the amount of useless network traffic. Print Manager requests the current status of the selected print queue whenever you expand the Print Manager icon to a window. It also requests updates at periodic intervals when the window remains expanded.

If you've connected a large number of PCs using Windows to the same network, you may discover that a measurable percentage of the network throughput is being consumed by this needless polling. By clearing the check box on the Update Network Display and clicking the OK button, you instruct Print Manager not to perform periodic polling. Unfortunately, the network queue status won't be updated again until this option is reenabled.

In many cases, the network server has the resources to schedule and control print jobs independently of your PC. In such cases, it's a waste of time and resources to get Print Manager involved. There is no simple way to determine whether to bypass Print Manager; you will simply have to experiment and select the option that works best for you. To bypass Print Manager, choose Network Settings in the Options menu, select the Print Net Jobs Direct check box, and click on the OK button.

The View Menu

The first two options in the View menu are automatically enabled when Windows is installed, and allow you to control the information displayed for each file in the queues. You can activate or deactivate each option by clicking on it. The option is active when a checkmark appears next to the entry. The Time/Date Sent option controls whether the time and the date when a print file was created will appear in the queue. If you usually have a couple of files in the queue and you want to minimize onscreen clutter, disable this feature.

The second option is Print File Size. If the total size of the print job is unimportant, you can disable this option to minimize clutter.

The next three options in the View menu are provided for network users. Use the Refresh option to retrieve fresh information from the network controller. To view the entire queue for a particular printer (some networks have more than one printer), choose the Selected Net Queue option. You can select the last option, Other Net Queue, to view network queues that you're not connected to. When you choose Other Net Queue, a dialog box requests the name and the location of the network queue to be viewed. Remember that viewing the status of a queue via the Other Net Queue option doesn't give you access to that queue for printing. If you wish to send a file to a queue other than the currently selected queue, first change the queue selection in the Network section of the Control Panel.

Intercepting Print Jobs

An earlier section about techniques for printer installation with the Control Panel discussed how you can select a file as an output device. The Print Manager provides the other half of the control structure to make this option work.

Imagine that you have a Windows-compatible application that prints files, and you want to modify your output before it goes to the printer. Follow these steps to set up your system to operate in this manner:

1. Start the Control Panel by double-clicking on the Control Panel icon in the Main group window.
2. Double-click on the Printers icon to bring up the Printers dialog box.
3. Select the printer you want to use.
4. Click the Connect button to display the dialog box shown in Figure 7.10.
5. Select the FILE: option from the Ports list box.
6. Confirm the changes by clicking the OK button.

▼ *Figure 7.10. Selecting the FILE: Output Device*

```
┌─────────────────────────────────────────────┐
│ ─              Connect                        │
│ HP LaserJet III PostScript          ┌──────┐ │
│                                     │  OK  │ │
│ Ports:                              └──────┘ │
│ ┌─────────────────────────────┐─┐   ┌──────┐ │
│ │COM3:  Local Port Not Present│▲│   │Cancel│ │
│ │COM4:  Local Port Not Present│ │   └──────┘ │
│ │EPT:                         │ │   ┌──────┐ │
│ │FILE:                        │ │   │Settings│ │
│ │LPT1.OS2                     │▼│   └──────┘ │
│ └─────────────────────────────┘─┘   ┌──────┐ │
│ ┌─Timeouts (seconds)───────┐        │Network│ │
│ │ Device Not Selected: ┌──┐│        └──────┘ │
│ │                      │15││        ┌──────┐ │
│ │ Transmission Retry:  ┌──┐│        │ Help │ │
│ │                      │90││        └──────┘ │
│ └──────────────────────────┘                 │
│ ⊠ Fast Printing Direct to Port               │
└─────────────────────────────────────────────┘
```

If you've installed multiple printers, make certain to set the printer connected to FILE: as the default printer. The easiest way to do this is to select the printer and click the Set As Default Printer button while you are in the Printers dialog box. Click the OK button to confirm your changes and return to the Control Panel window. Close the window and minimize the Main applications group back to an icon.

Run the application whose output you wish to intercept and initiate a print session. If you didn't designate the printer connected to FILE: as the default printer, select the printer using the Print Setup option of the File menu for your application. When Print Manager receives the print job, it detects that the job is destined to go to a file, and a dialog box (Figure 7.11) asks for the destination file name. You can also specify destination disk and path information.

Depending upon the attributes of the installed printer, you may need to use a text editor (such as Notepad) to modify the file. Of course, you can merge several of these files into one large file by using the DOS COPY command, as in this example:

```
COPY MYFILE1.PRN+MYFILE2.PRN ALLMYFIL.ZZZ
```

▼ *Figure 7.11. Printing to a File*

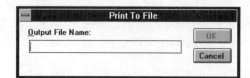

```
┌─────────────────────────────────────────────┐
│ ─              Print To File                  │
│ Output File Name:              ┌──────┐       │
│ ┌──────────────────────────┐   │  OK  │       │
│ │▌                         │   └──────┘       │
│ └──────────────────────────┘   ┌──────┐       │
│                                │Cancel│       │
│                                └──────┘       │
└─────────────────────────────────────────────┘
```

Here, the plus sign shows that the files are to be added in the order indicated, and then saved as the target file ALLMYFIL.ZZZ. This technique comes in handy when the network printer is located at a substantial distance away from your PC. By combining several printouts together, you can minimize the likelihood that a listing will be picked up accidentally by another user.

QUICK TASK SUMMARY

Task	Procedure
Install a new printer	Run Control Panel; select Printers option; use Install button
Select a printer as the default	Select printer; choose Set As Default button
Change printer settings	Select printer; choose Setup button
Remove an installed printer	Select printer; choose Remove button
Turn Print Manager on or off	Select Use Print Manager check box (Printers dialog box)
Run the Print Manager	Double-click Print Manager icon
View the files in the print queue	
Change the order of files in the queue	Click a file in the Print Manager queue and drag it to a different position
Remove a file from the queue	Select the file and click Delete button
Pause or resume printing a file	Select a file and click Pause or Resume button

PRACTICE WHAT YOU'VE LEARNED

In this chapter you've learned the basics of installing and setting up printers and techniques for using the Print Manager. We've covered the techniques for using queues, configuring the Print Manager, and using the Print Manager with the Installed Printers application of the Control Panel to divert printer output to a file for subsequent modification. Use these exercises to practice using the Print Manager.

1. Make sure the Print Manager is active by selecting the Use Print Manager check box in the Printers dialog box.

2. Start printing a file from the Notepad application.

3. Start the Print Manager, and disable the Time/Date Sent option from the View menu.

4. Pause the print job.

5. Print the file again, but this time send it to a file named SAMPLE.TXT.

ANSWERS

1. The Print Manager will be used by each Windows application when a file prints.

2. The file is managed by the Print Manager.

3. The print queue doesn't display the time or the date when the file is sent to the printer.

4. Your file stops printing until you select the Resume button.

5. The Print manager doesn't send your file to the active printer. Instead, your file is saved in the print file SAMPLE.TXT.

Working with Non-Windows Applications

If you're like many PC users, you've probably been running programs under DOS. Perhaps you have a large database that would be hard to convert to a format that could be used by a Windows application. In this chapter, we'll show you how to set up and run DOS programs (non-Windows applications) with Windows. Along the way, we'll discuss a number of technical issues about working with DOS and Windows. After you finish this chapter, you'll know:

▲ **The limitations of running non-Windows applications**

▲ **How to access the MS-DOS Prompt application**

▲ **How to use Program Information Files (PIF)**

▲ **How to use the PIF editor**

▲ **How to use some basic DOS commands**

Using Non-Windows Applications

Throughout this book, we've explored how Windows provides powerful features for running Windows applications, such as Write, Notepad, and Cardfile. Windows also allows you to run non-Windows applications—applications that were not specifically designed to run with Windows. You can run a non-Windows application in these ways:

▲ From the Program Manager

▲ From the File Manager

▲ From the MS-DOS Prompt application

As you'll see later in this chapter, you can also use special files, called Program Information Files (PIFs), to customize how Windows runs non-Windows applications. When a DOS application is started under Windows, Windows looks for the application's PIF to determine which settings should be used to run the application. If the application does not have its own PIF, Windows will use its default settings to run the application.

After we cover the basics of running non-Windows applications with the DOS Prompt, we'll show you how to install non-Windows applications so that they can be run from within Windows.

Options and Limitations

Windows can't compensate for the limitations of your hardware. If you run Windows on an 80286-based system in standard mode, you'll find that Windows can only run one non-Windows application at a time. These computers can't support the memory-management techniques offered by the 80386 and 80486 processors.

For example, if your computer runs Windows in the 386 enhanced mode, program execution can be split between the non-Windows active task and the background tasks, as specified in the

Control Panel's 386 Enhanced window (see Chapter 5). Thus, you can arrange for Windows to give 80 percent of the available execution time to your DOS word processor or database management program and to give only 20 percent to a background task, such as a communications program. If you are running Windows in standard mode, Windows must run the non-Windows foreground task 100 percent of the time.

Using Non-Windows Applications

For now, let's step away from the technical details of operating Windows and look at the general aspects of running DOS programs with the DOS prompt application.

CHECK YOURSELF

1. True or false? Non-Windows applications can be run on 80286-based machines.

2. True or false? Non-Windows applications can run as background tasks on 80386-based machines.

3. What is a PIF?

ANSWERS

1. True.

2. True.

3. A Program Information File. These files tell Windows how to run non-Windows applications.

Using the MS-DOS Prompt Application

When you open the Main program group window, you'll see an icon named MS-DOS Prompt. Double-click on this icon and the DOS environment appears. Notice that the screen is blank except for an instruction box and the standard message that identifies the version of MS-DOS you're running. (You will also see the usual DOS prompt (usually C:\WINDOWS> if you run Windows from a hard disk installed as the C drive). The command to return to the Windows environment is EXIT. Type this command at the DOS prompt, press Enter, and return to Windows.

TIP

If you are running Windows in 386 enhanced mode, you can run the MS-DOS Prompt application in a window, as shown in Figure 8.1, by pressing Alt+Enter. You'll then be able to use the mouse to scroll, resize, move, or minimize this window.

CHECK YOURSELF

Enter the command DIR and press the Enter key. What happens?

ANSWER

You see a listing of the files for the current directory.

You can run most non-Windows programs and DOS commands using the MS-DOS Prompt application. For example, if you had a text editor named QEDIT.EXE in the directory C:\TOOLS, you could run this program by entering the name of the program and its directory path,

```
C:\TOOLS\QEDIT
```

and then pressing the Enter key.

Keep in mind that DOS doesn't care whether the commands are in uppercase or lowercase. In fact, you can mix uppercase and lowercase letters on the same command line.

Unfortunately, when you run a non-Windows application in this manner, you have to start the MS-DOS Prompt application in

▼ *Figure 8.1. The MS-DOS Prompt Application Window*

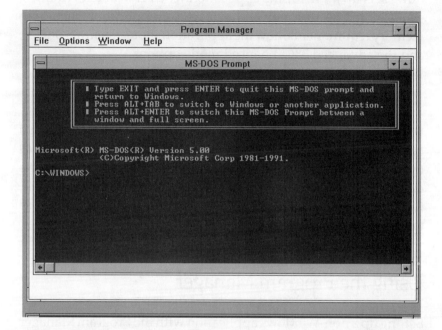

order to run the application. An easier way is to set up a non-Windows application as an icon so that you can start the application by clicking on its icon.

Setting Up a Non-Windows Application

To set up a non-Windows application as an icon, you can use either the Windows Setup application or the Program Manager. In either case, you'll first need to decide which group window you want to put the application's icon in. If you want to create a new group for the icon, use the techniques we explored in Chapter 3 for setting up a new group with the Program Manager.

When a non-Windows application is added to a group, Windows sets up a PIF for the application. The PIF will tell Windows everything it needs to run and manage the application, including memory requirements, how the application should share resources, and the advanced 386 enhanced mode options.

TIP

When a non-Windows application is set up, Windows will try to create a custom PIF if the application doesn't come with its own PIF. Windows will try to use information that it finds about your application to create the custom PIF. If Windows can't find the information it needs to create a PIF, it will use the default one named _DEFAULT.PIF. In either case, you can use the PIF editor to easily change the PIF.

Using the Program Manager

Setting up a non-Windows application with the Program Manager is not much different than setting up a Windows application. Once you've selected the group that you want to place the application in, choose the New command from the File menu. Next, select the Program Item option in the New Program Object dialog box to display the dialog box shown in Figure 8.2.

Type the label you want to assign to the application in the Description box and type the path and filename for the application in the Command Line box. As an option, you can specify a working directory and a shortcut key for the application. (If you need more information about how to use these features, see Chapter 3.)

▼ *Figure 8.2. Setting up an Application with Program Manager*

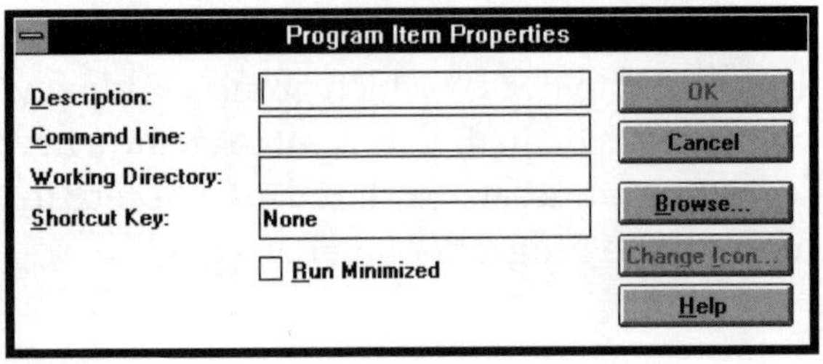

Program Item Properties		
Description:		OK
Command Line:		Cancel
Working Directory:		
Shortcut Key:	None	Browse...
	☐ Run Minimized	Change Icon...
		Help

When you have finished entering the necessary information, click the OK button to finish setting up the application. Your new icon appears in the desired program group window. The Program Manager assigns the default DOS icon for the non-Windows application.

To run the application, just double-click on your icon in the same way you start any of the other Windows applications.

TIP

Many applications come with their own PIFs. In such a case, Windows will locate the PIF and use it to set up the application and create its icon. If you want to change the icon, assign a new shortcut key, or change the working directory for the application, you can select the icon and use the Properties command in the File menu after the application has been set up.

Using Windows Setup

You can also use the Windows Setup application at any time to set up a non-Windows application. To use this application, open the Main group window and double-click on the Windows Setup icon. Choose the Set Up Applications command from the Options menu to access the dialog box shown in Figure 8.3. Notice that two options are provided. If you select the first option, Search for applications, Windows will search your computer's disk drive for applications. Select the other option if you want to specify the name of an application yourself without having Windows search your computer's disk drive.

▼ *Figure 8.3. Setting up an Application with Windows Setup*

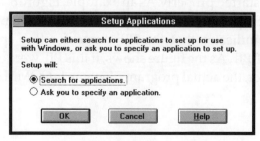

Working with PIFs

When you run an application, Windows determines how the program should be executed—and that's where the PIF comes into play. This file provides important technical information, such as:

▲ The actual DOS filename for the application

▲ The optional parameters used to run the application

▲ The startup directory for the application

▲ How much memory the application requires

▲ Whether the application should be run in a window

▲ Whether the application should be run in the background

▲ Whether the video mode for the application is text or graphics

▲ Whether the application modifies a communication port

If you run a program that doesn't have an associated PIF, Windows uses default settings that work for most programs. However, with a dedicated PIF, you can customize the environment for your application and improve its performance. The drawback to using PIFs is that you need to provide technical information about your application.

When a non-Windows application is started, Windows will use the PIF or program filename (COM, EXE, or BAT) specified in the application's Program Item Properties dialog box. If a PIF is specified, Windows will use the PIF to determine the actual DOS program filename and settings that should be used to run the application. Therefore, if a PIF is specified, the PIF must provide the DOS filename and parameters so that the program can be located and started properly. As an example, Figure 8.4 shows how the MS-DOS application is set up. The Program Item Properties dialog box indicates that the PIF name for this application is DOSPRMPT.PIF. As the figure shows, if this PIF were opened with the PIF Editor, the actual program filename is COMMAND.COM.

▼ *Figure 8.4. Linking a PIF to an Application*

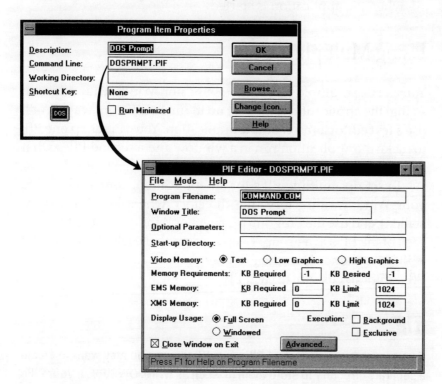

Using an Existing PIF

If you use an application that has its own PIF, you can easily install the PIF by following these steps:

1. Make sure the application is correctly installed on your hard disk. To perform the installation, follow the instructions provided with the application.

2. Copy the PIF provided with the application to your Windows directory or the directory where you installed Windows.

3. Start Windows and use the Program Manager or Windows Setup as we discussed in the previous section to set up the application in a group. Make sure you enter the name of the PIF in the Command Line text box in the Program Item Properties

dialog box. Windows needs this filename in order to use the PIF when the application is started.

Using Multiple PIFs

You can use multiple PIFs for the same non-Windows application so that the application can be set up to run in different ways. We'll use a text editor as an example application. You can set up one PIF to make the application run in a window and a second PIF so that the application will use the full screen.

To set up multiple PIFs for an application, copy each PIF to your Windows directory (the directory where Windows is installed), and use the Program Manager or Windows Setup to set up each of the PIFs in a group. Keep in mind that each PIF must have a different name. After the PIFs have been set up, you can use the PIF Editor to customize each PIF.

TIP

If you are using a number of PIFs with Windows, you may want to create a separate directory to store them in, such as \WINDOWS\PIF. If your PIFs are stored in a directory other than the default Windows directory, make sure you include the full path for the directory in the Program Item Properties dialog box so that Windows can find the PIFs.

Using the PIF Editor

The PIF Editor is used to view, create, or modify a PIF. To start the PIF Editor application, open the Main group window and double-click on the PIF Editor icon.

Figure 8.5 shows how the PIF Editor window looks when you run Windows in 386 enhanced mode. (If you are running Windows in standard mode, the application window will look slightly different.) The application consists of a simple menu bar with three menu items, File, Mode, and Help, and a data entry window that

▼ *Figure 8.5. The PIF Editor Window*

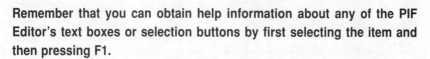

provides a number of text boxes and selection buttons. The File menu provides the basic commands for creating, opening, and saving PIFs. The Mode menu allows you to switch between standard and 386 enhanced modes. The Help menu provides a number of options for accessing help information for the PIF Editor.

TIP

Remember that you can obtain help information about any of the PIF Editor's text boxes or selection buttons by first selecting the item and then pressing F1.

Viewing a PIF

When the PIF Editor starts, the default Untitled window is displayed. To open an existing PIF, choose the Open command from the File menu. As Figure 8.6 shows, the Open dialog box lists files with the extension PIF that are stored in the Windows directory. Select the PIF you want to view, and click the OK button.

After the file is opened, the PIF Editor window will change to show you the settings for the PIF. Before you try to create a new PIF for a non-Windows application, you may want to open existing PIFs, to see how they are set up. You can also modify an existing PIF

▼ *Figure 8.6. Opening a PIF*

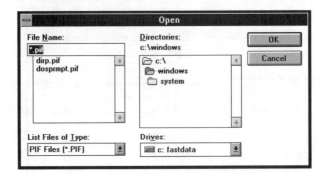

and then save it with a new name by choosing the Save As command from the File menu.

Creating a New PIF

To create a new PIF, enter the necessary information for the PIF and then save it by selecting the Save As command from the File menu. When the Save As dialog box is displayed, enter a filename for the PIF. Remember that Windows reserves the extension PIF for these files. Let's take a closer look at the basic components of a PIF.

TIP

Instead of creating a new PIF from scratch, you may want to use the default PIF named _DEFAULT.PIF, and then modify it to suit your needs. Remember to save the modified version using a different name. The default PIF provides settings that are designed to work with most non-Windows applications.

PIF Editor Basics

Although the PIF Editor may look confusing at first, you'll find that it is easy to use. The main data-entry components that you'll probably use to create or modify a PIF are listed first.

The first text box in the PIF Editor window, Program Filename, requests the name of the application that the PIF is being created for. (This entry should include the directory path where the application is stored.) The next text box, Window Title, requests the window title that will display in the title bar. (If your application uses the entire screen, this information will not be displayed.)

The Optional Parameters text box is used to provide information that would normally follow the program name on the command line. For example, if you wanted to run a program named QEDIT.EXE and load a text file named NOTES.TXT, you would enter QEDIT in the Program Filename text box and the text NOTES.TXT in the Optional Parameters text box.

Using the PIF Editor

TIP

If the parameter information is likely to change each time you run the application, enter a question mark in the Optional Parameters box. Windows will prompt you for an optional parameter, such as a filename, when the application starts.

The Start-up Directory box is used to define a default working directory for the application. This is the directory Windows will go to after the application starts so that you can access files for the application.

CHECK YOURSELF

1. What information do you enter into the text boxes Program Filename, Window Title, and Optional Parameters to run the application named WORD, which is stored in the directory C:\APPS? When the application starts, it should run in a window called MS WORD 5.5, and it should load the document file NOTES.DOC (which is stored in the directory C:\APPS \WORD\DOCS).

2. Enter a ? in the Optional Parameters text box. What will happen when you try to run the application?

3. True or false? All non-Windows applications must run in a window.

ANSWERS

1. (a) Program Filename: C:\APPS\WORD
   (b) Window Title: MS WORD 5.5
   (c) Optional Parameters: C:\APPS\WORD\DOCS

2. Windows prompts you for the name of a parameter before it starts to run the application.

3. False.

After you've provided information in these text boxes, you can choose from several groups of options. The options that you select will vary depending upon whether you run Windows in 386 Enhanced mode or Standard mode.

Using Standard Mode Options

If you don't have a 386- or 486-based PC, you can run Windows only in standard mode. If this is the case, the setup options are simpler than those provided for the 386 enhanced mode. Figure 8.7 shows the actual PIF Editor window that is displayed when you are running in standard mode.

First, you must decide if your application runs in Text mode or Graphics/Multiple Text mode. Unless you know that the application displays graphics and requires a graphics mode to operate, leave this setting in the Text position. Windows asks for this information because Graphics/Multiple Text mode requires more memory to run the application.

Use the Memory Requirements box to specify the amount of memory that must be available in the normal 640K DOS area for the program to operate successfully. It's usually best to leave this option at the default value of 128K unless you know that the program requires more memory. Windows gives the program all available memory in the 640K partition anyway, so this is usually not very important.

▼ *Figure 8.7. PIF Editor in Standard Mode*

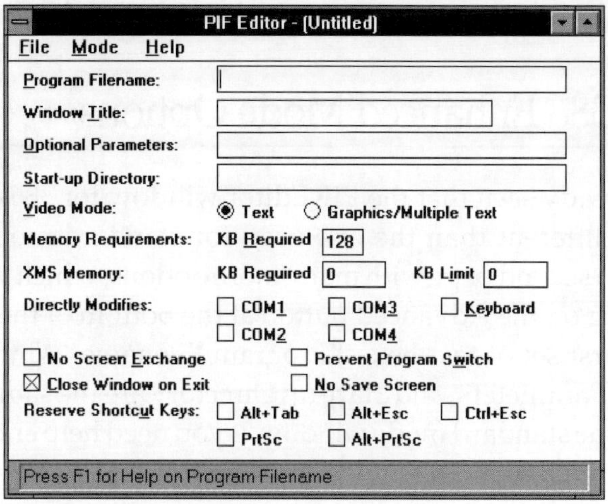

```
┌─────────────────────────────────────────────────────┐
│ ─          PIF Editor - [Untitled]            ▼ ▲   │
│ File   Mode   Help                                  │
│ Program Filename:    │                            │ │
│ Window Title:        │                            │ │
│ Optional Parameters: │                            │ │
│ Start-up Directory:  │                            │ │
│ Video Mode:          ⦿ Text   ○ Graphics/Multiple Text │
│ Memory Requirements: KB Required │128│            │
│ XMS Memory:          KB Required │0│   KB Limit │0│ │
│ Directly Modifies:   □ COM1   □ COM3   □ Keyboard  │
│                      □ COM2   □ COM4               │
│ □ No Screen Exchange    □ Prevent Program Switch   │
│ ⊠ Close Window on Exit  □ No Save Screen           │
│ Reserve Shortcut Keys: □ Alt+Tab  □ Alt+Esc  □ Ctrl+Esc │
│                        □ PrtSc    □ Alt+PrtSc      │
│ Press F1 for Help on Program Filename              │
└─────────────────────────────────────────────────────┘
```

The XMS Memory text boxes apply only to programs designed to directly utilize Extended Memory in PCs that don't have 386/486 microprocessors. Again, unless you run an application that specifically wants this additional memory (such as high-end database manager programs), leave this option at the default value of zero.

If your application directly accesses one or more hardware ports or the keyboard, click on the appropriate boxes in the Directly Modifies group to tell Windows which hardware components are needed by the application and should not be shared with other applications.

Select the check box associated with the No Screen Exchange to tell Windows that you won't be copying information from that screen into the Clipboard application. By selecting this option, you reduce the amount of memory consumed by the program. Use the Prevent Program Switch option to save additional memory by telling Windows that the only way to return to Windows after this application runs is to terminate the execution of the application.

The Close Window on Exit option tells Windows that whenever you exit the application (which normally would return you to the DOS prompt), Windows should close the window automatically and return you to the Windows environment. If you do not select Close Window on Exit, the application is terminated but the contents of its window remains on the screen.

Use the bottom section of the window to reserve certain key combinations used by Windows, so that your application can use them instead. Leave these boxes blank unless you have a conflict.

Using 386 Enhanced Mode Options

We've already seen that the PIF Editor window for 386 enhanced mode is different than the one used for standard mode. It also provides a second page with many more options, which you access by clicking on the Advanced button at the bottom of the window.

The first set of text boxes, Program Filename, Window Title, Optional Parameters, and Start-up Directory are the same as those found in the standard mode window. If you need help entering this information, review the previous section.

Video Memory Options

Use the Video Memory options to select among Text, Low Graphics, and High Graphics modes. Text mode is the least memory-hungry mode; it implies that all communications to the screen consist of the usual printable characters (including the symbols used by some programs to implement boxes around text, and so on). The second mode, Low Graphics, assumes that you use graphics images similar to those provided by a CGA card. Select the third option, High Graphics, if you expect to generate full-blown EGA/VGA graphics in the window.

Memory Options

When the PIF Editor opens a new PIF, it sets the KB Required option to 128 and the KB Desired option to 640. These numbers refer to the amount of conventional memory that should be allocated to your application. The KB Required option indicates the minimum amount of memory that Windows must have available before it can start the application. The default of 128K is a reasonable compromise; many DOS applications (excluding large word processors or database programs) fit in 128K.

The second box specifies 640K for the KB Desired option. This is your opportunity to tell Windows the maximum amount of conventional memory that should be provided to this window. If

640K is available, Windows allocates that much to the window (which keeps other tasks from using the memory). In cases where you run only a specific application in a window, you may wish to reduce the KB Desired figure to the maximum amount of memory that the application can use. This leaves more memory available for other windows.

Notice that the PIF Editor window also provides two groups of settings for allocating expanded and extended memory for your application. If your system is set up to use expanded or extended memory you may want to change the default values for these settings.

Display and Control Options

The next option, called Display Usage, allows you to specify whether the application should have the full screen to itself or should be run in a window. Select Full Screen to allow an application to operate the same way that it would if Windows were not present.

The main disadvantages of running an application in a window is that the application can't access the mouse (Windows keeps control), and the application consumes more memory than when running in Full Screen mode. These may be small penalties compared to the advantages of running in a window.

TIP

You may want to always select the Display Usage to Full Screen option, thereby saving resources and eliminating any potential problem with the mouse. If you want to run the application in a Window at any time, just press Alt+Enter.

Use the Close Window on Exit option to tell Windows what it should do once the application returns to DOS. If you select this check box, Windows automatically closes the window when the application program terminates.

Background and Foreground Options

To the right of the Display Usage options appear two check boxes that show how and when the application in the window executes. If you click on the Background option, Windows occasionally diverts execution time to this application when another nonexclusive application is running in the foreground. This option is particularly important when the application is performing a real-time function, such as communicating with another device through a port or waiting for a particular event to occur. If you don't select the check box, the task becomes completely dormant when another window is active.

The second option, Exclusive, specifies how execution time should be partitioned when this window is the active one. If you select this option, this application prevents any other non-Windows application from running.

Advanced PIF Options

Notice the button labeled Advanced located at the bottom of the PIF Editor window. Figure 8.8 shows the Advanced Options dialog box that appears if you click this button. The four main components of this window include multitasking, memory, display, and other options. Notice that same of the options in the Other Options group, such as Reserve Shortcut Keys, are similar to those provided with the standard mode PIF editor.

Multitasking Options

The first section in the dialog box allows you to set Background and Foreground Priorities for multitasking. (In reality, these should be called execution-time points.) Both boxes can receive numbers in the range of 0 to 10000. The default setting for Background Priority is 50 and the default setting for Foreground Priority is 100.

Windows sums the Foreground Priority number for the foreground application and the Background Priority values for the various background applications. The foreground application receives a percentage of the total available execution time, represented by its Foreground Priority number divided by the sum of the priorities. Each background application receives a percentage of the total available execution time, represented by its Background Priority number divided by the sum of the priorities. This sharing of execution time occurs if the Exclusive option isn't selected in the PIF of the foreground application.

▼ *Figure 8.8. PIF Editor's Advanced Options*

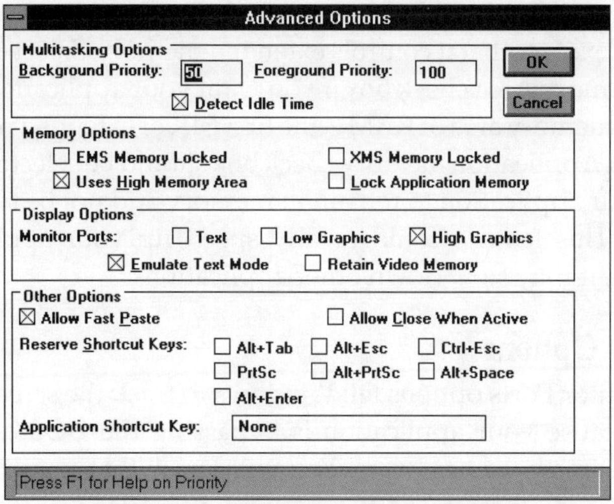

The Detect Idle Time option allows Windows to steal resources from the foreground application whenever it thinks that the foreground task is waiting for input from the user. For example, imagine that you're typing a letter using Windows Write. Unless you're an extremely fast thinker, you probably type a few sentences and then stop for a minute or two while composing the next set of sentences in your mind. While the computer is waiting for your next set of keystrokes, it can run other applications in the background (for example, send additional characters to a printer). When you select Detect Idle Time, Windows can best utilize the total execution time available. Of course, if you find that a particular application runs slowly under Windows, disable this option and try the program again.

Memory Options

The next set of options are grouped under the title Memory Options. If you run normal DOS applications (those that run in 640K of regular memory or less), then don't modify any of these options. If you run a memory-hungry application that tries to use more than 640K, read the user's manual for the application for more details about what the application needs to use.

Select the EMS Memory Locked check box to keep an application's expanded memory from being swapped to the hard disk. The XMS Memory Locked check box performs a similar function excepts that it controls extended memory. Select the Uses High Memory Area check box if you want your application to use the high memory area of RAM—the first 64K of extended memory. The Lock Application memory check box should be selected if you want your application to remain in memory and not be swapped to disk. This feature could greatly speed up your application; however, it may slow down other applications.

Display Options

The Monitor Ports options tell Windows to track the screen hardware because your application is bypassing the DOS calls and writing directly to hardware. You will know that you have this problem if you move to a different window, return to this application, and find that the screen has inexplicably changed or is garbled. You can tell Windows to monitor only for Text mode, for CGA-style Low Graphics, or for EGA/VGA High Graphics. Don't change these options for an application unless absolutely necessary, because the monitoring operation consumes additional computer execution time and slows down your application programs.

Use the last two options in the box, Emulate Text Mode and Retain Video Memory, to fine-tune your application. Select Emulate Text Mode (which is normally selected) to allow your application to display text more quickly. If your application won't run or you have troubles with screen operations (garbled text, cursor not operating properly, and so on), disable this feature and see if the problem goes away. Select the Retain Video Memory option to tell Windows not to release the extra video memory if your application shifts from a higher memory-consumption mode (such as EGA or VGA graphics) to a less memory-intensive mode (such as text-only mode). Some programs allow you to switch automatically from one mode to another; by activating this option, you can be certain that your application won't stop due to insufficient memory that results from a change in video mode.

Other Options

The last group, Other Options, contains several miscellaneous options. Allow Fast Paste is actually more of an inhibit than an enable option. If you don't select this check box, Windows uses a slower method of pasting information from the Clipboard into the non-Windows application. If you select the check box, Windows attempts to analyze the program that you're running, and uses the Fast Paste technique only if it thinks your application can handle it. Disable this option if you have trouble bringing in data from the Clipboard.

The Allow Close When Active check box tells Windows that it can just quit this application if you decide to exit the Windows environment with this application still open. If you don't select this option, Windows forces you to exit the task in the window before you can exit the environment.

Using the PIF Editor

TIP

If the application can open and modify files, leave this option off. Although DOS usually closes all files associated with an application automatically, there is a chance that something could go wrong (resulting in data loss). When it comes to data files, methodical and conservative techniques always pay off.

The Reserve Shortcut Keys option tells Windows to ignore the keystroke sequences selected and allow the command to go through to the application running in the window. This allows you to resolve conflicts where both Windows and the application program use the same command for different purposes.

Use the Application Shortcut Key to convert the application in this window into a pop-up program. To use this feature, you must specify a keystroke combination using either the Alt or Ctrl keys. For example, if you select Alt+7 as the shortcut, this window will immediately pop-up active whenever you press this combination of keys. The only disadvantage is that this combination of keys becomes reserved and can't be used in any other application. When defining shortcut key sequences, make certain that you won't have two separate windows with the same shortcut!

A Custom Directory Application

Now that you know how to set up a non-Windows application and use the PIF Editor to customize its PIF, let's look at an example. If you use the File Manager a great deal you know that it is difficult to locate a file if you can't remember its name or extension (type). Our example is an extremely simple tool that you run from the Program Manager by double-clicking on its icon. This program, written as a batch file (BAT), allows you to quickly find a file in any directory on any drive.

Figure 8.9 lists the batch file, called DIRP.BAT, which is invoked when you select the icon. The first line is a DOS command that disables the display of batch commands as they are executed. The second line does the actual work; it invokes the DOS directory command called DIR. The /P appended to the command is an option switch that requests that only enough information be displayed to fill one screen at a time. This "page" option means that DOS displays (at most) 23 file entries on the screen. The 24th line displays a message such as "Press any key to continue...", and on the 25th line, the cursor sits at column 1. After you've viewed the first page, you can continue by pressing a keyboard key. Each time you press the key, the next page appears.

Setting up the Application

Enter each line of this program by using an editor such as Write and then save it with the name DIRP.BAT. You'll then need to follow these steps to set up the application and its associated PIF.

1. Run the PIF Editor to create a PIF for the program. (Remember the PIF Editor is in the Main group.)

2. In the Program Filename text box, enter the path information and the name of the batch file you created (DIRP.BAT). For the Optional Parameters box, type a question mark. (You may also want to enter text in the Window Title box so that your application can have a title if you later run it in a window.)

▼ Figure 8.9. The DIRP.BAT File

```
echo off
rem dirp.bat program
dir/p %1
pause
```

A Custom Directory Application

3. Save the PIF with the name DIRP.PIF.

Once the PIF has been created, you can set up the non-Windows application as an icon in a group. Here are the steps required to set up the application in the Applications group.

1. Run the Program Manager and open the Applications group window.
2. Choose the New command from the File menu, select the Program Item option, and click the OK button.
3. In the Program Item Properties text box, enter the following information:

   Description: DIR Search
   Command Line: DIRP.PIF

   Notice that the file with the PIF extension is provided and not the BAT file.
4. Choose the OK button to complete the setup operation.

When you are finished, you should see a DOS icon with the label "Directory Search" in the Applications group.

Running the Application

To run the new application, double-click on its icon. Windows will then use its PIF and ask you to enter the parameters to be passed to the application. You can then provide a full path specification to the directory that you want to see, and provide either a full file-name or a file specification, including wildcards. For example, if you want to view all of the PIFs in the directory C:\WINDOWS, enter the parameter C:\WINDOWS*.PIF.

The parameter information is passed to the batch file, where DOS inserts it in place of the %1 symbol on the DIR/P line. This gives you flexibility to specify any directory and file combination using one icon.

Changing the PIF

If you've gotten this far successfully, you may wish to change the PIF so that you can run the application a little differently. For example, if you are running Windows in 386 Enhanced mode, you can change the PIF so that the application will run in a window instead of taking over the full screen. Figure 8.10 shows what the PIF would look like in the PIF Editor when this featured is selected. Notice that the Windowed option button in the Display Usage section is selected. After you've made a change, remember to choose the Save command from the File menu to save the changes.

▼ *Figure 8.10. Setting Up DIRP.PIF*

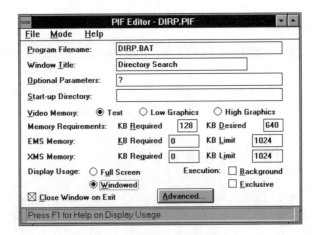

QUICK TASK SUMMARY

Task	Procedure
Run a non-Windows application	Use the MS-DOS Prompt application
Set up non-Windows application	Use Program Manager or Windows Setup
Create a PIF for an application	Use the PIF Editor
Set up application to run in a Window	Use PIF Editor; select Windowed option

PRACTICE WHAT YOU'VE LEARNED

In this chapter, you were introduced to the powerful features provided by Windows to access the DOS environment and run non-Windows applications. You also learned how set up non-Windows applications and use the PIF Editor to customize PIFs. Use these exercises to work more with non-Windows applications.

1. Create a PIF for a DOS application that you already have on your hard disk.

2. Include an optional parameter for your PIF.

3. Start the MS-DOS Prompt application and issue the DIR command.

4. Use the TYPE command to display a text file.

5. Issue the EXIT command.

ANSWERS

1. The PIF is assigned the same name as the program file that starts the application, but with a PIF extension. When you later double-click on the icon for the program, the PIF tells Windows how to run the application.

2. When the program starts, the parameter is executed.

3. A list displays for the files and subdirectories in the current directory.

4. The file is scrolled on the screen.

5. You return to the Windows environment.

9

Using Desktop Accessories

So far, we've explored the major components of Windows, such as the Program Manager, the Control Panel, and the File Manager. Windows also provides a useful set of accessory applications to help you perform tasks ranging from creating and editing notes to recording your schedules and appointments. In this chapter you'll learn how to:

▲ Display the clock

▲ Use the Notepad to create text files

▲ Use the Calendar to track your appointments

▲ Use the Calculator to perform calculations

▲ Use the Cardfile to set up a card index system

▲ Use the Recorder to record and play macros

▲ Use the Object Packager

Working with the Clock

The Clock application is the easiest accessory to use. When started, it displays the time by using your PC's system time. (If you need to correct your system time, you can do so from the Control Panel. This technique is explained in Chapter 5.)

To display the clock, double-click on the Clock icon in the Accessories group window. You can change the appearance of the clock by using the Settings menu, which provides two options: Analog and Digital. Figure 9.1 shows the clock that is displayed with each option. Notice that the Analog clock is a traditional clock with hour, minute, and second hands. If you choose the Digital option, you see a green digital display on a black background. The font used to display the time in the digital clock can be changed by choosing the Set Font command in the Settings menu.

The clock provides another handy feature: you can click on the minimize button at the top-right corner of the Clock's title bar to shrink it to a working icon. When minimized, the clock still displays the correct time.

TIP

By default, the clock also displays the current date. You can disable the display of the date by deselecting the Date option in the Settings menu.

▼ *Figure 9.1. The Analog and Digital Clock*

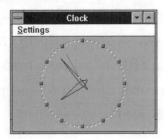 

Using the Notepad

Using the Notepad

The Notepad makes it easy for you to suspend an application that you're running, such as Excel, and compose a note. In fact, Notepad is intended to be a simple, easy-to-use text editor. Because the files that Notepad creates are simple ASCII files, you can print or view them with any text editor. These are some of the operations you can perform with Notepad:

▲ Compose notes and save them

▲ Edit text files created with Notepad or some other ASCII editor

▲ Search for text in a file

▲ Print a text file

▲ Copy sections of text files and paste them into other document files

Starting Notepad

As with all of the applications we'll explore in this chapter, Notepad is stored in the Accessories group window. To start Notepad, open this group and double-click on the Notepad icon. Figure 9.2 shows the Notepad window that appears. A blinking, vertical-bar cursor,

▼ *Figure 9.2. The Notepad Application*

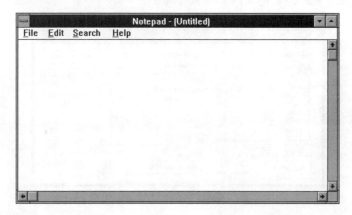

called the *insertion point*, displays in the top-left corner of the editing area. If you click on the File menu, you see the usual set of File commands—such as New, Open, Save, Print, and so on.

To begin using Notepad, simply enter text. The text will display to the left of the blinking cursor. Use the arrow keys or the mouse to perform navigation operations, such as moving the cursor to the left or down. When you are done creating a text file, save it by choosing the Save or Save As command from the File menu. When the dialog box appears (Figure 9.3 shows the Save As dialog box), type the filename in the File Name text box and choose the OK button. By default, Notepad uses the extension TXT to save its text files.

After you've saved your text file, the Notepad window's title changes to reflect the name of the saved file. For example, if you save a file using the name REPORT1.TXT, the window title becomes Notepad - REPORT1.TXT. After a text file has been created, you can change it and save the changes by choosing the Save command from the File menu.

Opening an Existing Text File

If you've previously created a Notepad file, or if you have an existing text file created by another text editor, you can open the file in Notepad by choosing the Open command from the File menu. This action brings up the dialog box shown in Figure 9.4. Notice

▼ *Figure 9.3. Saving a File in Notepad*

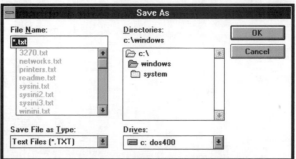

▼ *Figure 9.4. Opening a File in Notepad*

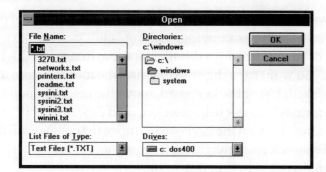

that this dialog box is similar to the Open dialog boxes provided with other Windows applications. The Directories list box allows you to select a directory, and the Files list provides a listing of the text files available in the currently selected directory. To open a file, either type the filename in the File Name text box, or click on one of the filenames provided in the Files list. Click the OK button to complete the operation.

CHECK YOURSELF

1. Create a Notepad file and add some text to the file.

2. Save the file with the name NOTES1.TXT and quit Notepad.

ANSWERS

1. (a) Start Notepad by double-clicking on its icon.
    (b) Position the cursor anywhere in the window and enter text.

2   (a) Choose the Save As command from the File menu.
    (b) Enter NOTES1.TXT in the File Name text box.
    (c) Press the Enter key to save the file.
    (d) Choose the Exit command from the File menu.

Editing Text

As we've mentioned, you can easily perform a number of editing operations—such as copying, cutting, and pasting text—with Notepad. To perform any editing operation, first select (highlight) the text you want to change by dragging the mouse across the text to be marked. Using the keyboard, move the insertion point to the left of the first character to be selected, hold down the Shift key, and use the arrow keys on the keyboard to move the cursor until the last desired character is highlighted. Release the Shift key when you've completed your selection operation.

TIP

To quickly select all of the text in a Notepad file, choose the Select All command from the Edit menu.

Using the Edit Menu

The Edit menu provides the basic editing commands. The first command, Undo, removes the latest editing operation performed.

The easiest way to remove a block of text is to first select the text and then press the Delete key or choose the Delete command from the Edit menu. To delete one character at a time, position the cursor to the right of the character and press the Backspace key.

TIP

To delete text and place it in the Clipboard, you must use the Cut command instead of Delete. In this case, the text is deleted but is moved into a temporary area called the Clipboard.

To remove the text from one location and insert it elsewhere, select the text to be moved, then choose the Cut command. Cut removes the selected text and places it into the Clipboard. You can then insert this text as many times as desired using the Paste command. Each insertion occurs at the present location of the insertion point. Another way to repeat a block of text is to select the block and then choose the Copy command. This copies the selected text into the Clipboard without removing it from the screen. The Clipboard can only hold one selection at a time; a second Cut or Copy command overwrites the previous contents of the temporary Clipboard buffer.

Basic Navigation Keys

Of course, you use the mouse and scroll bars to reposition your location within a Notepad file. However, you can also press Home, End, Ctrl+Home, and Ctrl+End to go to the beginning of a line, end of a line, beginning of a document, and end of a document, respectively. You can also use Ctrl+Left Arrow and Ctrl+Right Arrow to skip a word at a time to the left or the right, respectively.

Using the Word Wrap Feature

One problem with the Notepad editor stems from the fact that it follows ASCII conventions strictly. This means that you can enter up to 256 characters before Notepad will begin to wrap text to a new line. If you do not mind viewing several sentences of text on one extremely long line, this approach is fine. But for most Notepad documents that you create, you'll probably want to wrap text whenever Notepad reaches the end of the screen.

Fortunately, Notepad provides an option that allows you to wrap text. Simply choose the Word Wrap option from the Edit menu. When you choose Word Wrap (a checkmark appears when this option has been chosen), Notepad always makes the text fit inside the window. If you continue typing past the end of the current line, Notepad moves the words that don't fit down to the next line. If you later resize the window, your text reflows to reflect the window's new size. When you select Word Wrap, Notepad only changes the way text displays; the text is still stored on disk in lines of 256 ASCII characters. This means other text editors or ASCII applications can read Notepad documents with 100-percent compatibility.

Searching for Text

While you're editing a text file, you can search for specific text by using the Find command in the Search menu. When you choose this command, the dialog box shown in Figure 9.5 appears. Enter the character, word, or phrase you want to search for in the Find What text box. By default, Notepad will search for matching characters, regardless of case significance. (In other words, Notepad will ignore any distinction between uppercase and lowercase alphabetic characters.) To search for text that matches the exact uppercase and lowercase format that you specify, choose the Match Case option. For example, imagine that you wish to search for all occurrences of the word "Print" (where the letter P is always capitalized). Choose Search and enter the text "Print" into the text box and select the Match Case option.

Normally, Notepad starts its search at the current position of the text cursor and continues until it finds a match or reaches the end of the file. If the text you are searching for can't be found, a simple warning dialog box displays. To search backwards in a file, select the Up option in the Find dialog box.

Once a search has been performed successfully, you can repeat it by choosing the Find Next command in the Search menu or by pressing the F3 key.

TIP

Notepad doesn't allow you to perform a search-and-replace operation. If you need this feature, you'll have to use a word processing application, such as Write.

▼ *Figure 9.5. Searching for Text*

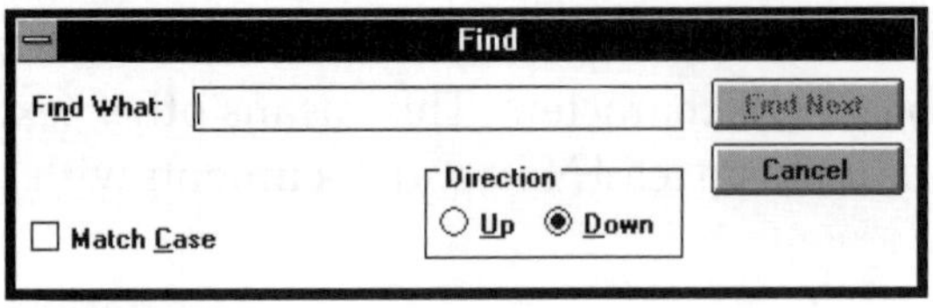

Find	
Fi**n**d What: [ ]	**Find Next**
	Cancel
☐ Match **C**ase — Direction — ○ **U**p ◉ **D**own	

Setting Up a Page

You can specify top, bottom, left, and right margins for Notepad files to be printed by choosing the Page Setup command from the File menu (see Figure 9.6). Notice that each of these margins is represented in inches. To change a margin, select the appropriate text box, delete the current value, and enter a new value. Keep in mind that fractions of an inch are represented to the right of the decimal point. For example, 0.5 represents 1/2 of an inch.

The Page Setup dialog box also allows you to define header and footer information for each page. Use the Help menu by choosing Contents and then the Print Headers and Footers entry, to view a list of options available for creating headers and footers. These header/footer controls are specified by two-character control codes. For example, when *&l*, *&c*, and *&r* precede the title information, Windows knows that you want the information printed left-justified, centered, or right-justified (respectively). The control code *&p* marks the location where the page number is placed, *&d* does the same for the date, and *&t* causes the current time to print. The *&f* control specifies the printing of the filename at a given location. In the default configuration, Notepad limits you to approximately 37 characters for the title.

CHECK YOURSELF

1. Set up a Notepad document so that it has a 1/2-inch left and right margin, a 3/4-inch top and bottom margin, and a header that displays the current date.

▼ *Figure 9.6. The Page Setup Dialog Box*

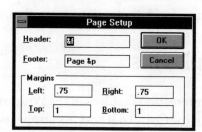

2. What text should be entered in the Header text box to print page numbers on each page?

ANSWERS

1. Display the Page Setup dialog box by choosing the Page Setup command from the File menu. Enter the following information:

   Header: &d
   Left: .5
   Right: .5
   Top: .75
   Bottom: .75

2. &p

Printing a File

After you set up your page configuration, print a text file by choosing the Print command from the File menu. A message box informs you that your file is being sent to the printer. The printed file appears exactly as it appears on the screen.

Using the Time/Date Feature

The Time/Date command inserts the current time and date at the present cursor position. You can automatically invoke this option by pressing the F5 key or choosing the Time/Date command from the Edit menu. This feature allows you to keep a time log so that you'll know how you spend your time while working with your computer. Each time you use Windows, you can bring up Notepad, choose the Time/Date command, and enter a note about your work.

Using Multiple Files

One of the more interesting features of the Windows environment is that you can Cut (or Copy) data across applications. This means that you can cut or copy some text from an application such as Cardfile, Terminal, Write, or Calculator, and insert it at the current cursor position in another application (such as Notepad) by simply using the Paste command.

Using the Calendar

The Calendar application provides a useful daily appointment book and a monthly calendar from 1980 through 2099. You can also use it to set an alarm to remind you of an important event, such as a meeting with your boss.

Starting Calendar

To start the Calendar, open the Accessories window and double-click on the Calendar icon. The untitled Calendar window (Figure 9.7) appears. Notice that this application provides File, Edit, and

▼ *Figure 9.7. The Calendar Application*

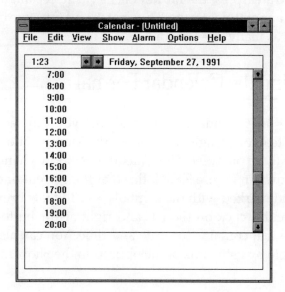

Help menus, which are similar to those found in other applications. In addition, the menus View, Show, Alarm, and Options are provided for setting an alarm or viewing different calendar dates and months in order to schedule appointments.

The Calendar window displays an appointment page for each date in one-hour time intervals. This format is called the *Day view*. At the top of the appointment page, a status bar provides the current time, scroll arrows, and the current date. Use the arrows to scroll through appointment pages. Click on the left arrow to see the previous day, or click on the right arrow to see the next day.

The appointment page area below the status bar contains the text for your appointments. Click to the right of each hour time interval to display the text cursor, and then enter a single-line message. For example, to remind yourself about a sales meeting in New York at 10:00 A.M. on September 21, select this day using the arrow buttons in the status bar, and then enter the text "Sales meeting in New York" at the 10:00 time slot. Calendar allows you to insert up to 80 characters per line. If you need more than this to hold a detailed mental note, use the Special Time command (discussed later in the chapter) to set up additional lines at one-minute increments.

The last component of the daily Calendar window is a scratch pad area where you can leave notes to yourself. To access this scratch pad area, press the Tab key or click in the rectangular region below the appointment page. The scratch pad can store up to three lines with as many as 44 characters per line.

Changing the Calendar Format

To change the Calendar window so that you can see an entire month instead of a single day, choose the Month option from the View menu, or press F9. The Calendar window changes to the format shown in Figure 9.8. Notice that the current date is highlighted and marked with the symbols > <. To view previous and future months, click on the left and right arrow buttons on the status line that contains the date and time. You can also select a specific date by using one of the options in the Show menu.

▼ *Figure 9.8. The Calendar's Month View*

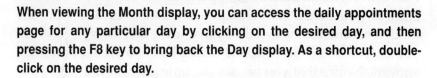

TIP

When viewing the Month display, you can access the daily appointments page for any particular day by clicking on the desired day, and then pressing the F8 key to bring back the Day display. As a shortcut, double-click on the desired day.

Selecting an Appointment Date

The Show menu allows you to immediately view today's appointments by choosing the Today option. You can also see the display for the previous day or the next day or month (depending on which calendar format you are viewing) by choosing Previous or Next. The shortcut keys for these options are Ctrl+PageUp and Ctrl+PageDn.

You can also use the Date command to enter a specific date to be viewed. When you choose this command, the Show Date dialog box appears (Figure 9.9). Type the date you want to display into the Show Date text box. When you choose the OK button, Calendar moves to the date you selected.

▼ *Figure 9.9. The Show Date Dialog Box*

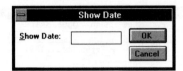

Setting Time Slots

By default, an appointment page in Day view lists time slots in one-hour intervals for a 12-hour period. However, you might need to schedule appointments on the half-hour or during a period that doesn't currently appear on the Calendar (7:00 A.M. to 7:00 P.M.). Fortunately, Calendar allows you to add, change, and delete time slots.

To alter the time slots in a Calendar page, use the Special Time and Day Settings commands that are available from the Options menu. Use the Day Settings command to select the time interval between entries on the Day view page, and to select between a 12- and a 24-hour format for the displayed times. Use it also to specify the default time for the first time entry on the Day view page. When you choose this command, the dialog box shown in Figure 9.10 appears. Notice that you can set the time interval to 15, 30, or 60 minutes. The options for the Hour Format group allow you to change the time indication between the 12-hour and the 24-hour (sometimes called military time) formats. The last option, Starting Time, provides a text box where you type the first entry on the appointment page.

Use the Special Time command to add a special time slot. For example, you may specify a 60-minute default interval for entries

▼ *Figure 9.10. Changing the Time Interval*

```
┌──────────────────────────────────────┐
│ ⊟           Day Settings              │
├──────────────────────────────────────┤
│ Interval:      ○ 15  ○ 30  ◉ 60       │
│                                        │
│ Hour Format:   ○ 12  ◉ 24    ┌──────┐ │
│                              │  OK  │ │
│ Starting Time:  7:00         └──────┘ │
│                              ┌──────┐ │
│                              │Cancel│ │
│                              └──────┘ │
└──────────────────────────────────────┘
```

▼ *Figure 9.11. Adding a Special Time Slot*

on a page, but you may want to mark a teleconference scheduled for 2:40 in the afternoon. Use the Special Time dialog box (Figure 9.11) to enter 2:40 P.M. (or 14:40 if you're defaulting to 24-hour time). Click on the Insert button to add that particular time to the Day view list. To remove a special time slot later, enter the time in the Special Time dialog box, and choose the Delete button.

CHECK YOURSELF

Set up the Calendar to display times on an appointment page in 12-hour (non-military time) format.

ANSWER

Choose the Day Settings command from the Options menu. Click on the 12 option button in the Hour Format group.

Marking Special Days

When you use the Calendar's Monthly view option, Calendar provides a special feature to help you keep track of birthdays, anniversaries, pay days, and other special-date categories. Use the Mark command listed in the Options menu to select one of five symbols to mark a date. (By default, the Month view marks the current date with the > < symbols.) To mark a day with a different symbol, select the date and choose the Mark command from the Options menu. When the dialog box shown in Figure 9.12 appears, select one of the five symbols and then click the OK button. Figure 9.13 shows a calendar in Month view that has dates marked with different symbols.

▼ *Figure 9.12. Selecting a Day Marker*

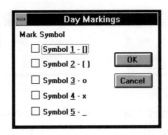

Setting an Alarm

You can use the Alarm feature to set an alarm for any day and time accessible from the Calendar. You can even set multiple alarms for one day.

To set an alarm for a specific time, follow these steps:

1. Display the calendar for the specific day using the Day view format. (Press the F8 key.)

▼ *Figure 9.13. Dates Marked with Different Symbols*

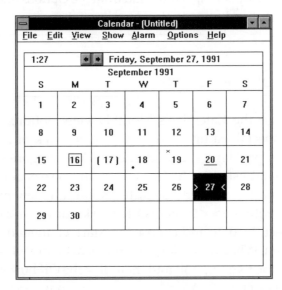

2. Click to the right of the desired time. To set an alarm for a time other than the ones listed, add a new time by choosing the Special Time command from the Options menu.

3. Choose the Set option from the Alarm menu, or press F5.

After you set an alarm, the alarm bell symbol appears next to the appointment time, and a checkmark is placed next to the Set command. Figure 9.14 shows an appointment page with an alarm set for 10:00 A.M.

If the alarm goes off while you're using Calendar, a dialog box reminds you about the appointment. If you're using another application, you hear the alarm chirp and may see the calendar icon blink. Click on the icon to view a dialog box that displays the information from the line in the calendar page that set off the alarm.

Once the alarm goes off, it continues to flash and beep until it's turned off. To turn off the alarm, display the Calendar window. When you see the Alarm dialog box, click the OK button to turn off the alarm.

Using the Calendar

▼ *Figure 9.14. An Alarm Set for 10:00*

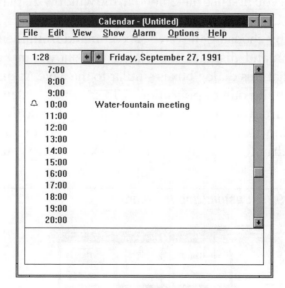

TIP

If you want to remove an alarm, click to the right of the time set for that alarm and choose the Set option from the Alarm menu. The checkmark next to Set disappears to indicate that the alarm is no longer set.

Alarm Options

You can also customize an alarm to sound early by 0 to 10 minutes. You can also enable or disable the audible alarm by clicking on the box next to the Sound label. To access these features, choose the Alarm Controls command from the Alarm menu. A dialog box appears (Figure 9.15) with the options Early Ring and Sound. To make an alarm go off earlier than its actual set times, enter a value from 1 to 10 in the Early Ring text box. If you disable the Sound check box, your alarms will not make a sound when they go off.

Creating and Saving Calendars

You can create and save different calendars for different activities. Thus, you can have one calendar for business appointments and another for personal activities.

When you first use the Calendar, the window displays with the filename Untitled). After you set appointment dates, save your calendar by choosing the Save As command from the File menu. This command displays the dialog box shown in Figure 9.16. (Notice that this dialog box is similar to the Save As dialog boxes provided with other applications.) To save your calendar, type a filename (from one to eight characters in length) into the File Name text box. Since Calendar uses the extension .CAL to store calendar files, it will automatically append this extension to your filename.

▼ *Figure 9.15. Customizing the Alarm*

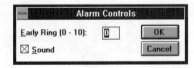

▼ *Figure 9.16. Saving a Calendar*

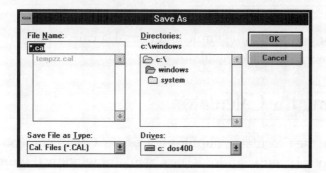

After you save and close a calendar file, you can open it later by choosing the Open command from the File menu. When the standard Open dialog box appears, select the desired file and click the OK button.

Printing a Calendar

You can print your important appointments by using the Print command from the File menu. This command displays the Print dialog box shown in Figure 9.17. Specify the start and end dates for the appointments you want to print using the From and To date boxes (respectively). For example, to print your appointments from December 12, 1991 to January 15, 1992, type 12/12/91 into the From box and 1/15/92 into the To box. Click OK to start the printer. (The printer that is currently active is used by the Print command to print your appointments.)

▼ *Figure 9.17. Printing a Calendar*

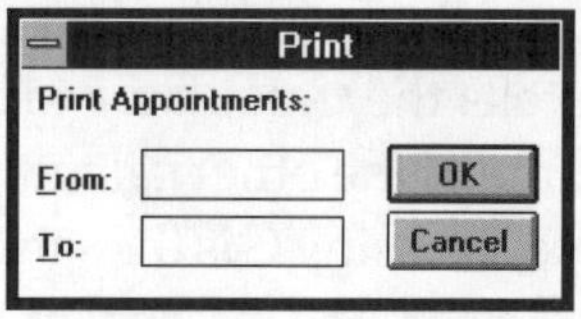

Working with the Calculator

You can perform both simple and complex calculations by using Windows' powerful Calculator accessory.

Starting the Calculator

To open the Calculator, double-click on the Calculator icon in the Accessories group window. The Calculator window (Figure 9.18) appears with three menu items (Edit, View, and Help), a basic single-line calculator display, and a set of calculator buttons. If you know how to use a hand-held calculator, you'll find this accessory very easy to operate.

The Calculator provides two operating modes: Standard and Scientific. For basic operations such as balancing a checkbook or calculating quarterly taxes, the Standard mode provides all of the features you'll need. If you need to perform more complex operations, such as logarithmic of trigonometric functions, use the Scientific mode. The calculator window shown in Figure 9.19 provides an extensive set of operator buttons and controls so that you can display and process numbers in different base systems. We'll explore this calculator in a little more detail later.

Setting Up and Using Your Keyboard

If your keyboard has a typical numeric keypad, you'll find that the basic calculator functions are easy to access. To use the numeric keypad, press the Num Lock key. Use the keypad area to enter numbers and perform the four standard functions of addition, subtraction, multiplication, and division (the asterisk represents multiplication, and the slash represents division). The Enter key at the lower-right corner of the keypad selects the equal-sign button on the screen (which tells the Calculator to compute the answer).

You can choose some of the other calculator functions from the keyboard. For example, pressing C is the same as activating the MC button on the screen; it clears the internal memory location. The M

▼ *Figure 9.18. The Calculator Application*

keyboard key, like the MS button, sends the number in the display box on the Calculator to the internal memory location. Pressing the P key activates the M+ button, which adds the number in the display box to the current value in the internal memory location. The R key activates the MR button, and recalls the contents of the internal memory location to the display box.

Other keys also choose calculator buttons. Pressing the % key on the keyboard is the same as clicking on the % key on the screen. The use of this percent function is not intuitive. If you want to calculate 30 percent of 600, you have to enter the following:

```
600*30%
```

▼ *Figure 9.19. The Scientific Calculator*

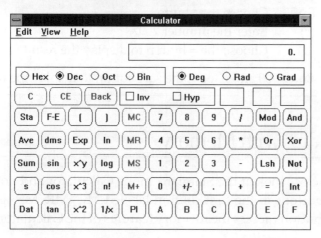

You can also press the @ keyboard key to calculate the square root of the number in the display box. Press the Delete key to clear the display box so that you can start a new calculation.

Performing a Calculation

In the Standard calculator mode, you perform calculations using the same technique that you use with a hand-held calculator: Enter a number, select an operation (such as multiplication or addition), enter another number, and select the = key. For example, to calculate how much you save on a $12,000 new car purchase if the dealer gives you a 15% discount, enter 12000, click on *, enter .15, and then click on =. The result appears in the single-line display. If you make a mistake while following these steps, select the C button to clear the calculation. Table 9.1 summarizes the basic mathematical functions that can be performed using the Standard-mode calculator.

CHECK YOURSELF

1. Multiply the numbers 275 and 2097.

2. Calculate the square root of 900.

ANSWERS

1. (a)   Enter the number 275.
   (b)   Choose the * button.
   (c)   Enter the number 2097.
   (d)   Choose the = button to display the result.

2. Enter 900 and choose the sqrt button to display the result.

Working with Memory

Take a close look at the Standard-mode Calculator and notice the set of buttons in the first column labeled MC, MR, MS, and M+. These buttons access the memory features of the Calculator. When

▼ *Table 9.1. Basic Mathematical Operations*

Keyboard	Button	Operation
+	+	Addition
-	-	Subtraction
*	*	Multiplication
/	/	Division
%	%	Calculate percent
@	sqrt	Square Root
R	1/x	Calculate reciprocal
F9	+/-	Change the sign of a value
=	=	Perform a calculation
Delete	CE	Clear the currently displayed number
Esc	C	Clear the current calculation

you put a number into memory, an M appears in the box directly below the display. To store a value, enter the number and choose the MS button. If you already stored a number in memory and you want to add the number in the display to the stored value, choose the M+ button. You can use this technique to easily keep a running total. Once a number has been stored, you can recall it at any time by choosing the MR button. If you want to clear the memory, choose the MC button. When the memory is empty, the M no longer appears in the memory-status box. If you want to replace a number in memory with another number, simply enter the new number and choose MS.

Using Calculated Results

You can cut and paste numbers between the Calculator and the Clipboard application. (Both operations are controlled through the Edit menu.) This allows you to move numbers between Windows applications without writing them on paper and reentering them in the target application. Using Windows, you transfer the results of calculations in the same way that you transfer text between applications.

To use this feature, calculate the value you want to use, and choose the Copy command from the Edit menu (or press Ctrl+Ins). The value stored in the Clipboard can then be pasted into another application at any time.

The Scientific Mode

The Standard mode is sufficient for most of the basic calculations that you'll need to perform. If you need to perform more complex operations, such as trigonometric functions, statistics, or logarithms, access the Scientific mode by choosing the Scientific option from the View menu. Figure 9.19 shows the Calculator in the scientific mode. Notice that this Calculator provides all of the components of the Standard-mode Calculator, such as the single-line display, memory buttons, numeric buttons, and standard operator buttons. In addition, you'll find an extended set of operator buttons for performing scientific calculations.

If you're accustomed to working with a scientific calculator capable of operating in various base-number systems, and you can perform statistical, trigonometric and logical operations, you'll find this calculator easy to use. To help you get acquainted with the Scientific mode, we'll discuss a few of its basic features.

Using Number Systems

The Standard mode Calculator only supports the decimal number system. The Scientific mode Calculator, on the other hand, converts numbers from one system to another, such as binary to hexadecimal. The four number systems supported are presented in Table 9.2, along with a column called Keyboard Select to show which quick key selects each number system.

Once you've selected a number system, you can enter numbers and perform calculations using the operator buttons. Keep in mind that the numbers entered must be appropriate for the selected number system. For example, the calculator won't allow you to type the number 234 into the binary system because only 1s and 0 values are valid.

▼ Table 9.2. The Scientific Calculator's Number Systems

Number System	Sample	Keyboard Select	Button
Binary	101100	F8	Bin
Octal	245623	F7	Oct
Decimal	129980	F6	Dec
Hexadecimal	A56EB0	F5	Hex

Working with the Calculator

To convert a number from one system to another, enter the value to be converted, then choose the button for the new number system.

Performing Statistics Calculations

The Scientific mode also provides features that let you perform statistics calculations. To use this feature, choose the Sta button to display the Statistics Box (Figure 9.20). At the bottom of the window, four buttons display for performing statistics operations. The RET button switches you back to the Calculator. LOAD instructs the calculator to display the selected number in the Statistics Box window. CD deletes the selected number in the window, and CAD deletes all numbers in the Statistics Box.

Using Cardfile

The Cardfile application allows you to build a limited database similar to the system you might keep on index cards. Each card

▼ Figure 9.20. Calculating Statistics

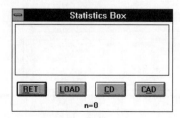

contains a title field and eleven lines, each of which can contain up to 40 characters. You can search for a particular title line, word, or phrase anywhere on the card. This application is excellent for keeping electronic mail/telephone books. (Each card file is separate, so you can keep one for friends and another for business contacts). You can even store pictures in Cardfile. This application is consistent with Windows' attempt to match as closely as possible what people do with the paper versions of desktop tools.

Starting Cardfile

To start Cardfile, double-click on the Cardfile icon stored in the Accessories window. Figure 9.21 shows the Untitled Cardfile window that appears, containing a blank card. Directly above the card appears a status line that indicates the view option selected. The default view is called *Card View*. The status line also contains a left and right scroll arrow so that you can easily select other cards. The status line also contains a card count. When you first start Cardfile, the card count is set to 1.

The index card itself contains an index line and an information area. The index line is used to store a word or phrase so that you can quickly identify a card. Enter the text or the graphics for a card into the information area.

▼ *Figure 9.21. The Cardfile Application*

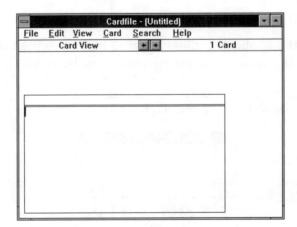

Creating a Card System

To create a new set of cards, consider which information you plan to place on the cards and in what order. Imagine that you want to create a card file of your ten-year collection of computer magazines that you intend to read when you retire. Since this collection is the first of a series of cards that will cover the large stacks of magazines in your garage, place the title of the magazine on the index line, and add the date and volume number on that line also. Use the body of the card to list the feature articles and other points of interest for a particular issue.

To create this simple record-keeping system, you don't have to retype the name of a magazine 120 times. Instead, you can create a template card that you can then duplicate many times. Double-click on the index line to bring up the Index dialog box. (If a card already has a filled index line, this dialog box allows you to alter the contents of the line.) Enter the index information into the text box. For the sake of our example, assume that you entered the text

```
PC TECHNIQUES Vol. 1 No. 1
```

into the Index Line text box. This is the text that will be displayed at the top of a card. (Keep in mind that you have to keep the index line brief because each line is only 40 characters wide.) Click the OK button to save the information. At this point, a single card appears in your window, with the index line containing the template information.

If you want any information to appear repeatedly on your cards, add it now before you begin making duplicates. As with other Windows applications, you can edit text with the mouse or the keyboard. Point and click where you want the information to appear (or use the keyboard arrow keys to position the cursor) and begin typing. Once you've typed your first card exactly the way you want it, choose Copy from the Edit menu (or use the shortcut key sequence Ctrl+Ins) to duplicate the card. At this point, you can duplicate the card several times to create a set of "preprinted" blank cards to fill in later.

TIP

You can also duplicate a card by bringing the card to the front of the stack and choosing the Duplicate command from the Card menu. The new card is then added to the front of the stack.

To complete a card, click on the left or right arrow button on the line below the menu bar to bring a new card to the front of the stack. Next, press the F6 function key to display the Index dialog box. Point and click at the location that you want to modify and insert the desired information. Use the Delete and Backspace keys to remove undesired characters. Note that when you activate the Index dialog box, the entire line is highlighted. Be careful to not start typing until you have moved the cursor or have clicked somewhere on the line. Otherwise, Windows will think that you wanted to type in a new Index line and will delete the previous contents.

Adding Additional Cards

To add a new card to a set (rather than duplicating a card), choose the Add command from the Card menu, or press F7. The Add dialog box provides a text box where you can enter an index line for the new card. After you choose OK, the new card moves to the front of the stack so that you can add information to it.

CHECK YOURSELF

1. Add a card, and give it the index title New Magazines.

2. Change the index line to New Magazines—1990.

ANSWERS

1. Choose the Add command from the Card menu. Enter the text *New Magazines* in the Add text box.

2. Double-click on the index line, and enter the new text when the Index dialog box appears.

Deleting Cards

If you want to delete a card, select the card so that it is in front, and then choose the Delete command from the Card menu. Cardfile will then display a dialog box requesting you to verify that you want to remove the card.

Editing Options

The Edit menu provides all of the operations for modifying the contents of your cards. The Undo command removes the most recent editing operation. The Cut, Copy, and Paste commands work the same way as the same commands in Notepad. The Index command (which can be activated by pressing the F6 function key) allows you to edit the contents of the card on the front of the stack.

Restoring a Card

While you're working with a card, it's easy to add or change information that you don't want to save. Cardfile provides a Restore command that restores a card to its original condition. To use this feature, choose the Restore command from the Edit menu. This command only works when the card remains at the top of the stack. When you move to another card, the changes become permanent.

Pasting a Picture

Normally, cards display in a text only mode and you can add only text information. When you choose the Picture option in the Edit menu, you switch Cardfile to a graphics mode so that a picture can be pasted to a card.

Adding a graphics picture involves the use of another application, such as Paintbrush or Excel. Use that application first to create a picture or a chart, and then paste the image to the Clipboard. Next, start Cardfile, select the card where you want the graphic image to appear, and make sure that the Picture option is selected.

To add the graphics, choose the Paste command from the Edit menu. You can then drag the mouse or use the arrow keys to position the image on the card.

The pasted image always displays in black and white. If it's larger than the card, the picture is cropped. After a picture is pasted, you can add text by choosing the Text option from the Edit menu and positioning the text cursor on the card. The text that you enter appears on top of the graphics image.

Saving, Opening, and Merging a Card Set

When you've created all of the cards for a set, use the Save or Save As commands from the File menu to store the card set on disk. When you save a card set, it's stored as a special file with the default extension CRD.

You can open the saved card file by using the Open command from the File menu. This command displays the standard Open dialog box, so that you can easily locate the file you want to open.

One of the more unique features of Cardfile is that it allows you to merge different card files. When you choose the Merge command from the File menu, the File Merge dialog box (Figure 9.22) requests the filename to be merged with the currently opened file. Provide the directory and file information (or provide the directory information, and use a file wildcard such as *.CRD) so that you can view the appropriate files in a selected subdirectory. Once you select a file, click the OK button to complete the operation.

▼ *Figure 9.22. Merging Two Cards*

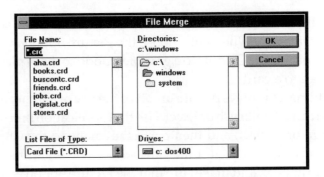

Tips for Viewing Cards

Cardfile organizes your cards by alphabetical and numeric order based on the contents of index lines. To sort the current set of cards (especially useful after a merge operation), choose the List option in the View menu. The cards disappear and are replaced by an alphabetized list of the index lines (Figure 9.23). Use this handy option to scroll down the list to find a particular card and choose the Card option from the View menu. The card highlighted in the List window appears as the top card on the screen. If you double-click on one of the index lines listed, Cardfile will allow you to change the index.

Searching for a Card

Use the Search menu to find information quickly in your card stack. Choose the Go To command (shortcut key is F4) to bring to the top of the stack the first card with an index line matching the information you provide in the Go To dialog box. Use the Find command in the Search menu to find a match with information in the body of the card (as opposed to just the index line). Choose the Find Next option (shortcut key F3) to repeat the search specified in the Find command and quickly search through multiple matches to find the one you want.

▼ *Figure 9.23. Viewing Cards as a List*

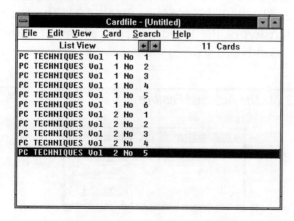

Using a Calling Card

You can use Cardfile to tell your PC to dial a phone number for you. To use this feature, follow these steps:

1. Highlight the phone number you want to call.
2. Choose the Autodial command from the Card menu.
3. Check the phone number in the Autodial dialog box (Figure 9.24) to make sure it's correct.
4. Enter a prefix (if one is required for your phone system) and choose the Use Prefix check box.
5. Click the OK button to dial the number.

For this feature to work properly, make sure your computer has a Hayes-compatible modem installed. To check your modem settings, choose the Setup button in the Autodial dialog box. Use the dialog box shown in Figure 9.25 to configure the baud rate, the port, and your phone type (pulse or tone). If you encounter problems when calling a number, check these settings.

Using the Recorder

You may have noticed an icon in the Accessories group that looks like a home video camera. This is the icon for the Recorder (sometimes also called the Macro Recorder). The Recorder is a logical extension of the Windows philosophy: it allows you to record your keyboard strokes *and/or your mouse strokes* so that you

▼ *Figure 9.24. The Autodial Feature*

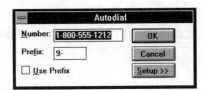

▼ *Figure 9.25. Setting up a Modem*

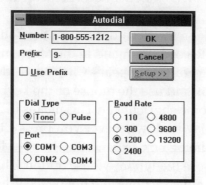

can play them back later. It doesn't just record simple commands within an application; it can be used to start an application such as Notepad and to perform particular actions within the application. The problem is that the mouse capture is very sensitive to factors such as window sizing or relative position of one item to another. For this reason, we will concentrate mostly on the techniques for capturing keyboard information.

Preparing the Target Application

In this example, we will cause the Notepad editor to insert certain words of text whenever you press Ctrl+Home. Begin by running the Recorder application (you should see the window shown in Figure 9.26) and then minimize the application so that it becomes

▼ *Figure 9.26. The Recorder Window*

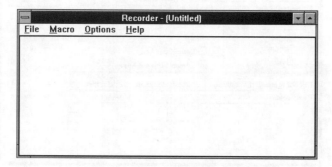

an icon at the bottom of the screen. Now run the Notepad application and position it so that the Recorder icon at the bottom of the screen is visible.

Double-click on the Recorder icon at the bottom of the screen and choose the Record command in the Macro menu. Figure 9.27 shows the dialog box that appears. Click on the down arrow in the Shortcut Key box and use the mouse or the keyboard arrow keys to choose the Home shortcut key. This means that the macro to be recorded will play back whenever you press Ctrl+Home. While you are in this dialog box, expand the Record Mouse drop-down list box and choose the Ignore Mouse option. This last action will guarantee that mouse actions will not be recorded. Press Enter or click on the Start button to save these selections and choose the record function. The Recorder window should disappear and you should be able to observe a blinking minimized Recorder symbol at the bottom of the screen. All keyboard commands from this point will be recorded until you click on the blinking Recorder icon.

When the Recorder window auto-minimizes, control should have returned to the Notepad application. Enter the words "three blind mice" and then click on the blinking Recorder icon. The dialog box in Figure 9.28 appears to request confirmation of completion of the recording. Click the OK button or press Enter to confirm the successful recording of the macro. Delete the text from the Notepad window and begin typing something else. Move the cursor to somewhere in the middle of the new text and press the

▼ *Figure 9.27. Recording a Macro*

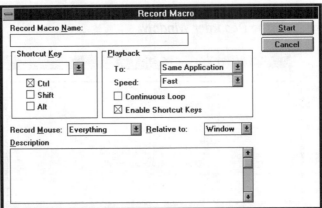

▼ *Figure 9.28. Completing a Macro*

*Using the
Recorder*

Ctrl key, then the Home key; the *three blind mice* text will appear as if it were pasted in from the Clipboard! You can now repeat this process several times with other Shortcut key combinations to build an inventory of stock phrases that can be inserted anywhere in a document by simply pressing the correct key sequence.

When you are done creating macros, use the Save As command in the File menu to save these definitions for future use. (The Open command is used to load previously created macro definitions).

Capturing Mouse Actions

Reliably capturing mouse commands using Recorder is rather difficult to do and is not a recommended way to use the Recorder. However, we will discuss this technique briefly. Begin by running the Paintbrush application and choosing the Line tool. Run the Recorder and choose the Record command in the Macro menu. Expand the Record Mouse drop-down list box again and choose the Everything option. Click the Start button to minimize the Recorder to an icon and to begin recording. Move the pointer to the drawing area in Paintbrush and draw three intersecting lines to form a rough triangle. Click on the Recorder icon to stop recording then choose New from the Paintbrush File menu to clear the entire drawing area. Now press the Ctrl and Home keys to observe Recorder drawing a copy of the triangle in the drawing area.

Problems with Capturing Mouse Commands

Depending on many separate variables, the previous mouse command exercise may or may not work for you. If it stops execution and gives you some sort of error dialog box, try positioning the mouse cursor in different parts of the screen before invoking the macro. If this doesn't work, you can delete the macro (see below) and try to define it again in a slightly different way. In general, you will probably find mouse command macros to be extremely unstable and unreliable.

Deleting Macro Definitions

If you are unhappy with a particular macro definition, expand the Recorder window and click on the offending macro (so that it is highlighted). Next, press the Delete key or choose the Delete command in the Macro menu.

The Object Packager

One of the more powerful features of Windows 3.1 is its ability to make documents that can contain information created by different applications. For example, you can create a text document using the Write application and then insert a Paintbrush picture in the document. Before Windows 3.1, documents that contained elements from different applications were created by pasting text or pictures to the Clipboard and then inserting the text or pictures in the document.

Windows 3.1 allows you to combine elements from different applications in a way that *links* or *embeds* the elements. This new feature, called *object linking and embedding*, allows you to easily view and edit information, and then have the edits updated or saved to all documents that are linked. For example, once a picture created with Paintbrush has been linked in a Write document, you can edit the Paintbrush picture from within the Write document. If the picture is changed from within Paintbrush, the changes will automatically be updated in the Write document. The basic Windows applications and accessories that support object linking and embedding include Cardfile, Paintbrush, Write, Sound Recorder, and Object Packager.

In Chapter 10, we'll present some useful object linking and embedding techniques by adding a Paintbrush picture to a Write document. For now, we'll explore the Object Packager, which serves as a tool for embedding information in documents in a unique way.

Understanding Objects and Packages

Windows 3.1 uses the term *object* to refer to information that has been created by an application, such as a Paintbrush picture, a paragraph of text composed with Write, or notes entered in a Cardfile document. Windows allows you to link or embed such objects in some applications. In addition, you can assign an icon to an object (information created by an application), and then insert the icon in a document. The icon is called a *package*. You use the Object Packager to create packages.

Once a package has been embedded in a document, you can access the information represented by the package (icon) by choosing the icon. For example, if you have turned a Paintbrush picture into a package (icon) and then embedded the package in a Write document, you can view the Paintbrush picture while reading the Write document, by double-clicking on its icon.

Using Object Packager

Object Packager can be used to package complete documents, parts of a document (such as a paragraph in a Write document or a section of a Paintbrush picture), or an MS-DOS command.

TIP

A package can only be embedded in an application, such as Write or Paintbrush, that supports Windows' new object linking and embedding feature.

To start Object Packager, open the Accessories group window and double-click on the Object Packager icon. Figure 9.29 shows

▼ *Figure 9.29. The Object Packager*

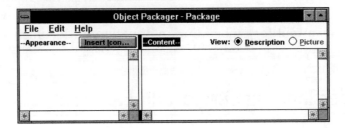

the application window that appears. Note that the window is divided into two sections: a Content window and an Appearance window. The Appearance window is used to display the icon that represents the linked or embedded object. The Content window, on the other hand, is used to display the name of the document that will contain the packaged object.

Packaging a Document

Packaging a complete document as an icon is a two-step process. First, you'll need to select an icon for the package, and then you'll need to select (import) a document.

To select an icon:

1. Open the Accessories window and choose the Object Packager.
2. Select the Appearance window by clicking on it.
3. Click the Insert Icon button and select an icon from the set of icons that are provided.

This completes the first step. To assign a document to the icon:

1. Select the Content window.
2. Choose the Import command from the File menu.
3. You can now select the desired file from the Import dialog box that is displayed.
4. After the file is selected, choose the OK button.

The filename that has been selected will appear in the Content window. This completes the process of creating the package, To use the package, you must first copy it to the Clipboard by choosing the Copy Package command from the Edit menu. You can then insert the package in a document (created by an application such as Write) by placing the insertion point at the desired location in the document and then choosing the Paste command from the application's Edit menu.

To view the contents of the package at any time, double-click on it.

The Object Packager

TIP

If you want to change the label assigned to an icon, select the icon in the Object Packager window and then choose the Label command from the Edit menu.

Packaging Part of a Document

If you don't need to package a complete document, you can select part of the document, assign it an icon, and then insert the icon into another document. When the icon is later chosen, only the previously selected part of the document will be available for viewing.

To package part of a document:

1. Open the document you want to use.

2. Select and copy only the desired part of the document.

3. Run the Object Packager and choose the Paste command from the Edit menu.

4. An icon will be displayed in the Appearance part of the window. To use the icon, choose the Copy Package command from the Edit menu.

5. Open the destination document (the document where you want to insert the icon), position the insertion point, and choose the Paste command from the Edit menu.

TIP

You can only package partial documents that have been created by an application whose objects can be embedded or linked into other applications.

Packaging a Command Line

You can also package a DOS command as an icon and insert it in a document. When the icon is selected, the command assigned to the icon will execute. This is a very powerful feature because it allows you to run another application while working within a document.

To package a DOS command:

1. Run the Object Packager and choose the Command Line command from the Edit menu.

2. Type the name of the command in the dialog box that is displayed.

3. Choose the OK button and the command will appear in the Content window.

4. Choose the Insert Icon button to assign an icon to the command.

5. After you have assigned an icon, copy the package to the Clipboard by choosing the Copy Package command from the Edit menu.

The package can be inserted into any document created by an application that supports the object linking feature. Open the document you want to insert the icon into and choose the Paste command from the application's Edit menu. To execute the command associated with the icon, double-click on the icon or select the icon and choose the Activate Contents command from the Package Object cascading menu (see the Edit menu).

QUICK TASK SUMMARY

Task	Procedure
Display the time	Run the Clock application (Accessories group)

Task	Procedure
Create a note	Run the Notepad application (Accessories group)
Search for text in Notepad file	Use Find command (Search menu)
Print a Notepad file	Use Print command (File menu)
Set an appointment	Use Calendar application
Set an alarm	Use Calendar; Choose Set command (Alarm menu)
Perform calculations	Use the Calculator application
Set up a card file database	Use Cardfile application
Merge Cardfile files	Use the Merge command (File menu)
Record a macro	Use the Recorder application

PRACTICE WHAT YOU'VE LEARNED

In this chapter, you've been introduced to the main Windows accessories. You learned how to display the time, create and print notes, perform calculations, create a card file system and how to record your own actions for later playback. Use these exercises to learn more about the accessory applications.

1. Start Clock, display it in the analog format, and reduce it to an icon.

2. Start Notepad, and open a file by selecting a TXT file with the Open dialog box.

3. Search for text in the file, using the Find dialog box.

4. Quit Notepad.

5. Open the Calendar, and set an alarm to go off in 5 minutes. (Look at the clock icon to determine the current time.)

6. Minimize the Calendar.

7. Start Cardfile and create a few index cards.

ANSWERS

1. The Clock displays in the lower-left corner, keeping the correct time.

2. The file opens and the window's title changes to reflect the name of the file.

3. If the text you search for is found, it is highlighted; otherwise, a dialog box warns you that the text cannot be found.

4. Control returns to the Program Manager.

5. The alarm icon displays next to the time set. You may have to use the Special Time command to add the time slot you need.

6. Calendar turns into an icon, and control returns to the Program Manager.

7. If you use the application for five minutes, the alarm that you set goes off.

10

Working with Write

This chapter introduces the Windows document editor called Write. Write is a powerful word-processing program that you can use to create documents that contain both text and graphics. After you finish this chapter, you'll know how to:

▲ Start Write

▲ Define page attributes for a document

▲ Set and clear text and decimal tabs

▲ Select different character fonts and sizes

▲ Control paragraph formatting

▲ Define document headers and footers

▲ Search for and replace text

▲ Combine text and graphics

About Write

Write is a sophisticated word-processing program that supports most of the features needed to create letters, small to medium-sized documents, and even newsletters. Write's ability to import text, data, and graphics from other Windows applications makes it extremely useful and flexible. Write also allows you to define and control character fonts, line spacing, paragraph indentation, and more.

In many respects, Write operates like Notepad: the basic techniques for entering and editing text are the same. However, Write adds a number of powerful features that you won't find in Notepad, such as tab control, full text headers and footers, and the capability to import graphics.

Starting Write

To start Write, double-click on the Write icon in the Accessories group window. The Untitled window shown in Figure 10.1 appears. This window provides a title, seven menu items, scroll bars,

▼ *Figure 10.1. Write Application Window*

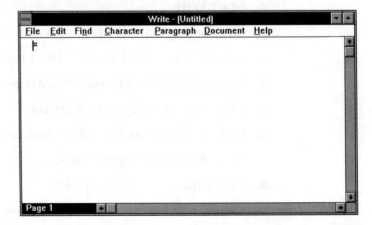

minimize and maximize buttons, the Control menu, and a status bar in the lower-left corner that indicates the current page number. A blinking vertical bar cursor and a star symbol also appear within the work area. The vertical bar cursor (also called the insertion point) marks the place where text appears when you type. The star symbol indicates the physical end of the file.

Setting Up a Document

Each time you use a word processing application to create a new document, you'll need to make sure that your document is properly set up. Figure 10.2 shows the dialog box that appears if you choose Page Layout from the Document menu. This dialog box allows you to define the starting page number as well as the document's margins. You can select dimensions in inches or centimeters (whichever is most convenient). Usually a document should have a minimum of 0.5 inches for each margin. The default left and right margins are 1.25 inches and the default top and bottom margins are 1 inch.

Defining Paper Size

You'll also want to define a document's paper size. Choose the Print Setup command from the File menu. Figure 10.3 shows the dialog box that is displayed. If you want to select a different printer,

▼ *Figure 10.2. Page Layout Dialog Box*

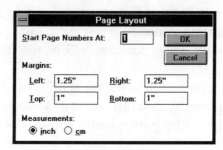

▼ *Figure 10.3. Setting Up a Printer*

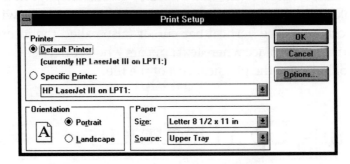

do so by clicking on the down arrow button to expand the printer list and then select a printer from the list of available printers. If you are planning to print sideways on a standard sheet of paper, click on the Landscape button in the Orientation group.

If you are using a paper size other than 8 1/2" by 11", click on the down arrow button in the Size box to view the available settings. Once you have made your selections, click the OK button.

Using the Ruler

If you were to begin typing text at this point, you would find that it is very difficult to determine the number of characters in a line or to visualize the tab stops positions. For this reason, Write provides a ruler. To view the ruler, choose the Ruler On option from the Document menu. Figure 10.4 shows the additional information presented when the ruler is displayed. Notice that several icons appear immediately below the menu bar. These icons (from left to right) stand for tab, decimal Tab, single space, 1-1/2 space, double space, left paragraph, centered paragraph, right paragraph, and justified paragraph. These features will be discussed in detail a little later.

The ruler is represented in the same units used to define your paper size (in inches by default) and is as wide as the active text area on the paper (the paper width minus the left and right borders).

▼ *Figure 10.4. Displaying the Ruler*

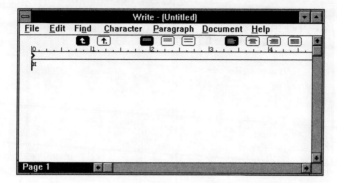

Directly below the ruler you'll see a right-pointing arrow, which indicates the left margin. When you scroll the window horizontally, an arrow points in the other direction to indicate the right margin. Embedded in the left margin marker is a small dot that represents the indent marker. To left-indent the first line of a paragraph, mark the paragraph, and then slide the indent marker to the desired starting position.

Defining Tab Positions

Two types of tabs are supported by Write: text and decimal. The text tab is used in the same way tabs are used with a typewriter. The decimal tab is used to define number fields where it is desirable to align the decimal points (such as in money columns).

Setting Text Tabs

Write automatically defines tabs at intervals of 1/2 inch, but these tabs are not visible on the ruler. To define a text tab, first select your text. Then click on the left-most tab icon to make certain it is active. Move the pointer so that it is between the two long horizontal lines on the ruler and click at the desired location. You'll then see a tab symbol displayed inside the ruler.

Figure 10.5 shows a ruler with text tabs set at 1.25, 1.5, 1.75, and 2.0 inches. If you choose the Tabs command in the Document menu, you will see the dialog box shown in Figure 10.6. You can

▼ *Figure 10.5. Setting Text Tabs*

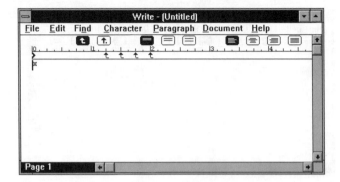

select one of the entries, such as 1.25, and change it. When you return to the Write window, you'll see each of the tab settings that you have changed. The Write ruler is graduated in eighths of an inch. The dialog box shown in Figure 10.6 is quite useful when you wish to set tabs at precise positions.

TIP

Keep in mind that only the text you have marked is affected by the tabs. If you want to tab an entire document using one set of tabs, mark the document by placing the cursor at the beginning of the document and pressing Ctrl+Shift+End, and then set your tabs.

Deleting or Moving a Tab

Move the pointer to a tab arrow that has been set, then click and drag it to the left until it disappears. Observe that your text

▼ *Figure 10.6. Tabs Dialog Box*

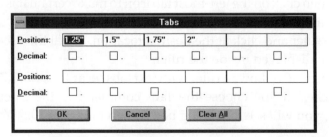

immediately shifts because the tab is removed. Choose the Tabs command again and you'll see that the tab entry is gone from the dialog box. You can also remove a tab by clicking on the tab arrow and dragging it down below the ruler so that it disappears.

A tab can be moved by clicking and dragging the tab arrow to its new location or by changing the position value in the Tabs dialog box.

Using the Ruler

TIP

You can remove all the tabs set in a document by clicking on the Clear All button in the Tabs dialog box.

Setting Decimal Tabs

Decimal tabs are set, moved, and removed similar to the techniques you use with text tabs. To define a decimal tab, click on the decimal tab icon. Next, click the desired location on the ruler to set the tab. You can also use the Tabs dialog box, enter the desired position as you would for a text tab, then press the tab key once so that the decimal point below the position entry is surrounded by a dashed box (see Figure 10.7). Press the spacebar once so that the small square to the left of the decimal point is filled with an X. When you are done making changes, choose the OK button. Decimal tabs appear on the ruler (on a VGA screen) as a straight arrow to the left of a decimal point.

Try defining one decimal tab at the 2-inch mark, and then press the tab key once to move the cursor to that position. Enter the number 123456789.12345 and observe what happens on the screen.

▼ *Figure 10.7. Setting a Decimal Tab*

Tabs					
Positions: 1.2	1.4	1.6	1.8		
Decimal: □ .	☒ .	□⬚.	□ .	□ .	□ .
Positions:					
Decimal: □ .	□ .	□ .	□ .	□ .	□ .
OK		Cancel		Clear All	

Write will shift the number so that the decimal point is located at the decimal tab position. Press Enter then Tab and experiment with other numbers. This is obviously a great way to enter financial or scientific data in a column format.

Setting Line Spacing

Another formatting option that can be defined on a per paragraph basis is line spacing. You can select single spacing, 1-1/2-spacing, or double spacing by first selecting your text and then clicking the appropriate line-spacing icon above the ruler. You can also choose one of these spacing options from the Paragraph menu. If you look carefully at the three spacing buttons, you will note that each shows a pair of parallel lines; the left-most button (with the two lines very close together) represents single-spaced text.

Setting Paragraph Alignment

The four right-most buttons in the ruler can be used to select left-aligned, centered, right-aligned, or justified text in a paragraph. The left-alignment button aligns your text at the left margin, leaving the right margin ragged. The right-alignment button justifies the right margin and leaves the left margin ragged.

The center-alignment button centers your text. This formatting option can be used for setting the title for a document. The last option button justifies your text. It inserts "soft-spaces" between the words on a line so that the left and right margins are always justified, except for the last line of a paragraph.

Setting Paragraph Margins

Write allows you to easily indent paragraphs by using the Indents command in the Paragraph menu. Test this feature by entering the two lines shown in Figure 10.8. You will need to press the Enter key at the end of the first line to begin the second one at the left edge. (Whenever you press the Enter key, Write starts a new paragraph.)

▼ *Figure 10.8. Entering Two Lines*

Using the Ruler

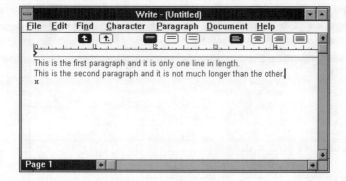

Make certain that the cursor is somewhere on the second line before choosing the Indents command.

Figure 10.9 shows that three separate formatting attributes are available from the Indents dialog box. The first and third entries are associated with the left and right indents (respectively). They define the paragraph limits relative to the left and right page borders defined earlier. The middle entry is used to define the amount of additional indentation for the first line of the paragraph.

Enter 0.5 and 4.0 for the left and right indent values (respectively) and choose the OK button. The second paragraph should be reformatted (see Figure 10.10) so that it is narrower than the first one. Of course, you can combine this formatting with the line spacing control and paragraph alignment to obtain a distinctive appearance for a particular paragraph. To change the formatting of a single paragraph, position the cursor at any point within the paragraph and select the desired formatting option. To change multiple paragraphs, highlight the paragraphs with the mouse or the keyboard before changing a format setting.

▼ *Figure 10.9. Setting Indents*

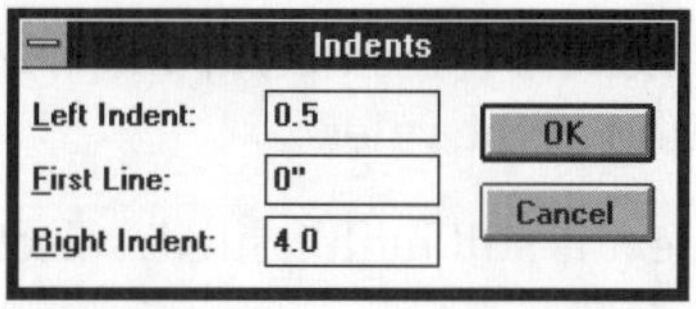

▼ *Figure 10.10. Indenting a Paragraph*

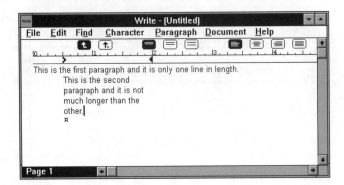

Another way to set the indentation for the first line of the paragraph is to click on the paragraph and drag the indent marker on the ruler. (The indent marker is represented as a small dot with the left margin arrow.)

CHECK YOURSELF

Run Write and display the ruler by choosing the Ruler On command.

1. Scroll the window to the left. What is the default setting for the right margin?

2. Change the right margin to 5".

3. Enter a few sentences and double space your text.

4. Center-align the text.

ANSWERS

1. The Right margin default is 6".

2. Click on the right margin marker, and drag to the 5" mark.

3. Highlight the text you entered, and select the fifth icon from the left on top of the ruler.

4. While the text is still highlighted, select the seventh icon.

Using Fonts and Styles

Write provides a number of options for formatting characters and selecting font styles. These formatting options are selected form the Character menu, as shown in Figure 10.11. The first group of options allows you to change the style of text to bold, italic, underline, superscript, and subscript. When you choose a style option, a checkmark appears to the left of the style. By default, Write sets all type to the Normal style. You can change the style by marking the text and then selecting one or more of the options. For example, you can set type as bold and italic. If you are working from the keyboard, you can change the style of text by first selecting the text to be changed and then using one of these keyboard shortcuts:

Bold   Ctrl+B

Italic   Ctrl+I

Underline   Ctrl+U

Shortcut keys are not available for superscript and subscript types. Figure 10.12 shows lines of text displayed in all five of these formats.

▼ *Figure 10.11. Formatting Options*

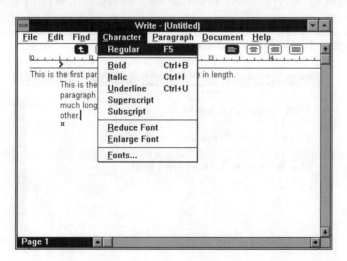

▼ *Figure 10.12. Text in Different Styles*

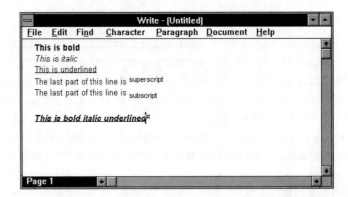

About Fonts

You can also select fonts by using the Character menu. Figure 10.13 shows lines of text displayed in different fonts. To select a new font, choose the Fonts command. When the dialog box (Figure 10.14) appears, select a font, font style, and a point size.

If you look carefully at the list of fonts, you will see that some are preceded by the letters TT. These letters indicate a TrueType font. TrueType fonts are scalable, which means they can be defined to be almost any standard size. By contrast, other bitmapped fonts may not look as good. As a general rule, you will probably want to use the TrueType fonts because of their improved appearance.

▼ *Figure 10.13. Text in Different Fonts*

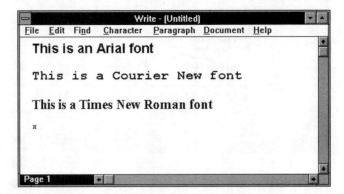

▼ *Figure 10.14. The Font Dialog Box*

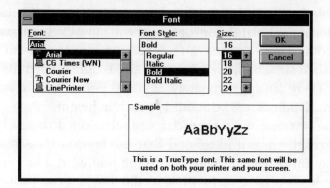

Note that the box at the lower right of the dialog box illustrates the appearance of the type for the selected size.

CHECK YOURSELF

Type some text into the Write window and highlight it.

1. Set the text as 12-point Script.

2. What changes appear in the Character menu after you set your text to Script?

3. Select Normal in the Character menu. What happens to your text?

ANSWERS

1. (a) Open the Character menu.
   (b) Choose the Fonts command.
   (c) Click on the Script entry in the Fonts menu.
   (d) Double-click on 12 in the Size menu.

2. The Script font is listed in the menu.

3. Nothing. The Normal option does not change the font—it only changes the type style. The type was not in bold, italic, or otherwise altered, so it does not change.

The Reduce Font and Enlarge Font commands in the Character menu decrease or increase the currently selected text to the next available font size. For example, if you select text that is 12 point and choose the Enlarge Font option, it will most likely be increased to 14 point. These options can be chosen multiple times to obtain the desired size character. Character size is defined in units called *points*. There are approximately 72 points per inch. So, characters that are 12 points will be about 1/6 inch in height.

One warning about character size selection: if you pick small font sizes, there is a likelihood that the text on the screen will become unreadable. This is due to the limited resolution of the screen; however, the text will be readable when you print it on a sufficiently capable device, such as a laser printer.

Formatting Documents

So far, you've learned how to format individual words and paragraphs. This section shows you how to control the overall appearance of your document by creating headers and footers and setting page breaks.

Creating Headers and Footers

When you print your documents, you can include a header or a footer on each page. A *header* is a line or more of text placed at the top of each page. A typical header is the name of the document and a page number or date. A *footer*, on the other hand, is a line of text placed at the bottom of each page.

To create a header, choose the Header command from the Document menu. Write will change to a Header window (Figure 10.15a) and will also display a dialog box (Figure 10.15b). Type text into the window and use the ruler to set the header margins. If you want the header to display a page number, move the cursor in the window to the desired location before selecting the Insert Page # button in the Page Header dialog box. Use this dialog box also to

▼ *Figure 10.15. Setting a Header*

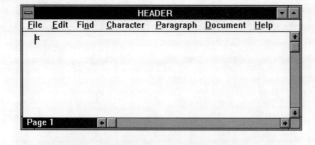

(a)

(b)

specify where the header should appear (distance from the top of the page) and whether the header should be placed on the first page. When you are done defining the header, choose the Return to Document button.

After you create a header, you can remove it at any time by choosing the Header command, and then clicking the Clear button to erase the Header window.

You create a page footer using the same technique just presented for headers. The only difference is that you must first choose the Footer command from the Document menu. As Figures 10.16a and 10.16b show, the Footer window and the Page Footer dialog box look just like those provided for creating a header. When you finish entering text for the footer, choose the Return to Document button.

Setting Page Breaks

Before printing a document, make sure that all of your page breaks are in the right place. Unlike many other Windows word processors, Write doesn't provide a print preview (which allows you to view, page by page, how your document will print). However, you can repaginate your document and manually check or change each

▼ *Figure 10.16. Creating a Footer*

(a)

(b)

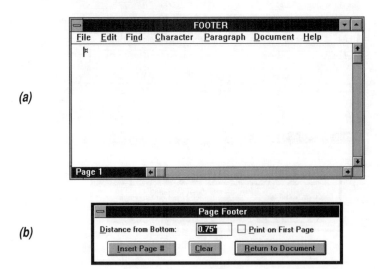

page break. To use this feature, choose the Repaginate command from the File menu. When the dialog box (Figure 10.17) appears, select the Confirm Page Breaks check box and click OK. Write shows you each page break, and then prompts you with the dialog box shown in Figure 10.18 so that you can confirm the break or change it. Choose the Up button to move the page break up one line, or select the Down button to move the break down one line.

A manual page break can also be set from the keyboard. Position the cursor on the line where you want the break to occur and press Ctrl+Enter. A single dotted line appears, representing the manual page break. To remove a page break at any time, highlight the dotted line and press the Delete key. Write displays a manual page break with a single dotted line, and an automatic page break with a chevron character.

▼ *Figure 10.17. Repaginating a Document*

▼ *Figure 10.18. Setting a Page Break*

```
┌─────────────────────────────────────┐
│ ─        Repaginating Document       │
│ Use up and down buttons  ┌──────┐ ┌────────┐
│ to move page break       │  Up  │ │ Confirm │
│ if necessary,            └──────┘ └────────┘
│ then confirm.            ┌──────┐ ┌────────┐
│                          │ Down │ │ Cancel  │
│                          └──────┘ └────────┘
└─────────────────────────────────────┘
```

Searching and Replacing Text

Sometimes you need to find a particular occurrence of a word or group of letters or numbers. You can use the options in the Search menu to do these tasks. Figure 10.19 shows the dialog box that will appear if you choose the Find command in the Find menu. The main point of interest is the box where the search text is inserted.

If you select the Match Whole Word Only option, the selected group of letters must be preceded and followed by spaces or punctuation marks. For example, type some random sentences including the word "father" and choose the Find command in the Find menu. Enter the three letters "the" in the search box and repeatedly click on the Find Next button. At some point, the search will highlight the letters contained within the word father. Now move the cursor to the top of the paragraph and select the Match Whole Word Only option before performing the search; the program will skip over the word father because the text you are searching for is embedded in other letters.

The other option of the Find dialog box is Match Case. When this is selected, the text to be found must match exactly the uppercase/lowercase style of the search sample.

▼ *Figure 10.19. The Find Dialog Box*

```
┌─────────────────────────────────────────────────┐
│ ─                    Find                         │
│ Find What: [                    ]  ┌──────────┐  │
│                                    │ Find Next │  │
│ ☐ Match Whole Word Only            └──────────┘  │
│                                    ┌──────────┐  │
│ ☐ Match Case                       │  Cancel  │  │
│                                    └──────────┘  │
└─────────────────────────────────────────────────┘
```

Once a search has been successful at least once, the Repeat Last Find option in the Find menu becomes operational. This allows you to search for repeated instances without having to deal with the Find dialog box. You can also access this command by pressing F3.

Replacing Text

Figure 10.20 shows the dialog box that appears when you invoke the third command in the Find menu: Replace. The top box allows you to define the text being searched for and the second box allows you to define what the specified text will be replaced with. The button in the upper-right corner acts just like the one in the Find dialog box; the text is found but is not replaced. If you click on the Replace button, the currently highlighted instance will be changed to the replacement text and the next instance will be searched for. The Replace All button tells Write to substitute all matches without asking for confirmation.

The last option in the Find menu, Go To Page, is useful when you have a large document and wish to move to a specific page in the document. Simply enter the desired page in the dialog box and click the OK button to jump to that location.

Combining Text and Graphics

One of the powerful features of the Windows environment is the ability for applications to share information from documents that

▼ *Figure 10.20. The Replace Dialog Box*

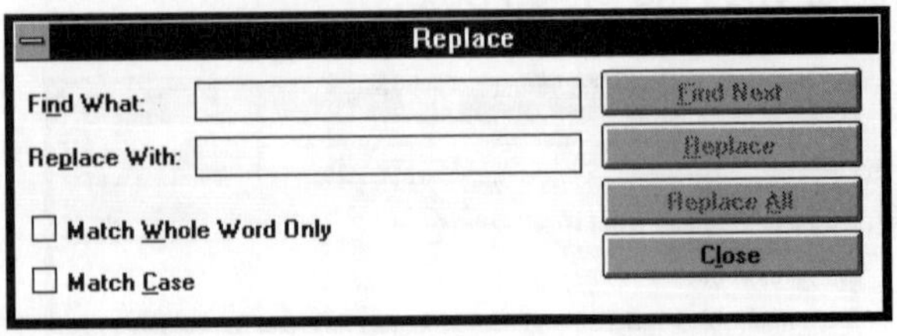

you create in other applications. Also, applications can share more than just text; they can also share and transfer pictures through the Clipboard. By importing graphics from Paintbrush or other picture sources, you can add illustrations to your documents or newsletters.

To see how this feature works, begin by drawing a simple object using Paintbrush. (A square inside another square is fine for this example.) Clip the object using the Pick tool, and then choose the Copy command from the Edit menu to place a copy of the picture in the Clipboard. If you're done with Paintbrush, either double-click on the control box or select the Exit command. If you want to keep Paintbrush active while working with Write, minimize Paintbrush to an icon before calling Write.

Switch back to Write. After you've typed a few lines of text, press the Enter key at least once to move the cursor to a new line below the text. Choose Paste from the Edit menu. The picture that you sent to the Clipboard now appears on the screen immediately below the text. Figure 10.21 shows how your screen might look. Depending upon your printer selection, you may notice some distortion of the picture. (It may appear as if it has been squeezed from the sides.) This distortion results from the internal representation of the page information in Write. If your printer is capable of producing graphics, the picture will appear just as it did in the Paintbrush program.

▼ *Figure 10.21. Pasting a Picture*

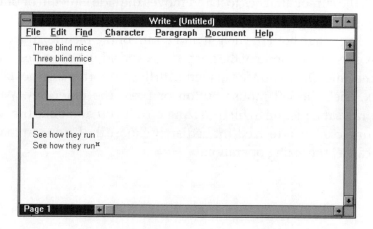

Moving a Picture

Write always inserts a Paintbrush picture at the left margin. To move a picture toward the right (to center it on the page), follow these simple steps:

1. Click on the picture with the mouse, or use the up and down arrow keys to select the picture. (The picture appears in reverse video when it is selected.)

2. Choose the Move Picture command from the Edit menu to release the picture from the page. (A dotted square appears around the picture.)

3. Move the pointer without clicking the left button to move the picture to the new location. (You can also use the left and right arrow keys to do this.)

4. When the picture is properly positioned, click the left mouse button or press the Enter key.

Changing the Size of a Picture

You can change the size of a picture by selecting it and choosing the Size Picture command from the Edit menu. The cursor will change to a box cursor. Next, move the pointer (without clicking the left mouse button) to the center of one of the sides of the dashed square that surrounds the picture. Once the box cursor touches the dashed box, the cursor attaches to it and moves the side either in or out to adjust the size of the square.

To change both the height and width of the picture, move the box cursor to a corner of the dashed box and adjust two sides at the same time. Once you are satisfied with the proportions of the sizing box, click the left mouse button or press the Enter key. Write redraws the picture to fill the sizing box. If you don't like the way your picture was resized, immediately choose the Undo command to cancel the sizing operation.

Saving Files

Saving Files

To save a Write document for the first time, choose the Save As command from the File menu. Use the Save As dialog box to assign your file a name. This dialog box also provides a pull-down menu in the lower-left corner so that you can save the file as a Write file (with the extension WRI), a Microsoft Word for DOS file, a Word for DOS text-only file, or a text-only file. If you save the file as text only, you'll lose the formatting features you've used. After you save the file for the first time, you can save it after changes are made by choosing the Save command. If you click on the box next to Backup, later editing sessions will always save the previous version as a backup file before saving the modified copy.

Special Linking Features

Windows 3.1 provides certain powerful new linking features to make documents easier to maintain. Several of these features allow you to build links to other documents and pictures so that when they are updated, your document is updated also. We'll cover some of the basics here and then we'll show you how to link documents created with the Paintbrush application.

Pasting a Picture with Links

Earlier, we showed you how to paste a Paintbrush picture in a Write document. You can also paste a picture in a Write document in such a way that the two documents become linked. After they are linked, you can edit the Paintbrush document and the changes you make will automatically be reflected in the Write document where the picture is pasted.

To paste a document with a link, you'll need to use the Paste Link command in the Edit menu. Here are the steps for linking a picture:

1. Move the Write cursor to the location where you want the picture to be pasted.

2. Run Paintbrush.

3. Create the desired drawing and save it with a unique name.

4. Select the drawing using the scissors tool and move a copy of the drawing into the Clipboard using the Copy command.

5. Switch back to Write and choose Paste Link from the Edit menu.

6. The drawing will appear in your Write document.

7. Save the Write file.

To see that the Paintbrush file is linked to the Write document, switch to Paintbrush again, load the file you linked to the Write document, and make some minor modifications (such as changing some of the colors). Use the Save command to store the modified file to disk using the same name. Now, switch to Write and open the Write document that contains the linked picture and observe that the drawing reflects the *modified* version that you just saved using Paintbrush.

This pasting and linking technique is extremely useful when you are creating a document where the illustrations may need to change over time. It allows the graphics to be updated separately from the text, thus assuring that the most recent illustrations are printed with the document.

TIP

If you want to paste and link a Paintbrush picture in a different format other than the standard BMP format, use the Paste Special command instead of the Paste Link command.

Using the Links Command

The Links command in the Edit menu is used to modify the graphics links created using the Paste Link command we just explored. Figure 10.22 appears when you choose the Links command in the Edit menu. This dialog box lists all of the documents that are currently linked to your Write document. You can select one of the linked documents in the Links scroll box and then use one of the buttons at the bottom of the dialog box to change how the document is linked.

By default, all documents are linked so that they will automatically be updated if they are modified. You can change this setting by selecting the linked document and then choosing the Manual option in the Update group. If a linked document is set up in this manner, you can update it at any time by choosing the Update Now button.

The Cancel Link button allows you to remove a link. To change a link, choose the Change Link button. A dialog box will be displayed so that you can select another file to link to. If you want to edit a picture that has been pasted with a link, you can select the picture (file) in the Links dialog box and choose the Edit button. You can also edit a linked picture by double-clicking on the picture.

Embedding a Picture

In addition to linking and pasting pictures, you can embed a Paintbrush picture in a Write document. An embedded picture is not physically linked to a Write document; however, the picture can easily be edited from within the Write document.

To embed a picture, click on the location where you want to place the picture and choose the Insert Object command in the Edit

▼ *Figure 10.22. The Links Dialog Box*

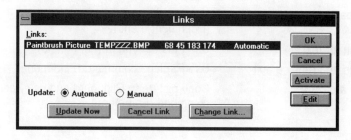

**Special Linking
Features**

▼ *Figure 10.23. Embedding a Paintbrush Picture*

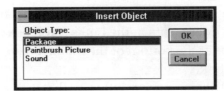

menu. The dialog box shown in Figure 10.23 will appear so that you can select the type of object you want to embed. Select Paintbrush Picture to embed a paintbrush picture and click OK. The Paintbrush application will automatically begin execution so that you can create a new picture or open an existing Paintbrush file. When you are finished with the picture, choose the Update command from the File menu and exit Paintbrush. The drawing will now appear within your Write document at the location where the cursor was when you chose the Insert Object command.

QUICK SUMMARY

Task	Procedure
Start Write	Double-click Write icon in Accessories group
Set page margins	Use Page Layout command (Document menu)
Change printed paper size	Use Print Setup command (File menu)
Display ruler	Select Ruler On option (Document menu)
Set text or decimal tabs	Use Tabs command (Document menu); or Use tab icons above ruler
Indent a paragraph	Use ruler
Change font or font style	Select text and use Fonts command (Character menu)
Set header or footer	Use Header or Footer command (Document menu)
Search for text	Use Find command (Find menu)
Search and replace text	Use Replace command (Find menu)
Paste a picture	Copy picture to Clipboard and use Paste command (Edit menu)

PRACTICE WHAT YOU'VE LEARNED

In this chapter, we've provided a close look at Write. You learned how to control the width and line spacing of individual paragraphs; how to define the size, style, and font of individual characters; how to format documents by adding headers and footers; and how to import and manipulate pictures imported from the Clipboard. Use these exercises to learn more about Write.

1. Start Write.

2. Open a text file or a .WRI file.

3. Mark the entire file by pressing Ctrl+ Shift+End.

4. Justify the text.

5. Mark a block of text and copy it to the Clipboard.

6. Paste the block of text at a different location.

7. Exit Write without saving your document.

ANSWERS

1. The Write application window appears.

2. If you open a text file, Write converts it to its own internal format. A .WRI file is opened without any conversion.

3. The entire document is highlighted.

4. The text appears justified between the default left and right margins.

5. First, select the text by holding down the mouse button and dragging the mouse. Then choose the Copy command from the Edit menu.

6. Move the pointer to the desired location and click the mouse button.

7. Control returns to the Program Manager.

Working with Paintbrush

This chapter presents the Paintbrush application—a graphics drawing and painting program that allows you to create and modify all sorts of pictures. If you have a printer that supports graphics (such as a dot-matrix, ink-jet, or laser printer), you can easily print the pictures you create. In addition, pictures created with Paintbrush can be included within documents created by other Windows applications, such as Write. In this chapter you'll learn how to:

▲ Size your drawing area and select foreground/background colors

▲ Use the basic drawing tools provided with Paintbrush

▲ Create and save pictures

▲ Use the Clipboard to replicate and transfer images

▲ Customize the palette colors

▲ Print black-and-white pictures

Notes about Using Paintbrush

Because Windows supports many displays and graphics cards, it's impossible to cover all of Paintbrush's modes of operation. In this book, we assume you are running Paintbrush with a color VGA display. If you use different display hardware, some of the options we cover won't be available to you. For example, if you use a monochrome system, the discussion about adjusting the Paintbrush colors won't apply. We'll try to keep our coverage of Paintbrush as general as possible.

Starting Paintbrush

To start Paintbrush, open the Accessories group and double-click on the Paintbrush icon. Figure 11.1 shows the untitled window you'll see when the application starts. Notice that Paintbrush provides three sets of tools along the left and the bottom of the viewing area. To the left are the various drawing and painting tools available for creating and modifying pictures. At the bottom of the viewing area is the color palette—a group of colored squares. In the lower-left

▼ *Figure 11.1. Paintbrush Application*

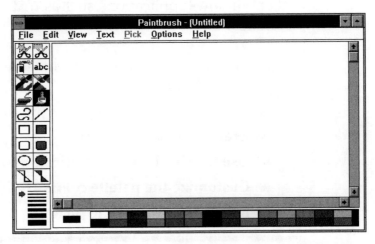

corner is a group of horizontal lines of varying widths, which are used to define the widths for lines, drawing tools, erasers, and so on.

Setting Up Paintbrush

Paintbrush is designed to imitate, as closely as possible, the experience of drawing pictures using paper, pencil, and paint. You'll need to define the size of your drawing area much in the same way that an artist sets up a sheet of canvas. The drawing area can also be set up like a colored posterboard. In addition to freehand drawing, you can select tools that draw lines, rectangles, circles, and ellipses. You can also redefine the colors in your palette in the same way an artist mixes paints to obtain a desired hue.

Defining the Drawing Region

After you start Paintbrush, you'll want to verify that the drawing region is the right size for your project. Figure 11.2 shows the dialog box that appears when you choose Image Attributes from the Options menu. This feature allows you to define your drawing area in inches, centimeters, or picture elements (often called *pixels* or *pels*). Once you have selected the units of measure, you can click on the width and height fields to define these dimensions. Notice that this dialog box also allows you to specify whether your drawing will be in color or in black and white.

▼ *Figure 11.2. Setting Up Page Attributes*

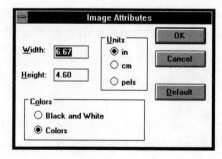

Click OK to confirm your selections and return to the Paint-brush window. If you haven't drawn anything in the Untitled window, your new attributes will take effect immediately. If you try to change the attributes of a picture that has been started, Paintbrush will ask you if you want to save the current picture before it changes the attributes.

Selecting the Active Color

Unless you have been experimenting with Paintbrush, the box to the left of the color palette should consist of a black rectangle surrounded by a larger white rectangle. The smaller rectangle represents the foreground color. You can change the foreground color (the drawing color) by clicking on the desired color in the palette with the left mouse button. The larger rectangle represents the background color and is selected by clicking on the desired palette color using the right mouse button. For now we'll use a white background to avoid confusion.

Clearing the Screen

Now that you've defined your drawing attributes, you're ready to clear the drawing area. To do this, choose New from the File menu. If a dialog box appears to ask you if you want to save the current image, choose No. After a few moments the screen will be reset and all of the setup options that you selected will be used.

TIP

A fast way to choose the New command and clear the screen is to double-click on the Eraser tool. (The Eraser tool is the third icon in the second column of the tools palette.) Keep in mind that this will clear the entire screen.

Where's the Cursor?

You should now have a clear screen set to the dimensions you selected in the Image Attributes dialog box. As you start to draw and paint, how can you tell the relative position of the cursor to the top corner of the window? Paintbrush provides this information through the Cursor Position option, which is available from the View menu. When it is active, a small box appears with two numbers representing the horizontal and vertical distances from the top-left corner of the drawing.

If your drawing is dimensioned in inches, the numbers represent hundredths of an inch. For example, the value 150 for a horizontal dimension represents 1.5 inches. You can move this box in the window by clicking on its title bar and dragging it. You can also remove it by either double-clicking on its Control menu icon or by choosing Cursor Position again.

Setting Up Paintbrush

The Paintbrush Tools

Figure 11.3 illustrates the Paintbrush toolbox area and identifies the various tools available. The two items in the top row, called Scissors and Pick, extract parts of a picture by removing the picture or making copies of it. These options are equivalent to highlighting text with the mouse and then using the Cut and Paste commands to remove and insert text. The spray-can icon represents the Airbrush tool, which allows you to "fade" one color over another, just as you would with a real airbrush or paint sprayer.

▼ *Figure 11.3. Paintbrush's Toolbox*

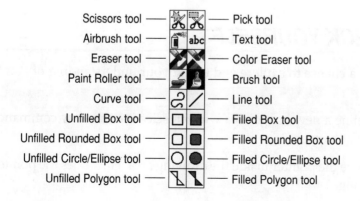

Scissors tool — Pick tool
Airbrush tool — Text tool
Eraser tool — Color Eraser tool
Paint Roller tool — Brush tool
Curve tool — Line tool
Unfilled Box tool — Filled Box tool
Unfilled Rounded Box tool — Filled Rounded Box tool
Unfilled Circle/Ellipse tool — Filled Circle/Ellipse tool
Unfilled Polygon tool — Filled Polygon tool

Use the Text tool to enter text on your drawing. The Color Eraser and simple Eraser erase portions of an existing drawing. The Paint Roller tool fills an area with a particular color or pattern; the Brush paints the current foreground color on the visible window. The Curve and Line tools create controlled curves and straight lines on the screen between two defined points. (The Curve tool is especially handy if you're not skilled at drawing smooth freehand curves using a mouse.) Finally, the Box, Rounded Box, Circle/Ellipse, and Polygon tools create closed objects. As indicated, these region-drawing tools come in two flavors: filled and unfilled.

Selecting the Active Tool

To select a drawing tool, click on the appropriate icon. With some tools, such as Paint Roller, the pointer actually changes to represent the active tool. In other cases, such as Line, the drawing cursor area is represented as a crosshair (like a + sign), where the cursor position is denoted by the intersection of the two lines in the crosshair.

Sizing the Active Tool

Most of Paintbrush's tools are affected in some way by the size selector located in the lower-left corner of the window. To change a tool's size, first select the tool and then click on the desired width value (the lower the position, the larger the width). When you click on a new size, notice that the arrow to the left of the lines moves to point to the new selection.

CHECK YOURSELF

Here's a chance to explore and to test your understanding of Paintbrush.

1. Define a new image area without selecting the New command. What happens?

2. Move the pointer inside the drawing area. How does the pointer change?

ANSWERS

1. You will get a confirmation dialog box asking you if you want to save the current image.

2. The pointer is represented as a small dot.

Using the Line Tool

The simplest tool in Paintbrush is the Line tool. Try it out. Make certain that you have selected black for the active color (the smaller rectangle) and white for the background color (the larger rectangle). Click on the Line icon, and then move down to the width selector and click on the third line from the top. Move the drawing cursor to a position in the top-left part of the screen, press and hold the left mouse button, and drag the mouse toward the lower-right corner. A line will appear from the starting position to the crosshair pointer. Notice that the line will track the cursor as you move the mouse around the screen. After you are satisfied with the position of your line, release the mouse button.

A Drawing Example

You might now be wondering whether there's an easy way to draw vertical and horizontal lines? Yes. The trick is to press the Shift key while drawing a line. To test this feature, make sure your drawing region is set up using the default settings of 6.67 for your image's width and 4.6 for the height. Next, choose the Cursor Position command, if it is not already in view, then move the cursor so that it is in the upper center of the drawing area. Perform these steps:

1. Keep the Shift key pressed.
2. Click and drag the mouse from location 200,25 to 300, 125.

3. Release the mouse then click again from 300, 125 and move it to 200, 225.

4. Repeat the procedure moving to 100, 125 and finally back to 200, 25.

5. Release the Shift key and you'll end up with a diamond.

The Shift key makes it easy to position the drawing cursor but you may have accidentally moved the cursor when you started the next line segment (which led to a space between the endpoint of one line and the starting point of the next line). There is a way to avoid this: use the Polygon tool.

The Polygon Tool

The Polygon tool operates like the Line tool except that it draws a *closed object*. This means that the last line must always return to the beginning point of the first line. To try out this tool, draw the first three segments of the diamond per the earlier exercise. After you move the cursor to the 100, 125 location and release the mouse to draw the line segment, hold the mouse steady and double-click the left button. Polygon will automatically draw the last line segment from the ending point to the starting point.

Undoing Mistakes

If you make a mistake while drawing a line, you can choose the Undo command from the Edit menu. This will erase your most recent drawing work as long as you haven't clicked the mouse on anything else (such as selecting a different drawing tool or beginning to draw a new line or object).

If you make a mistake at the beginning of a drawing operation (such as clicking on the wrong spot to start a line), you can cancel the operation by pressing the right mouse button while the left button down is still pressed. The line or object will disappear and you can then release both buttons.

Undoing Mistakes

TIP

You should save your drawing work frequently. This approach reduces the chance that Undo will undo more of the drawing than you really want to correct.

Using the Eraser

The Eraser tool works like you might think except for one detail: It replaces the area swept by its cursor with the *current background color*. To try out the eraser, draw several thin horizontal lines on the usual white background drawing area. Click the Eraser. When the pointer is moved inside the drawing area, the pointer changes to a small square. This square represents the actual size of the area to be erased. Move the Eraser cursor to the beginning of the area to be erased, then click and drag the Eraser.

To change the size of the eraser, click on a line in the size selector. To erase large parts of the screen, you will want to use the widest eraser.

The Color Eraser

The Color Eraser changes the foreground color into the background color, where the cursor is dragged. It also allows you to replace all occurrences of one color within the window with a different color. For example, you might draw lines or shapes of various colors (including red) in the drawing area. You could then elect red as the foreground and yellow for the background. If you now double-click on the Color Eraser icon in the Toolbox while carefully observing the red areas, the Color Eraser changes all of the red areas to the background color (yellow) but will not affect the other colored objects.

Painting with the Brush

The next tool we'll explore is the Brush. If you click and drag the Brush, you'll get a painted line or curve created in the active drawing color. As you would expect, the Brush tool's size is controlled by the size selector.

The Brush tool also supports different *brush shapes*. Figure 11.4 illustrates the dialog box that appears when Brush Shapes is chosen from the Options menu (the default shape is the square at the left). One shape that may be of particular interest is the tool shape that looks like a normal slash (/). This tool can be used to hand-print calligraphy (Old English) letters. Since the Brush tool responds to the Shift key for vertical and horizontal lines (sorry, no 45-degree angles), you can really keep your letters straight.

CHECK YOURSELF

What steps would you perform to draw a red, Old-English H?

ANSWER

1. Select the solid blue on the top row of the color palette as the foreground color.

2. Select the Line tool and set the line size to the thinnest value.

3. Draw two blue horizontal lines separated by about 3/4 inch.

4. Select the Brush tool.

5. Select the Brush shape that looks like a slash.

6. Select Red as the foreground color.

7. Select the third line width from the bottom.

8. Move the cursor to the top blue line, press Shift, and drag the cursor down.

9. Repeat the process for the other vertical and horizontal segments of the H.

▼ *Figure 11.4. Selecting a Brush Shape*

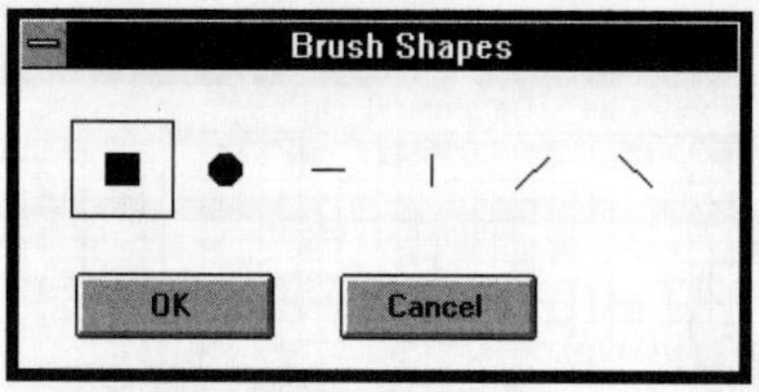

More about Colors

In Windows, pure colors such as blue, red, and green are easily displayed because they are supported by your display hardware. Windows' second method for creating colors is to intermix dots of two or more pure colors to fool the eye into thinking that the two colors are actually a single, third color. The easiest way to see this is to use the Zoom In feature to look at individual pixels.

Select the Brush, set the width to a middle value, and make certain that the tool shape is a square. Select the dark blue color in the middle of the top row of the color palette as the drawing color and draw a vertical stripe. Now select the blue color that is located third from the right on the lower row as the drawing color and draw a second stripe next to the first one. Choose the Zoom In command from the View menu and note that the pointer has turned into a transparent rectangle. Move the cursor so that it overlays both color stripes and click the mouse. The regular drawing area will disappear and the window in Figure 11.5 will appear.

The Zoom In feature acts like a magnifying glass; it allows you to see the individual pixels or pels that make up an image. As you can see, the pixels in the first stripe are all of the same color, those in the second stripe are composed of a regular pattern of two separate colors.

Saving Files

You now know how to draw simple lines, closed polygons, and freehand curves. But how do you save your work? Unlike most of

▼ *Figure 11.5. Zooming in on a Picture*

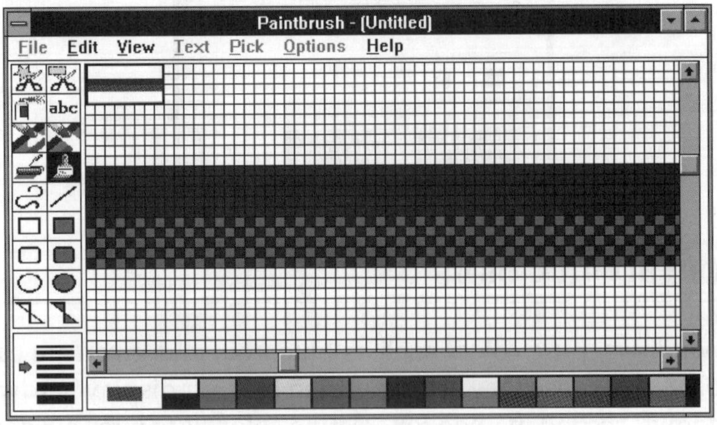

the other Windows tools, Paintbrush allows you to save a file in five possible formats:

1. PCX file

2. Monochrome bitmap

3. 16 Color bitmap

4. 256 Color bitmap

5. 24-bit bitmap

The first option is probably the most efficient because PCX files are stored in a compressed format. Monochrome and 16 Color bitmap files tend to be larger than PCX but are still smaller than 256 Color files. You would typically select either Monochrome or 16 Color if you have a monochrome or EGA display.

You'll want to use the 256 Color bitmap if you're running Windows with a VGA (or better) display. The disadvantage with this format is that it requires one entire byte for each pixel in the drawing area. As an example, a drawing area of 640 by 480 pixels requires at least 307,200 bytes (640 multiplied times 480) just to hold the picture values!

Figure 11.6 shows the dialog box that appears when you choose the Save As command from the File menu. The drop-down menu in the lower-left corner allows you to choose between the various

▼ *Figure 11.6. Saving a Paintbrush File*

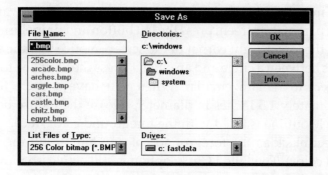

file formats just explained. Enter the filename then select the desired file format; choose the OK button when you are done.

Opening Files

Paintbrush allows you to open three different types of files: PCX, BMP, and MSP. To open a file, use the Open command (File menu), enter the path information and filename. One of the interesting quirks of Paintbrush is that it is capable of importing and correctly displaying a 256 Color BMP file, yet it cannot accommodate the larger palette so that all of the colors in the image can be modified.

TIP

To get a feel for the quality of graphics that can be presented using Paint-brush, open the various BMP files provided in the main Windows directory.

Using the Closed Shape Tools

Paintbrush provides several tools for drawing common geometric shapes such as circles, ellipses, and rectangles. Let's start by drawing concentric circles to form a target. Select red as the foreground color, white as the background color, and click on the Filled Circle tool (the one on the right). Move the cursor toward the top-left part of the screen, press the left button and drag the mouse toward the lower-right corner of the screen. Notice that the shape changes between a circle and an ellipse. Press the Shift key to force the object to remain circular. When you have a circle that is approximately 1.5 inches in diameter, release the mouse button. The circle outline is filled with the foreground color (red).

Select black as the foreground color (white is still the background color). The Filled Circle option is still active, so move the crosshairs to a point in the upper-left side of the red circle, press the Shift key, and click and drag again toward the lower-right side to create a smaller circle inside the first one. (Don't worry that the circles aren't concentric; this isn't important in this example.)

When you've drawn a circle inside the red one, release the mouse button to freeze the shape and fill it with black (Figure 11.7). Look carefully to observe a thin band of white around the black circle. This occurred because Paintbrush always draws an edge around the filled objects, using the background color. The width of the edge is controlled by the line width selector. If you don't want this edge to be drawn, make the background color the same as the foreground color before you draw the object. Experiment with this by making the foreground and background colors red, then draw a small circle inside the black one.

▼ *Figure 11.7. Drawing a Target*

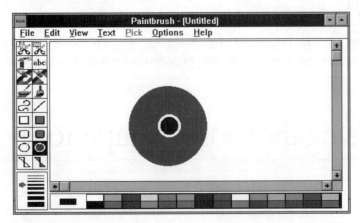

Using The Roller Tool

If you followed the previous example, you should now have a large red circle, containing a smaller black circle bordered by a white edge. (It doesn't matter whether you drew the third circle.) Select red for the foreground color and select white for the background again. Choose Zoom In from the View menu (or use the Ctrl+Z shortcut). Move the magnifier rectangle to the top of the black circle so that the white edge divides the rectangle into approximately equal-sized pieces. When the rectangle reaches the correct location, click the left mouse button to expand the region (Figure 11.8).

Click on the Paint Roller icon and move the pointer so that the point of the icon is inside one of the white squares that make up the arc in the main viewing area. Click the mouse button to perform a fill operation; all of the white squares in the viewable area change to red. Now choose the Zoom Out command (or use the Ctrl+O shortcut) to return to the normal screen. Notice that the only part of the white edge that is altered is the area that was visible in the zoom window. To change the rest of the white arc to red, position the point of the Roller tool inside the white arc. Click the left mouse button to activate the fill operation again.

▼ *Figure 11.8. Zooming in on the Target*

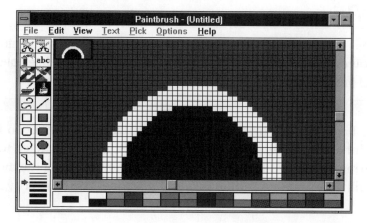

CHECK YOURSELF

1. While your picture is in the viewing area, choose the View Picture command from the View menu. What happens?

2. How many times can you select the Zoom In command to zoom in on your picture?

ANSWERS

1. The picture expands to fit the entire screen. Click the mouse to return to the drawing window.

2. Only one time.

Setting Pixels

Using the Zoom In feature, you can easily change the color of a pixel. To experiment with this technique, select the Line tool and draw a simple triangle. Choose Zoom In, move the magnifier rectangle over one of the end points, and click once. Select the background color for that area on the screen as the current foreground color and choose the Brush tool. Note that the pointer remains a white arrow when operating in the Zoom In mode.

TIP

When you paint individual pixels, you can create extremely intricate textures in your drawings; this technique just requires a little patience and imagination.

Begin clicking on squares (pixels) that may extend beyond the point of the triangle, and notice that each square is changed to the currently selected foreground color. You can also drag the mouse to fill groups of individual pixels at one time. You can verify how the true-size object will look by inspecting the contents of the rectangle in the top-let corner of the zoomed area (it contains a miniature view of what you are currently working on). When you are done, Zoom Out to inspect your handiwork and to select a different area if necessary.

Defining Custom Colors

Until now we've treated the color palette as an unchanging part of the Paintbrush window. In reality you can change any of the colors in the palette to values that suit your needs. Figure 11.9 shows the dialog box that will appear if you choose Edit Colors from the Options menu. Once the dialog box is visible, click on one of the colors in the palette so that it appears in the large rectangle to the right of the slide bars. Change the red, green, or blue settings to observe how different mixtures of the primary colors result in different pure or mixed colors.

After you are finished editing a color, click the OK button to actually change the color in the palette. You can then continue to edit different colors, using the Edit Colors dialog box.

Once you have modified the palette to suit your needs, save these settings using the Save Colors command (Options menu). To retrieve the custom palette at a later time, choose Get Colors (Options menu) and then select the desired palette from the scrollable list of PAL files.

▼ *Figure 11.9. Editing a Color*

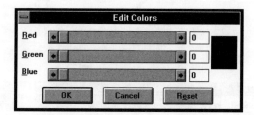

The Curve Tool

The Curve tool operates in a similar manner as the Line tool and allows you to curve a line. Anchor both endpoints as you would for the Line tool, move the cursor to some point on or near the line (but away from the endpoints), and click and drag the cursor. The flexible line curves in the direction you're dragging the cursor. Once you've moved the curve to the right location, release the left mouse button. If you want a simple curve, move the cursor to the second endpoint and click on it. Figure 11.10 shows some of the types of curves you can create.

To make an "S" curve, anchor the two endpoints as before, then move the pointer to a location approximately one-third of the way along the line and deform it as described above. Once you have released the mouse button, move the cursor to the other end of the line and then click and drag to deform it in the other direction. If you wish to cancel and start over at any point in this operation, press the right button once to cancel the line. If you release the mouse button for the second time and decide that you don't like the shape of the line, immediately choose Undo (Edit menu) to remove the line.

▼ *Figure 11.10. Drawing Curves*

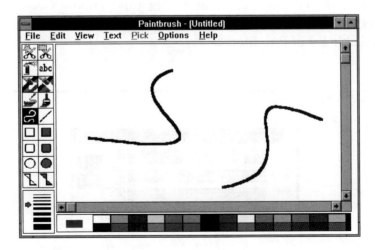

CHECK YOURSELF

1. Select the Line tool. Click and drag the crosshair pointer in the drawing area. While you're dragging, click the right button. What happens?

2. Select the Curve tool, and double-click the crosshair pointer in the drawing area. Move the pointer to a second position and click once. Move the pointer to a third position and click again. What happens?

3. Hold the mouse button down on the third click and drag the mouse. What happens?

ANSWERS

1. The line disappears.

2. A curved, closed shape is drawn.

3. You will be able to reshape the closed, curved figure.

The Airbrush Tool

The last tool in the drawing and painting category is the Airbrush. This powerful tool uses the foreground color to cover an area with a random concentric pattern similar to what you might get from a can of spray paint. If you click on the mouse and move it quickly, only a sprinkling of paint dots is visible. If you drag the Airbrush pointer very slowly, the area becomes completely saturated with the currently selected foreground color. Figure 11.11 shows a window painted with the Airbrush tool. Notice that many different types of patterns can be created. The line width selector at the lower-left corner of the window defines the size of the spray pattern. The Airbrush tool takes some practice but once you get familiar with it you'll be able to create many interesting effects.

▼ *Figure 11.11. Using the Airbrush Tool*

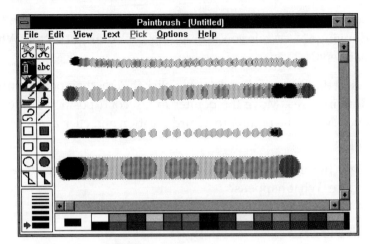

CHECK YOURSELF

Experiment with the Airbrush tool to change the size of the brush spray.

ANSWER

Change the size by selecting a different line width from the palette in the lower-left corner.

Editing Techniques with Scissors and Pick

Scissors and Pick are extremely useful when you plan on doing anything that is repeated, or if you want to include drawings in your Write documents. Scissors and Pick generally work in the same way: use them to select a graphics area so that it can be moved, duplicated, or sent to the Windows Clipboard for use by another application.

Select Pick to define a rectangular-cut perimeter. This is quite handy when you work with objects that have a substantial amount of separation from other objects. If the area that you wish to cut contains some background objects that you want to leave in place, don't use Pick. Instead, choose the Scissors tool.

The Scissors tool is used to define an elaborate perimeter around the area to be cut. This is ideal for extracting an irregularly shaped object. The only requirement is that you must drag completely around the object to the point where you began the cut operation.

Both tools define a dashed line that allows you to verify what is to be cut. The cutting perimeter is defined by moving the pointer to the beginning location, pressing the left mouse button, dragging the mouse to define a closed cutting perimeter, and releasing the left mouse button. Pick works like the unfilled rectangle tool, and Scissors works similarly to Brush. Figure 11.12 shows an image area selected with the Scissors tool.

When you release the left mouse button to perform the cut operation, you have a few options. You can choose the Cut or Copy command in the Edit menu to move a copy of the object into the Clipboard. You can then use the Paste command to bring in multiple copies of the object. Another option is to simply drag the item to a different part of the screen. If the background of the object is the same color as the currently selected background, you can

Editing Techniques with Scissors and Pick

▼ *Figure 11.12. Image Selected with the Scissors Tool*

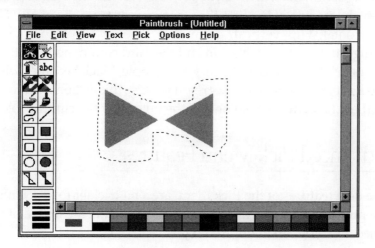

move the object transparently: the object can overlay other objects on the screen so that the objects underneath are visible.

Moving an Object

To move an object, first define a cut perimeter using either tool. Next, move the pointer inside the cut perimeter, press the left mouse button, and drag the object across the screen to the new location.

If you want to use the Cut and Paste commands to make multiple copies, define the cut perimeter and choose Cut. Next, choose Paste to bring the object back (usually to the top-left corner of the viewing area). Move the pointer to the center of the object (as defined by the dashed perimeter) and drag it to the new position. If you're not happy with the object position, move the cursor inside the dashed perimeter, press the left mouse button again, and move the object. When you're satisfied, move the pointer outside of the dashed area and click the left mouse button once to paste it. (The dashed perimeter disappears.)

Using the Pick Menu

The Pick menu provides a number of options for changing how an object is displayed. For example, you can use the Flip Horizontal command to flip an object horizontally. To try out some of these editing commands, draw an object, select it with the Pick tool, and then choose one of the first three commands from the menu: Flip Horizontal, Flip Vertical, or Inverse. The first two commands change an object's orientation and the third command inverts the colors inside the selected area. For example, black becomes white and light grey becomes dark grey. If you use this option with colors on the screen, the new colors are the inverse of the current colors.

Advanced Pick Menu Features

The next features of the Pick menu are a bit trickier to use. Unlike the previous features, these allow you to distort the image of the object that you are manipulating.

Shrink + Grow

The Shrink+Grow option is used to resize an object. As an example, assume that you want to draw a group of dominoes disappearing into the distance (as in Figure 11.13). Draw the first object, select the Pick tool, mark the object, and use the Copy command to place it in the Clipboard. Now perform the following steps several times:

1. Choose Paste (Edit menu) to bring a copy of the object to the top-left corner of the screen.

2. Choose the Shrink + Grow option from the Pick menu.

3. Click on the location where the top-left corner of the object should go and drag the mouse down while holding down the Shift key.

4. Release the mouse button, then the Shift key, to observe a miniature object created.

One interesting feature of Shrink + Grow is that you must choose it again whenever you select a new object. You can also resize an existing object (without making a duplicate in the Clipboard) by performing the following steps:

1. Define a cut perimeter using either Pick or Scissors.

*Editing
Techniques
with Scissors
and Pick*

▼ *Figure 11.13. Using the Pick Options*

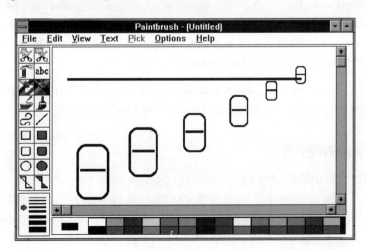

2. Choose the Clear command and then choose Shrink + Grow (two separate operations).

3. Move the pointer to where the top-left corner of the modified object should appear.

4. Drag the mouse to define a rectangle inside of which the object will appear (if you want to avoid distorting the object, hold the Shift key while dragging).

5. Release the mouse button and the Shift key to cause the resized object to appear.

Tilt

Tilt is used to laterally distort an image. Erase the screen and paste a domino object from the previous exercise. Drag it to the center of the drawing area, and choose the Clear option (Pick menu) and then choose Tilt. Move the pointer to the location where you want the top left corner of the object to appear, then drag to the left or right; a parallelogram will be drawn that follows your movements. Release the mouse button to see the distorted object on the screen. Click on a tool to paste the image.

CHECK YOURSELF

1. Draw a red square with a blue border on a white background and use the Pick tool to cut the object and a border around it. Hold the Shift key down while dragging a copy to a different part of the screen. Release the left mouse button (but not the Shift key) and move the mouse to a third location. Click the left mouse button momentarily. What happens?

2. How would you create a shadowed box (called a drop shadow) like those seen in desktop publishing applications?

ANSWERS

1. Another copy of the object appears each time that you click the mouse button at the location of the pointer. Clicking using the left mouse button will result in transparent copying; using the right button will result in opaque copying.

2. Assuming a white drawing area, select a white foreground and a grey background. Draw a square or rectangle of the desired size. Set the background to black and then cut the object carefully using the Pick tool. Move the pointer to the center of the object and drag it upwards and to the left by the desired amount; the area underneath the original square will appear black. Use the Paint Roller tool to fill in the interior of the box to grey.

Editing Techniques with Scissors and Pick

Copy To and Paste From Commands

One interesting feature of the Edit menu is that it allows you to import or export selected portions of an image to disk. For example, you could use the Open command (Edit menu) to open a file that has some scenery, and then import a picture of an elephant from another file using the Copy To and Paste From commands (Edit menu). This is probably best illustrated by an example:

1. Draw a black rectangle with a grey border.

2. Use Pick to carefully cut the object from the white background.

3. Choose Copy To (Edit menu) and give it the name OBELISK.BMP; click OK.

4. Select green for the background color and double-click on the Eraser icon.

5. Select brown for the background color.

6. Select the largest possible eraser and paint the lower third of drawing area brown.

7. Choose Paste From (Edit menu) and select the file OBELISK.BMP.

8. Drag the object so that it is part way in the brown area and mostly in the green.

9. Click on any tool to paste the image.

The Text Tool

The last tool we'll cover is the Text tool, which you can use to insert various styles of text anywhere in the drawing area. Select the Text icon, and choose the Fonts command in the Text menu to view a list of the fonts available. Click on the name of the desired font to change the selection. The Size scroll menu indicates the point sizes available for the currently selected font (the larger the number, the larger the letters).

You can select different style options at the same time. The main options in the Style menu are Regular, Bold, Italic, and Bold Italic. Bold makes the letters appear to have been drawn with thicker lines. Italic slants the letters and makes each letter a bit narrower.

CHECK YOURSELF

1. What is the minimum font size available for the Arial font? What is the maximum size?

2. Enter some text and change its font size. What happens?

3. Enter some text and select the Undo command. What happens?

ANSWERS

1. The minimum size is 8 points, and the maximum is 72 points.

2. As long as you don't reposition the cursor after typing the text, you can change its size. You can also use this technique to change the style of the text.

3. Nothing. This command is not supported with the Text tool.

The Outline and Shadow options in the Text menu allow you to change the way your text is displayed. These options work only when the currently selected background color is different from the background color of the viewing area. Outline draws a band of color around the outside and the inside of each letter. The color of this band is the currently selected background color. Shadow draws an outline of the letter using the current background color, so that the letter is shadowed as if a high-intensity light source is shining on it from the top-right corner of the screen. Only one of the Normal, Outline, or Shadow options can be selected at a time. Selecting Normal also resets the other options.

The Text Tool

Once you've made your selections, move the pointer to where you want the text to appear. Click the left mouse button and begin typing text; if you make a mistake, use the backspace key to remove the characters to the left of the cursor, one at a time. If you type past the right side of the view window, Paintbrush won't beep or otherwise warn you, and ignores the additional letters. To get around this, move the viewing window to the right using the scroll bar and type the additional text.

QUICK SUMMARY

Task	Procedure
Start Paintbrush	Double-click Paintbrush icon (Accessories group)
Set up a picture's page size	Use Image Attributes (Options menu)
Display cursor position	Use Cursor Position (View menu)
Select a foreground color	Click left mouse button on a color in the palette
Select a background color	Click right mouse button on a color in the palette
Select a Paintbrush tool	Click on a tool in the palette
Draw a 45 or 90 degree line	Use Line tool and press Shift key
Change the drawing width for a tool	Select a line width in the lower-left corner
Clear the drawing area	Double-click on the Eraser tool
Create a custom color	Use the Edit Colors command (Options menu)
Cut an object	Select the object using the Scissors or Pick tool and choose the Cut command (Edit menu)
Zoom in on a drawing area	Use the Zoom In command (View menu)

PRACTICE WHAT YOU'VE LEARNED

In this chapter, we've taken a close look at the key Windows application Paintbrush. We learned how to use Paintbrush to create pictures and make alterations using the basic drawing and painting tools. Use these exercises to learn more about Paintbrush.

1. Start Paintbrush by double-clicking on the Paintbrush icon.

2. Select the largest line size available.

3. Select the box drawing tool, and move the cursor inside the drawing window.

4. Hold down the Shift key and click and drag the mouse.

5. Select the Scissors tool, and draw a region around the box.

6. Click and drag the mouse.

7. Choose the Cut command.

8. Exit Paintbrush.

ANSWERS

1. The Paintbrush application displays with the Untitled window.

2. The line size pointer moves to the bottom line size in the palette.

3. The box icon is highlighted, and the cursor changes to a crosshair.

4. A square is drawn.

5. A dashed line appears around the box, and the cursor changes to an arrow.

6. The box moves around on the screen.

7. The box is deleted.

8. Control returns to the Program Manager.

12

Using
Terminal

This chapter introduces the Windows communications program called Terminal. Terminal allows you to communicate with other computers and on-line communication systems, such as bulletin boards. After you finish this chapter, you'll know how to:

▲ Start Terminal

▲ Configure Terminal to connect with other computers

▲ Set up a modem

▲ Call other computers

▲ Customize Terminal's function keys to your needs

▲ Troubleshoot your connections

▲ Transfer and receive files using Terminal

About Terminal

Terminal is a full-featured communications program that allows you to connect to another computer or network, such as CompuServe or an on-line bulletin board. Terminal uses the serial communications ports (such as COM1 or COM2) in your PC to send or receive information.

If you need to connect two PCs that are in the same room (without using a phone connection), you must use a *null modem* cable so that the send wire of one machine becomes the receive connection of the other machine, and vice versa.

To use Terminal to communicate via a telephone line, you need either an external modem connected to a serial port or an internal modem card that plugs into your PC. In either case, the modem then connects to the outside world through a standard telephone line.

TIP

Many built-in modem cards have two connectors: one to connect the line between the PC and a telephone wall outlet, and a second connection that allows you to plug in a telephone. With the second connection, you can use Terminal as an automatic dialer for your voice calls!

Starting Terminal

To start Terminal, open the Accessories window and double-click on the Terminal icon. The application window (Figure 12.1) contains a menu bar with the following menu items:

File	Provides a set of commands for opening, saving, and printing files
Edit	Provides basic editing commands and allows you to clear the screen

▼ *Figure 12.1. The Terminal Application*

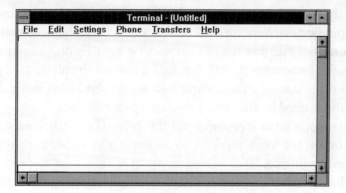

Settings	Provides options for configuring communication settings
Phone	Provides commands for dialing and hanging up
Transfers	Provides commands for transferring and receiving files
Help	Provides commands for accessing Help information

If you have experience using a communications program, you'll find Terminal easy to use. If you are unfamiliar with communications programs, you should consult a book that covers the basics. The discussion in this chapter will assume that you are using a Hayes-compatible modem to communicate with another computer.

About Communication Parameters

Computer communications can be confusing. Before you dial and connect with another computer, you must make certain that your system is configured properly. First, you need to set the communication parameters, such as the baud rate, number of data bits, stop bits, and parity, and flow control.

Computers use 1 and 0 values to represent all of their information—this is also true for communications. With the serial ports on a PC, the 1 and 0 digits are represented as the presence or absence of a voltage or current on a wire. A modem converts these voltages into unique, audible tones that can be sent through telephone wires. For two computers to send information simultaneously, the frequencies used by the calling modem to send data must differ from those used by the answering computer's modem. Thus, data is sent on one set of frequencies and received on a different set. So, it is important for a modem to be set up as either a calling or answering device.

Modems that connect to regular telephone lines are available in different speeds: 1200 baud, 2400 baud, 4800 baud, and so on. These speeds indicate the number of bits (1 and 0 digits) that can be sent or received by the modem each second. Usually, a relatively fast modem, such as a 2400 baud modem, can also send and receive data at a slower rate, such as 1200 baud.

For reasons that are too complex to explain in this book, the data bits transmitted by a PC serial port are sent in bunches. This leads to the specification of the number of *data bits*, *parity bit*, and *stop bits*.

TIP

If you subscribe to a commercial service like CompuServe or Prodigy, the required communications parameters are specified in the membership documentation. If you are dealing with local bulletin boards, the most prevalent settings are 1200 baud, eight data bits, no parity bit, one stop bit, and flow control (Xon/Xoff) enabled.

Setting Up Communications Parameters

To define the communication parameters for a particular session, choose the Communications command from the Settings menu. When the dialog box (Figure 12.2) displays, check each communication parameter to verify that the correct value is selected. For example, if you use a 1200-baud modem, select the 1200 option button in the Baud Rate group.

▼ *Figure 12.2. Setting up Communication Parameters*

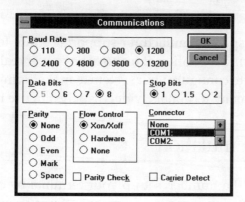

The Data Bits option specifies the number of data bits in each packet sent between two computers. Usually this setting is assigned a value of 7 or 8. The Stop Bits option specifies the time interval between transmitted characters, and is typically set at 1.

The Parity option specifies the technique used for checking your data when it is being sent; parity is typically set to None. The Flow Control option specifies what will happen if the buffer receiving data at your computer becomes full. The Xon/Xoff setting is standard, and tells your computer to send a pause signal to the other computer. This allows your computer time to clear its data buffer. When the buffer is fairly empty, the receiving machine will send an OK-to-send signal to the other machine so that it will recontinue transmitting data.

The Connector option specifies which serial port your modem is connected to. Select the COM port that is connected to your modem. If you are using a mouse with Windows, usually the mouse is connected to COM1 and the modem is connected to COM2.

TIP

You can save all of the settings you select so that you won't have to reconfigure Terminal each time you use it. To save your settings, choose the Save As command from the File menu. Next, enter a name in the Save As dialog box and click OK.

Setting up Your Terminal

Each video display manufacturer supports certain features (and not others). Standardization of features has never really occurred, so you'll need to configure your system to make Terminal compatible with the many terminals (videl displays) in use today.

Terminal Emulation

Before you dial a number, set up your terminal by choosing the Terminal Emulation command from the Settings menu. The dialog box (Figure 12.3) displays, and provides three options. If you are connecting to another PC or a standard on-line service (such as CompuServe), select the TTY (Generic) option. The other two options enable your computer to emulate a terminal (such as the Digital Equipment Corp. VT-100) when connecting your PC to mainframe computers. Click OK to select the new setting.

Terminal Preferences

After you've selected an option for terminal emulation, you must specify your terminal settings. For this task, choose the Terminal Preferences command from the Settings menu. You'll then see the dialog box shown in Figure 12.4.

The first group of options, Terminal Modes, allows you to select how your terminal displays data. Select the Line Wrap check box if you want incoming characters to wrap from one line to the next on your display. (If you don't select this option, you may lose characters that extend past the right edge of the screen.)

▼ *Figure 12.3. Selecting a Terminal*

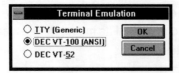

▼ *Figure 12.4. Setting up Terminal Preferences*

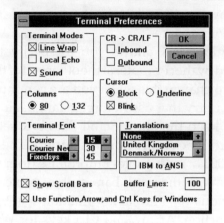

The Local Echo option allows you to display the characters that you enter through the keyboard. Because some systems automatically echo characters after they are sent, enabling this option may produce duplicate characters on the screen. Enable this option only if the keys that you press do not appear on screen.

The Sound option turns on your system bell. It allows the system you're connected with to send a special code (a nonprintable character) that is then intercepted by Terminal to sound a beep.

To save transmission time, some computer systems only send a carriage return (CR) character at the end of each line, but not a line feed (LF) character. The cursor will move to the first column of the *next* line when the CR is detected. Some devices, however, will not advance the cursor to the next line unless a line feed character is detected. The options in the CR -> CR/LF box allow you to automatically replace each CR with CR and LF for both transmitted and received information. Select Inbound to convert the data you receive, and Outbound to convert the data you send.

The Columns box allows you to specify 80 or 132 columns. Unless you are using a VGA display in 132-character mode, leave this setting at 80.

Use the Cursor box to select either a block (upright rectangle) or underline for the cursor that displays in the Terminal window. You can also make the cursor blink by selecting the Blink check box.

The Terminal Font box is used to select the display font for both incoming data in the Terminal window and the text that you enter. This feature allows you to select the most readable font available for your display hardware.

The Translations box allows you to specify the particular character set used by the computer at the other end of the connection. You only need to change this when you are communicating with someone in a country that uses a foreign language.

You should keep the Show Scroll Bars box selected since it allows you to scroll back to previously sent data. The default Buffer Lines value of 100 is a reasonable compromise (four to five screens of information). With the scroll bars visible, you can scroll up to review the previous 100 lines of information sent to your PC.

The Use Function, Arrow, and Ctrl keys for Windows check box should be selected if you want Windows or the remote computer to recognize these keys.

Selecting a Modem

Most PC-based modems are designed to be Hayes-compatible, and this is the default configuration for Terminal. If you have a different type of modem installed, choose Modem Commands from the Settings menu and then select the appropriate modem. Figure 12.5 shows the four options provided in the Modem Defaults group. After you select the correct option, click the OK button.

When one of the modem options is selected in the Modem Defaults group, the settings in the Commands section are auto-

▼ *Figure 12.5. Setting up the Modem*

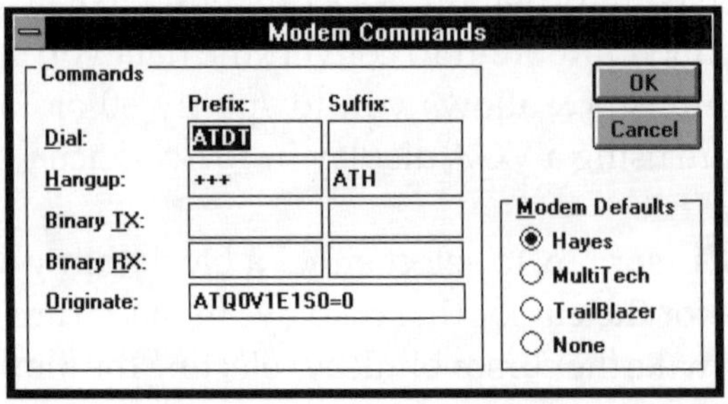

matically updated. These settings specify the commands that your modem uses to perform such operations as dialing a number or hanging up the phone line. If you are using a Hayes-compatible modem, you should not need to change any of these settings.

Selecting a Number

After you set the basic parameters and terminal preferences, you're ready to dial a number and connect with another computer. Choose the Phone Number command from the Settings menu. When the dialog box (Figure 12.6) displays, you can use the Dial text box to enter a phone number (and an area code, if required). You can use parentheses and hyphens to separate the parts of the phone number. To insert a delay between numbers, use a comma. If Terminal encounters a comma when dialing a number, it pauses for two seconds before dialing the next digit. Here are a few examples of valid numbers:

(212)483-2165

1-800-922-7541

9,455-3223

8,,402-351-8754

The Phone Number dialog box also lets you set three options: specify a timeout value, specify that your number will be redialed if it can't be connected on the first try, and specify that Terminal should signal you when it connects to the remote computer. For the first option, Timeout If Not Connected In, you can enter a value to increase the number of seconds Terminal waits for a connect signal.

▼ *Figure 12.6. Entering a Phone Number*

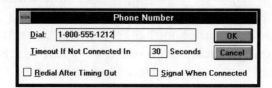

After a number has been dialed, Terminal waits until it "times out" or until it receives a connect signal. By default, Terminal's timeout limit is 30 seconds. If your telephone company is particularly slow to make a connection or if you are dialing a large computer system that is slow to answer and respond, increase the timeout value.

If you are calling a system that is often busy, such as an on-line bulletin board, select the Redial After Timing Out option. This option tells Terminal to keep dialing the number until it connects. If you also select the Signal When Connected option, you can leave your computer; Terminal will beep when it connects.

Understanding Your Modem

Before making your first phone call, we should cover some basic information involved in modem communications. For example, there are two ways to dial a telephone number: pulse and tone. If you are using a Hayes-compatible modem, it probably defaults to tone dialing. However, a few areas of the country only accept pulse dialing signals. In these situations, commands can be sent to the modem to tell it to pulse the line (like the old rotary phones) rather than use tones. To do this, you type *ATDP* in the Dial Prefix box in the Modem Commands dialog box, and then press Enter. The letters AT tell the modem that you are trying to send it a special command, while the DP specifies pulse dialing. Of course, you can also switch back to tone by typing *ATDT*.

Another useful command controls the loudness of the speaker in the modem. If you would like to hear the dialing activity on the line and the ringing of the telephone on the other end, issue the command *ATL3* (the loudest setting). You can also reduce the speaker volume by entering *ATL2* or *ATL1*. (*ATL0* turns off the speaker entirely.)

If you are having trouble establishing communication, your first reaction might be to pick up a telephone and listen to the modem traffic. Unfortunatly, most modems have a circuit that detects when a regular phone has been picked up and responds to this condition by interrupting modem service. Thus, it is important that the modem be connected to an independent line or that you make certain no one picks up the phone while you are using the modem. Some modems allow you to override this feature through the ATH command, which alternately commands the modem to go off-hook or on-hook (pick-up the phone or hang up, respectively).

One last caution: never use a modem on a line with call waiting or other interruption services; the beeps or clicks caused by these services will disrupt your modem communications. See your modem owner's manual or contact the manufacturer for a complete list of valid AT commands for your unit.

Understanding Your Modem

TIP

If you do not yet own a modem, consider carefully the tradeoffs in speed and packaging (internal versus external). In the long term, a high-speed internal modem is probably best since it has less cabling and can usually be set to several popular speeds. An internal modem requires a card slot in your computer.

Using Function Keys

Terminal allows you to assign often-used modem commands to function keys so that you can play the commands back later. The function keys can be used to carry out simple commands such as turning the speaker volume to loud, or they can execute longer sequences of instruction, such as dialing frequently used phone numbers.

To define a function key, choose the Function Keys command from the Settings menu. (The dialog box in Figure 12.7 will appear.) Click on one of the long text boxes under the word Command and enter the command. Click on the short text box to the left and type a descriptive name for the command. After you have entered your commands, click OK to save the function key definitions. If you do not see the function keys along the bottom of the screen when you return to the Terminal window, choose Show Function Keys at the bottom of the Settings menu.

▼ *Figure 12.7. Assigning Function Keys*

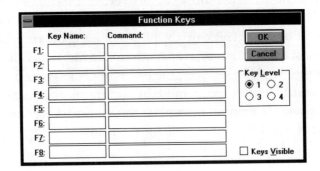

If you return to the Function Keys dialog box, you will notice a set of option buttons labeled Key Level. These buttons allow you to define different function keys in up to four separate levels (Terminal always defaults to 1). Since you can define 8 different function keys in each level, assigning different levels to function keys allows you to define up to 32 unique function keys for a given Terminal setup.

TIP

Use the Terminal function keys to hold frequently called numbers. If you are dialing from an office that has a PBX system (one that requires you to dial a 9 to get an outside line) insert one or two commas between the 9 and the rest of the number to allow time to connect to the outside line and the telephone company switching equipment. Another way to overcome this problem is to program one key with the command ATL3 ATPD 9 so that the speaker will be enabled before the 9 is dialed. You can then listen for the dial tone, which indicates that you have been assigned an outside line.

Making a Call

When you choose the Dial command from the Phone menu, Terminal begins dialing the number provided earlier in the Phone Number dialog box. If you didn't provide a number yet, the Phone

Number dialog box will appear to ask you for the number. If your modem has a speaker and it is enabled, you'll hear your number as it is being dialed. You will also hear the ringing and response tone from the other modem.

What If You Can't Connect?

If your computer doesn't connect after Terminal dials the number, and you suspect that your communication parameters are not set properly, return to the Communications dialog box by selecting the Communications command from the Settings menu. If your computer doesn't connect, here are some possible reasons:

▲ Your modem might not be turned on (external modem only)

▲ Your computer might not be hooked up to the modem with the proper cable or this cable may be faulty (intermittent)

▲ You might not have selected the correct modem in the Modem Commands dialog box; to check this, select Modem Commands from the Settings menu

▲ You might be dialing the wrong number

▲ The number you are calling may be busy or the system you are trying to connect to may be down for maintenance

▲ You might have selected the wrong COM port

▲ You might have selected the wrong baud rate

▲ The cable between your modem and the wall may be faulty (intermittent)

Preparing to Transfer a File

Before you attempt to send a text or binary file, you should check the file transfer settings. You can view or change transfer settings by using the Text Transfers or Binary Transfers command from the

Settings menu. Text transfers are normally used with files that contain pure ASCII data (such as notes written using the Windows Notepad application). Binary transfers are used to move information that does not conform to ASCII standards (such as program files). If you are not certain whether a file is pure ASCII text, send it as a binary file.

Note that the Text Transfers dialog box (Figure 12.8) provides three options for sending your data: Standard Flow Control, Character at a Time, and Line at a Time. The dialog box also indicates whether Xon/Xoff flow control has been selected. Select the options you need and click OK to save your settings.

The Binary Transfers dialog box (Figure 12.9) allows you to select Xmodem/CRC transfer or the Kermit transfer. These are by far the most popular binary transfer protocols in use today. Click on the appropriate option button, then click OK to save the selection.

Sending or Receiving a Binary File

Once you have established communication with a remote computer and have logged on using the appropriate password (if necessary), you can set up both systems for a transfer. Usually you first have to tell the remote computer what action you wish to take (send or receive a specific file). After you have provided this information, the remote system will enter a waiting state. At this point, you must inform Terminal of what is to happen.

▼ *Figure 12.8. Selecting Text Transfer Options*

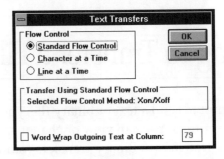

▼ *Figure 12.9. Selecting Binary Transfer Options*

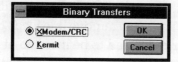

To send or receive a Binary file, select the Send Binary File or the Receive Binary File command from the Transfers menu. A dialog box similar to Figure 12.10 displays so that you can identify the file to be transferred. Select the desired file and then click the OK button. Terminal will open the specified file or create a new file, if necessary, and will signal the remote computer to begin the transfer. A line will appear at the bottom of the screen for the duration of the transfer. This line includes a Stop button so that you can abort the operation, and includes fields that will indicate the name of the file being transferred and the number of bytes or percent of the total file transferred so far. When the transfer has been completed, this special line will disappear.

Sending or Receiving a Text File

The process of sending or receiving a text file is similar to the procedure used for binary files. The only major difference is that

▼ *Figure 12.10. Sending a Binary File*

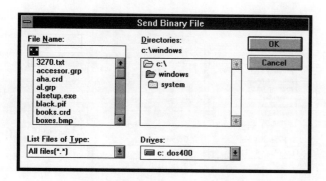

you may need to select additional options. Figure 12.11 illustrates the dialog box that appears when you choose Send Text Files from the Transfer menu. If you are sending a text file, you will need to decide whether you wish to remove line feeds that follow carriage returns or whether they need to be inserted at transmission time.

If you are receiving a text file, you will need to specify whether the new information should be appended to the back of an existing file and whether the information being received should be treated as tabular data. While your computer is performing a file transfer, a status bar displays at the bottom of the Terminal window. This status bar contains a Stop button as well as the name of the file being transferred, and the number of bytes or percentage of the file transferred so far.

CHECK YOURSELF

Use Terminal to connect to a computer or an on-line bulletin board. Send a text file, one character at a time.

ANSWER

Choose the Text Transfers command from the Settings menu. Choose the Character at a Time option button, and click the OK button. Choose the Send Text File command from the Transfers menu, select the file, and click the OK button.

▼ *Figure 12.11. Sending a Text File*

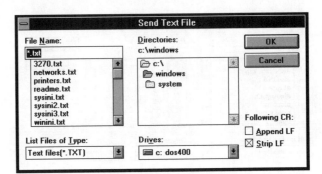

Disconnecting

Disconnecting

After you finish your communication session with another computer, hang up by choosing the Hangup command from the Phone menu. Before you choose this command, make sure you've logged off the remote computer. Otherwise, the remote computer might still think that you're connected.

Saving Terminal Settings

To save your communications settings and function key definitions before exiting Terminal, choose the Save As command from the File menu. When the standard Save As dialog box displays, enter the name of a new file. Terminal uses the extension TRM to store its terminal settings. When you later start Terminal, you can use the Open command (File menu) to load the settings that you saved in a previous session so that you can later use them.

QUICK TASK SUMMARY

Task	Procedure
Start Terminal	Choose the Terminal icon (Accessories group)
Setup Communication Settings	Use Communications command (Settings menu)
Setup the terminal	Use Terminal Preferences command (Settings menu)
Select a modem	Use Modem Commands (Settings menu)
Dial a phone number	Use Dial command (Phone menu)
Send a text file	Use the Send Text File command (Transfers menu)
Disconnect	Use Hangup command (Phone menu)
Save Terminal settings	Use the Save As command (File menu)
Use saved terminal settings	Use the Open command (File menu)

PRACTICE WHAT YOU'VE LEARNED

You have now learned to use Terminal to configure your communications hardware and to connect to other computers. Here are some exercises to help you learn more about Terminal.

1. Start Terminal

2. Set the communications parameters using the Communications dialog box.

3. Dial a number.

4. Hang up your modem.

ANSWERS

1. The Terminal application window appears.

2. If your modem is installed correctly and you selected the correct options, Terminal is ready for you to call a number.

3. Choose the Dial command in the Phone menu and type a phone number in the Phone Number dialog box. If your system is set up properly, your modem should connect.

4. Choose the Hangup command from the Phone menu.

A

Installing and Setting Up Windows

To perform several tasks at once, Windows must know about the capabilities of your PC hardware. Fortunately, the installation process for Windows 3.1 has been greatly simplified over previous versions of Windows. This appendix will cover the basics that you'll need to know to install and set up Windows 3.1, including:

▲ Information that you need in order to successfully install Windows

▲ How to install Windows

▲ How to use the Windows Setup application to change the way Windows is set up

▲ How to start and exit Windows

Getting Started

The Windows Setup program provides two installation options: Express Setup and Custom Setup. The Express Setup option is the easiest one to use because it automatically identifies the hardware and software you are using and it installs Windows to work with your current configuration. This is the option you should use if you are unfamiliar with your computer hardware or with other setup information.

The Custom Setup option allows you to control the way Windows is installed on your hard disk. You can override the default installation options and tell Windows which hardware components your computer has installed, such as the keyboard, screen, and the mouse. In addition, the Custom Setup option allows you to choose which optional Windows accessories should be installed.

TIP

Both the Express and Custom setup options will select the directory \WINDOWS by default for storing the Windows 3.1 program files. If you have previously installed Windows 3.1 or you are upgrading from an earlier version, such as Windows 3.0, the Setup program will display a special screen so that you can install Windows 3.1 in a different directory or replace the currently installed version of Windows. We'll explain how Windows 3.0 can be upgraded in more detail in the section "Upgrading Windows 3.0."

Using Express Setup

To use the Express Setup option, you need to know which printer, if any, is connected to your PC. The Setup program will also ask you which port your printer is connected to. The other installation details will be taken care of by the Setup program.

To install Windows using Express Setup, follow these steps:

1. Insert the first Windows 3.1 installation disk in drive A.

2. Move to drive A by typing A: at the DOS prompt and then pressing Enter.

3. Type Setup and press Enter.

4. Choose the Express Setup option shown on the screen.

5. The Setup program will then prompt you to insert each of the required installation disks.

The Setup program starts running in the DOS environment and switches to the Windows environment after it has copied the critical Windows files to your hard disk. Setup also automatically updates your PC's system files (AUTOEXEC.BAT and CONFIG.SYS) so that Windows 3.1 will run properly.

TIP

Express Setup will attempt to install all of the Windows accessories and applications. If the Setup program determines that your hard disk does not have enough memory for the complete installation, it will allow you to select the applications and accessories that you want to install. Once Windows has been installed, you can use the Windows Setup application to change how your system is set up or to add new applications.

Using Custom Setup

The Custom Setup option is provided for Windows users who want full control over how Windows is installed. With this option, you'll be able to select which optional Windows files are copied to your hard disk. This feature is especially useful if you have limited hard disk space available. The Custom Setup installation also allows you to view and change your PC's sytem files, AUTOEXEC.BAT and CONFIG.SYS.

What You Need to Know

Unless you know a great deal about your PC, you'll need to do some research before using the Custom Setup installation. You will be asked for the following information:

▲ The type of PC you have

▲ The type of display adapter and monitor in your system

▲ The type of printer you have (if any) and which port it's connected to

▲ The type of mouse you have (if any)

▲ The name of the directory where you want the Windows files stored

▲ Information about a PC network, if you're connected to one

▲ Information about your keyboard

▲ The applications currently on your hard disk that you want to set up to run under Windows

▲ The optional Windows applications you want to install

▲ The changes you want made to the system files AUTOEXEC.BAT and CONFIG.SYS

You'll find most of this information in the owner's manuals that came with your PC. If you don't have this documentation, you may need to do a bit of detective work. For example, Windows needs to know the type of display adapter card in your system because different display cards provide different capabilities.

To install Windows using Custom Setup:

1. Insert the first Windows 3.1 installation disk in the A drive.

2. Move to the A drive by typing A: at the DOS prompt and then pressing Enter.

3. Type SETUP and press Enter.

4. Select the Custom Setup option on the screen.

5. The Setup program will then prompt you to insert each of the required installation disks.

The Setup program will also prompt you to select different hardware options so that it can install Windows 3.1 on your sytem.

Upgrading Windows 3.0

If Windows 3.0 is currently installed on your system, you can use the Setup program to upgrade to Windows 3.1. The Setup program will replace the necessary Windows system files, device drivers, and accessories. Before you run Setup, however, make sure that you back up the data files and programs on your hard disk.

The Setup program will preserve Program Manager groups, system hardware settings, desktop settings, color settings, memory management settings, and other settings that are in use for Windows 3.0. If the Setup program detects that any of the drivers installed with your version of Windows 3.0 have been updated, it will automatically install the new drivers.

TIP

If your computer has Windows 3.0 drivers that were supplied by vendors other than Microsoft, the Setup program will not automatically change them. You can, however, use the Custom Setup program to replace the driver with one of the new Windows 3.1 drivers.

Changing Your Setup

After Windows has been installed, you can later add or change drivers, add applications, or change other setup options by using a program called Windows Setup.

To use this feature, double-click on the Windows Setup icon in the Main group window. Figure A.1 shows the startup window for Windows Setup. Use this application to modify the Windows configuration, or to install additional applications.

Use the first option to modify the Windows configuration when you upgrade your hardware. For example, you might change

▼ *Figure A.1. The Windows Setup Dialog*

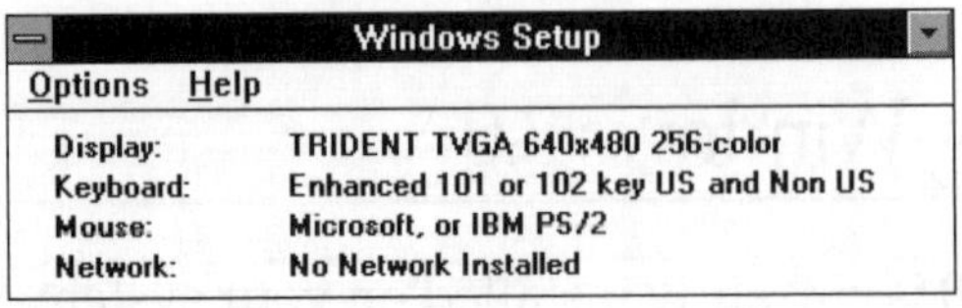

```
┌─────────────────────────────────────────────────────┐
│ ─           Windows Setup                         ▼ │
├─────────────────────────────────────────────────────┤
│ Options  Help                                       │
├─────────────────────────────────────────────────────┤
│ Display:    TRIDENT TVGA 640x480 256-color          │
│ Keyboard:   Enhanced 101 or 102 key US and Non US   │
│ Mouse:      Microsoft, or IBM PS/2                   │
│ Network:    No Network Installed                     │
└─────────────────────────────────────────────────────┘
```

your standard VGA display hardware to a super VGA or you may add a PC network card.

Open the Options menu by clicking on the Options item or pressing Alt+O. To modify the configuration, select the Change System Settings command. The dialog box in Figure A.2 appears. Notice that pull-down boxes are provided for the display, the keyboard, the mouse, and the network. Click on the down scroll arrow to the right of a particular group, and open the menu to view several entries at once. Use the scroll arrows to view all possible options. Make your selection by clicking on the option.

After you've made your configuration selections, click on the OK button in the dialog box to tell Windows to reconfigure itself. This approach is much faster than going through the entire setup procedure again. If you use this feature, keep the installation disks available, because Windows will ask you to insert one or more disks into the disk drive to obtain any files required to change the configuration.

If you select the Windows Setup option to install an additional application, a new window will request more information, such as the location of the application's starup file.

▼ *Figure A.2. Changing the System Settings*

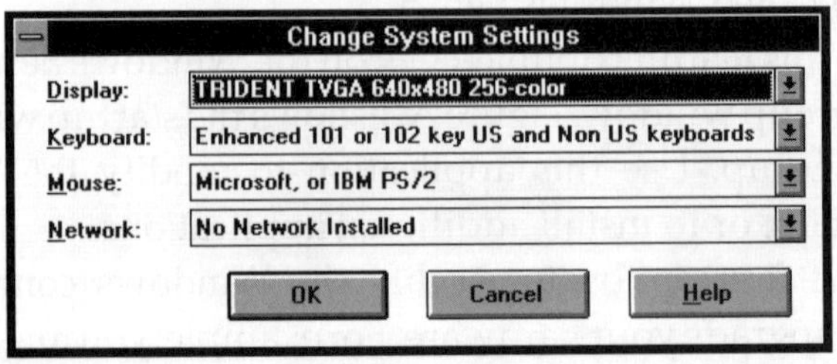

```
┌───────────────────────────────────────────────────────────┐
│ ─              Change System Settings                      │
├───────────────────────────────────────────────────────────┤
│ Display:    [TRIDENT TVGA 640x480 256-color           ▼]  │
│                                                            │
│ Keyboard:   [Enhanced 101 or 102 key US and Non US ...▼]  │
│                                                            │
│ Mouse:      [Microsoft, or IBM PS/2                    ▼]  │
│                                                            │
│ Network:    [No Network Installed                      ▼]  │
│                                                            │
│       [   OK   ]    [  Cancel  ]    [   Help   ]           │
└───────────────────────────────────────────────────────────┘
```

Starting Windows

Starting Windows

Before you can start Windows, your PC must first successfully boot-up its Disk Operating System (DOS) software. When the DOS prompt appears (it will look similar to C:\>), invoke the Windows environment by entering this command:

```
WIN
```

If Windows has been installed correctly, the Program Manager window appears. This window contains a second window, called Main, which displays icons for each of the main applications. To access one of these applications, double-click on the corresponding icon. To open one of the menus listed in the Program Manager window (File, Options, Window, Help), click on the menu item.

TIP

If you don't have a mouse, you can access a menu bar item by holding down the Alt key and pressing the first letter of that menu item. For example, select the File menu by pressing Alt+F. You can activate an icon by pressing the arrow keys until the icon is highlighted, pressing Alt+F to open the File menu, and then pressing O to choose the Open command in the menu.

Options for Starting Windows

When the WIN command is executed, Windows automatically determines whether it should start in the standard or 386 enhanced operating mode. If you want to use a mode other than the default mode, type WIN followed by an option. Two options are supported:

```
WIN/S
WIN/3
```

The first command invokes Windows in standard 286 mode, and the second command invokes Windows in the 386 enhanced mode. If you have an AT-class system with an 80286 microprocessor, you must run in the standard mode. If your system uses either an 80386 or 80486 microprocessor, you can run Windows in the 386 enhanced mode to take advantage of Window's advanced memory-management and task-scheduling features.

TIP

To run Windows 3.1 automatically whenever your PC is powered-up, append the command WIN to the AUTOEXEC.BAT file. Your computer will complete its normal cold-start procedure, and then automatically invoke Windows.

Starting Windows with an Application

You can specify a command to start Windows and tell it to automatically run an application. As an example, the following command starts Windows and executes Microsoft's Word for Windows application (which, for our example, is stored in the directory DOCS):

```
WIN \DOCS\WINWORD
```

Quitting Windows

Windows can be terminated using a number of different techniques, but you must use the Program Manager window to exit Windows.

The quickest way to exit Windows from within the Program Manager is to press Alt+F4. This action brings up the Exit Windows dialog box, which allows you to either quit Windows or cancel the operation and return to the Program Manager. To quit Windows, click the OK button in the dialog box.

To exit Windows by using the mouse, either open the File Menu and select the Exit Windows command, or open the Control menu and select the Close command. To access the Control menu, click on the small box in the upper-left corner of the Program Manager window.

Index